7

D0667230

DATE			

DISCARD

African Population and Capitalism

AFRICAN MODERNIZATION
AND DEVELOPMENT
Paul Lovejoy, York University
Series Editor

Forthcoming in This Series

Patriarchy and Class: African Women in the Home and Workforce, edited by Sharon Stichter and Jane Parpart

South African Labor Migration and the South African Gold Mines: 1960-1984, Jonathan Crush, Alan Jeeves, and David Yudelman

The Precarious Balance: State and Society in Africa, edited by Donald Rothchild and Naomi Chazan

African Population and Capitalism

Historical Perspectives

edited by
**Dennis D. Cordell
and Joel W. Gregory**

Sponsored by the Joint Committee on African Studies
of the American Council of Learned Societies
and the Social Science Research Council

Westview Press / Boulder and London

African Modernization and Development

Copyright © 1987 by Westview Press, Inc.

Published in 1987 in the United States of America by Westview Press, Inc.; Frederick A. Praeger, Publisher; 5500 Central Avenue, Boulder, Colorado 80301

Library of Congress Catalog Card Number: 85-26181
ISBN: 0-8133-7408-1

This book was produced without formal editing by the publisher.

Printed and bound in the United States of America

⊚ The paper used in this publication meets the requirements of the American National Standard for Permanence of Paper for Printed Library Materials Z39.48-1984.

6   5   4   3   2   1

Contents

About the Contributors

CHARLES BECKER is a Researcher of the Centre national des recherches scientifiques (Paris), based in Senegal since 1970. His fields of interest include protohistory, demographic history, and history in general. He has published numerous articles on these topics, alone and in collaboration with Senegalese and French scholars.

DENNIS D. CORDELL, Associate Professor of History, Southern Methodist University, Dallas, Texas, has also been an invited researcher at the Département de démographie, Université de Montréal. His book, *Dar al-Kuti: The Last Years of the Trans-Saharan Slave Trade* (University of Wisconsin Press), appeared in 1985; he has also written articles on the history of Central Africa and African historical demography. His current research focuses on history and subfertility in Central Africa.

MARC H. DAWSON, Assistant Professor of History, Union College, Schenectady, New York, has done research on the relationship between socioeconomic and epidemiological changes in Kenya during the colonial period. His publications include articles in *Social Science and Medicine, African Economic History,* and *African Historical Demography II.*

MAMADOU DIOUF is Maître-Assistant in the Département d'histoire at the Université de Dakar. Since completing a doctoral thesis on the history of Senegal in the nineteenth century, he has become interested in the history of relations between the United States and Africa, African historical demography, urban history, and the impact of technological change.

MYRON ECHENBERG is an Associate Professor of History and former Associate Dean of Graduate Studies at McGill University. A former editor of the *Canadian Journal of African Studies,* he has published numerous articles on French military policy in West Africa and is completing a book-length study on the same topic.

RAYMOND GERVAIS has completed an M.A. in African history at the University of Birmingham and an M.Sc. in demography at the Université de Montréal. He is a coauthor of *African Historical Demography: A Multidisciplinary Bibliography* (with Joel W. Gregory and Dennis D. Cordell). At present he is preparing a doctorate at the Université de Paris VII on French colonial policy, agriculture, and population among the Mosi of Burkina Faso.

JOEL W. GREGORY is Professor of Demography, Université de Montréal, Montréal, Québec. Most recently he has compiled *African Historical Demography: A Multidisciplinary Bibliography,* in collaboration with Dennis Cordell and Raymond Gervais, and coedited a collection of essays, *Démographie et sous-développment* (McGill, 1986). His current research focuses on African historical demography and household strategies and demographic change in Africa and the Caribbean.

LINDA HEYWOOD is an Assistant Professor of History at Howard University. Her publications include an essay in *The Workers of African Trade,* edited by Paul E. Lovejoy and Catherine Coquery-Vidrovitch (Sage Publications, 1985). Another article is included in the collection *The Ending of Slavery in Africa,* edited by Suzanne Meirs, Richard Roberts, and Igor Kopytoff (in press). Her current research focuses on the modern economic history of Angola.

J. E. INIKORI has recently completed a term as Head of Department in the Department of History at Ahmadu Bello University, where he is also Professor. He has edited two collections on the slave trade, *Forced Migration: The Impact of the Export Trade on African Societies* (Hutchison, 1982) and *The African Slave Trade from the Fifteenth to the Nineteenth Century* (UNESCO, 1979). In addition, he has published numerous articles on the topic.

BOGUMIL JEWSIEWICKI is Professor of History, Université Laval, Québec. He has published numerous articles on the economic history of Zaire in the colonial period. He has also edited several essay collections, including one on Zaire, and another entitled *Mode of Production: The Challenge of Africa,* both originally published as theme issues by the *Canadian Journal of African Studies,* of which he is an editor. Current research focuses on social history and historiography.

MARTIN A. KLEIN is an historian of Africa who teaches at the University of Toronto. He has been involved for many years in the study of slavery and French colonial rule. His most recent book is *Women and Slavery in Africa,* edited with Claire Robertson.

LUTUTALA MUMPASI has been a research and teaching assistant at the Université de Kinshasa since 1978. He is currently preparing a doctoral thesis at the Université de Montréal entitled "La dynamique des migrations au Zaire." In his thesis he uses a sample survey of 1853 households in Kinshasa in 1983 financed by the International Development Research Centre in Ottawa. Apart from migration, he pursues work in the historical demography and social demography of Zaire.

ABDULLAHI MAHADI is Lecturer in the Department of History at Ahmadu Bello University. He completed his Ph.D. dissertation, "The State and Economy, the Sarauta System and Its Role in Shaping the Society and Economy of Kano, with Particular Reference to the Eighteenth and Nineteenth Centuries," in 1982 at the same institution. His subsequent writings include "Population Growth and the Urbanisation Process in *Kasar* Kano in the Nineteenth Century," a paper presented at the annual congress of the Historical Society of Nigeria at Ilorin in 1983.

ELIAS MANDALA is Assistant Professor of History at the University of Rochester. He has published on the economic history of the peasantry in Malawi and the sexual division of labor in *African Economic History* and the *African Studies Review.* His Ph.D. is from the University of Minnesota.

PATRICK MANNING is an Assistant Professor in the Departments of History and African-American Studies at Northeastern University. His publications include *Slavery, Colonialism, and Economic Growth in Dahomey, 1640-1960* (Cambridge University Press, 1982) and diverse articles on African slavery such as "Contours of Slavery and Social Change in Africa" (*American Historical Review,* 1983).

MOHAMED MBODJ is Maître-Assistant in the Département d'histoire, Université de Dakar. Since completing a thesis on the impact of peanut cultivation in Sine-Saloum in the twentieth century, he has become interested in economic networks in central Senegambia, African historical demography, and the evolution of technology. Along with Charles Becker and Mamadou Diouf, he belongs to a research group, "Recherches en Démographie Historique du Sénégal," attached to the Laboratoire d'histoire économique et sociale at the Université de Dakar.

JAY O' BRIEN teaches in the Department of Anthropology and Sociology at Lawrence University in Appleton, Wisconsin. His Ph.D. thesis was entitled "Agricultural Labor and Development in Sudan" (University of Connecticut, 1980). From 1974 to 1979 he conducted research in Sudan and taught at the University of Khartoum and the University of Gezira. He has published a number of articles and book chapters on agriculture and labor in Sudan.

THOMAS M. PAINTER is a Research Associate at the Institute for Development Anthropology in Binghampton, New York. He has just completed his Ph.D. dissertation in sociology and development anthropology at the State University of New York, Binghampton, on peasant migrations and rural social change in southwestern Niger, and the ways both relate to capitalist development within a larger region including much of the Sahel and Guinea Coast.

VICTOR PICHÉ, Professor of Demography, Université de Montréal, has published numerous articles on African and Haitian demography, including "African Return Migration: Past, Present, and Future" (*Contemporary Marxism,* 1983; with Joel W. Gregory) and "Emigration et immigration: les Haitiens au Québec" (*Sociologie et sociétés,* 1983; with Micheline Labelle and Serge Larose). His current research focuses on the family, work, and migration networks in Haiti and demography and social classes in Guadeloupe.

MICHAEL P. PROCTOR is currently affiliated with the Department of Geography and Environmental Studies at the University of the Witwatersrand, Johannesburg, where he also received his Ph.D. His research interests include local urban forms and processes.

JOHN K. THORNTON is a Fellow at the Carter Woodson Institute at the University of Virginia. His principal research deals with historical demography in Central Africa from the sixteenth century to the eighteenth century, the slave trade, and relationships between the slave trade and population. He has published a book, *The Kingdom of Kongo: Civil War and Transition, 1641-1718* (Cambridge University Press, 1982).

MEREDETH TURSHEN received her doctorate in politics from the University of Sussex in England. Her book, *The Political Ecology of Disease in Tanzania* (Rutgers University Press), was published in 1984. She teaches at the Rutgers University School of Urban and Regional Policy and at the University of Medicine and Dentistry of New Jersey-Rutgers Medical School.

Acknowledgments

Over the half decade that this collection has been in progress we have received the encouragement, advice, and support of numerous individuals and institutions. It is impossible to thank everyone who contributed to the project: the colleagues who attended panels on African historical demography at a variety of national and international meetings in Canada, Great Britain, and the United States; the students, ranging from freshpersons at Southern Methodist University (Dallas) to graduate students both there and at the Université de Montréal, who listened to us talk about the importance of demographic research for a more complete understanding of the history of Africa; the archivists, librarians, and government officials in Africa, Europe, Canada, and the United States who helped us locate documents.

But there are those who offered special aid and support whose contributions we would like to acknowledge. First, we are grateful to the Institut du Sahel (Bamako), the Ford Foundation (Dakar), the International Development Research Centre (Dakar), the Social Science Research Council (New York), the Fund for Faculty Excellence of Dedman College and the Stan Sharp Trust in the Department of History at Southern Methodist University (Dallas), and the département de démographie at the Université de Montréal, all of which provided financial assistance for this volume as well as a workshop held in Montréal in May 1985, which brought together contributors and a variety of commentators.

We also wish to thank the chairpersons and commentators who offered new insights and raised new questions about our common effort to create a collection of essays and our individual chapters. These people include Odile Frank of the Population Council (New York), Nancy Howell of the University of Toronto, Papa-Syr Diagne of the Institut du Sahel (Bamako), Sidiki Coulibaly of the International Development Research Centre (Dakar), and Victor Piché of the Université de Montréal.

The names of the people who commented on individual essays are included in acknowledgments at the end of chapters. However, for their wide-ranging comments and intellectual support since the beginning of this project we would like to express appreciation to Bogumil Jewsiewicki, Université Laval (Québec); Jean Poirier, the Université de Montréal; Saliou Mbaye, Directeur des Archives nationales du Sénégal (Dakar), and Danielle Gauvreau of the Université du Québec (Chicoutimi).

In addition, there were those who helped with the actual production of the manuscript whose accurate and dependable work made our task as editors immensely easier: Lise Massé and Francine Robert of the département de démographie at the Université de Montréal as well as Mona Wildman of the Department of History and Susi Meyn of the Dedman College Dean's Office, both at Southern Methodist University.

Finally, we wish to acknowledge the contributions of Sabakinu Kivilu (Université de Kinshasa) and Mumbanza mwa Bawele (Université de Lubumbashi) who, along with Bogumil Jewsiewicki, were to have prepared another chapter for this volume, but for logistical and financial reasons were unable to do so. We hope that their stimulating ideas will be published in the near future.

Dennis D. Cordell
Joel W. Gregory

1

AFRICAN HISTORICAL DEMOGRAPHY
The Search for a Theoretical Framework

DENNIS D. CORDELL
JOEL W. GREGORY
VICTOR PICHÉ

   Demographers and historians have largely ignored the past of African populations. Yet, much heat and some light are being generated by studies of high birthrates; less heat and more light have been focused on the all-too-slow improvement in infant, child, and general survivorship. And the massive movements of African populations—from fields and pastures to towns and cities, from the interior to the coasts, not to mention intercontinental migration and refugee flight—figure prominently in descriptions of African economic and political crises.

   The passionate discussion of the present, however, is being pursued in ignorance of the past. The most dramatic example of overly simplistic analysis is the facile linking of the African food crisis—and more generally the crisis of international confidence in Africa's ability to "develop"—to the rapid growth of Africa's population.

   This collection of case studies provides historical background for the understanding of African demography. The chapters call for greater historical sophistication: From these essays it is clear that African demography evolved in diverse ways, according to the specificity of local conditions and outside pressures (see Jewsiewicki, Chapter 17, this collection). They also take issue with the simplistic assumptions that African fertility and mortality have always been high and that mortality necessarily declined as a result of European intervention, thus creating the conditions for Africa's much decried "population explosion."

This overly simplistic and ahistorical view has provided fertile soil for the propagation of demographic transition theory as the appropriate paradigm—implicit or explicit—for the understanding of African demography in the recent past. The demographic transition is a descriptive model of the historical evolution of some European populations. Its basic phases are:

(1) *At the beginning of the transition:* high fertility and high mortality, with a very slow rate of natural increase (births minus deaths).
(2) *In the first phase of change:* mortality begins to decline, while fertility remains high; the rate of natural increase accelerates.
(3) *After a phase of increasing and rapid population growth:* fertility begins to decline; the rate of natural increase thus begins to diminish.
(4) *A the end of the transaction:* a new equilibrium is established, again characterized by a very slow rate of natural increase, this time at low levels of fertility and mortality.

The model specifies neither the timing of the phases nor the causes for the decline in mortality and fertility. Those who have used the paradigm to describe various societies have attempted to date the timing and the length of the transition and to identify the causes of decline (see O'Brien, Chapter 11, in this volume, for further discussion). The causes for improved survivorship are the subject of debate: better socioeconomic conditions in general or improved health and sanitation? The relative importance of reasons for the eventual decline in fertility is also open to question: changes in the economic costs and benefits of children or shifts in the value system of parents?

Demographic transition theory, born of European experience, has profoundly influenced thinking about population change in the Third World. In particular, the rapid rates of population growth in many Africans societies are perceived in terms of a "delayed" transition. The high rates of natural increase are interpreted as a confirmation that mortality decline has commenced but that fertility decline remains in eclipse. Implicitly or explicitly, the major question about African demography becomes, "How can fertility decline be induced?" This model of orderly and predictable decline in death and birth rates precludes a more complex and varied analysis of what is happening and how it came about.

The principal goal of this collection is *not to refute demographic transition* theory, but rather to show that population changes are historical processes, which vary from one period and one society to another. Population change is the combined result of births and deaths, and of immigration and emigration, two sets of additions and two of subtractions, from the total numbers of a society. This process is only a part of the *demographic regime,* which also includes the strategies that allow families and households, women and men, successive generations, and competing social classes to ensure their survival. The demographic regime is based on the necessity—and the authors of the essays would agree that these necessities are fundamentally material—for societies to reproduce and to produce if they are to survive. Reproduction begins with the necessary creation and recreation of labor; production begins with food and shelter.

There is no single pattern that explains demographic change. As we have maintained elsewhere (Gregory, Cordell, Gervais, 1984: viii), population is neither an independent nor a dependent variable, but a thread that must be interwoven with many others to produce a tapestry that accurately depicts a society's past.

Beyond this general objective, a specific concern of this collection is to show the links between the evolution of the demographic regime and the history of capitalist penetration in Africa over the past two or three centuries. For example, many of the case studies (Cordell, Lututala, Turshen, Dawson, Heywood and Thornton, etc.) show that mortality increased—sometimes dramatically—during the first half of the colonial period. When mortality did begin to decline, the curves depicting the change are marked by peaks and valleys that differ from one society to another. Even where the peaks and valleys are similar, the studies suggest that explanations for them may be strikingly different (compare, for example, Turshen, Chapter 12, with Heywood and Thornton, Chapter 15).

Second, the empirical evidence indicates that among some societies, capitalist penetration may have occasioned *increases* in fertility. Dawson's case study of the Kikuyu (Chapter 13), whose fertility is today the highest of any society in Africa, dramatically illustrates that a drop in mortality was probably much less important than a rise in fertility during the colonial era. O'Brien (Chapter 11) illustrates that African societies "fine-tuned" fertility to match differing patterns of demands for labor.

Third, several chapters (Becker, Diouf, and Mbodj, Chapter 5; Painter, Chapter 8; Cordell, Chapter 9; Lututala, Chapter 10; Gregory and Mandala, Chapter 14; and Proctor, Chapter 16) offer compelling evidence of the need to include migration in any study of the African demographic regime. Natural increase (births minus deaths) is important, but its analysis is incomplete without the additions and subtractions caused by immigration and emigration.

Failure to place contemporary questions about African population into an historical context has led to an oversimplified diagnosis of the so-called demographic crisis in Africa, emphasizing the dangers of further delay in fertility decline. Yet few policy alternatives to fertility control have been generated, even by those who criticize the ahistorical, conventional wisdom. A historical rereading of the African demographic record calls for an alternative conceptual framework beyond the tradition of transition theory.

It is not surprising that many who criticize the conventional wisdom have turned to Marxism and feminism. The practice of historical and dialectical materialism has generated a wide-ranging set of hypotheses about the effects of capitalist penetration in Africa. The study of African and colonial patriarchy and the dynamic of the sexual division of labor has produced a potentially complementary set of hypotheses about reproduction and production. Yet little of this conceptually rich work has influenced the study of African demography. The strengths of such analysis, with its emphasis on conflict and discontinuity, its inclusion of irregularity and disequilibrium, and the historical and material basis of its perspective, are potentially productive antidotes to the limits of the static equilibrium model of homogeneous, harmonious, and regular change described by transition theory.

MATERIALIST ANALYSIS AND HISTORICAL DEMOGRAPHY

In fact, demographic theory in general is dramatically underdeveloped. In demography there is no explicit body of theory equivalent to Parsonian functionalism in sociology or to liberal and neoclassical theory in economics. Within demography, specific subjects have benefitted from the theoretical byproducts of other disciplines. Urbanization and intraurban migration, for example, have been analysed using the concepts of the "human ecology" school of Chicago sociology (Duchac, 1974). Fertility has been scrutinized with the aid of "middle-level" theory drawn from sociology (Davis and Blake, 1956, for example) and from economics (Becker, 1960, or Easterlin, 1968). And mathematical models have had considerable impact on demographic methods (Dublin and Lotka, 1925, for example).

Yet a general theory of demography simply does not exist. While most demographers would probably say that the object of their discipline is to study the renewal of human populations, they would be hard pressed to explain why this renewal is significant and important. Most would hesitate when asked how this renewal of human populations is related to other social processes. Preoccupation with links between specific demographic events (a set of births for example) and specific nondemographic events (a recession, for example) is common to much of "social demography." But a holistic view of demographic renewal in relation to that which is "nondemographic" is almost nonexistent. This is not surprising, given that a holistic view of demographic renewal itself is rare.

Materialist Analysis and the Externalization of Demography

Even within the theoretically inclined materialist tradition, demographic theory has not flourished. Demographic renewal, or, in materialist vocabulary, demographic reproduction, has been externalized. In historical materialist analysis—preoccupied by relations of production and the production of material goods—the production and reproduction of human beings has, until recently, almost always been relegated to biology, as if this dynamic and dialectic process could be transformed into a simple, exogenous variable.

To illustrate our point, we refer to major materialist authors who have worked on Africa. Samir Amin (1972), in "L'Afrique sous-peuplée," takes a strong anti-Malthusian position (consistent with at least one school of orthodox Marxist theory), asserting that African underdevelopment is the result of "underpopulation" (on this topic, see Chapter 4 by Mahadi and Inikori). No theoretical significance is attached to the concept of underpopulation; it is an exogenous empirical fact that "explains," in part, why African development is so slow. And this, in spite of Marx's succinct but careful definition of "overpopulation" (Marx, 1954: I).

Catherine Coquery-Vidrovitch (1972), in her seminal work on Central Africa, leaves demography to others. Yet the specificity of North Central African demographic history is a fundamental part of any comprehensive understanding of these societies. The relatively low fertility, population density, and high mobility (and perhaps extremely high mortality) are part of a unique demographic regime that was only marginally able to renew itself in the late nineteenth and the early twentieth centuries.

At least two important new developments in materialist analysis have, however, reintegrated parts of the demographic regime. The production and reproduction of human beings is the focus of some of the work of economic anthropologists working on the "domestic mode of production" in precapitalist Africa (Meillassoux, 1975b;

Rey, 1978; Dupré, 1982; *Canadian Journal of African Studies,* 1985). It is likewise the focus of feminist materialists interested in the sexual division of labor and household and domestic labor in capitalist social formations *(Critique de l'Économie Politique,* 1981; *Sociologie et Sociétés,* 1981). However, these feminist contributions are often limited to fertility and nuptiality and have little to say about migration; neither set of contributions has much to say about morbidity and mortality, which are other essential parts of the demographic regime.

A second recent development in materialist analysis does focus on mobility and migration. The elaboration of a theory of labor mobility in advanced capitalism emphasizes the need for a highly mobile labor force in order to combat the law of the decreasing rate of profit (deGaudemar, 1976; Nikolinakos, 1975). Two forms of mobility are identified: spatial and sectoral. The first refers to what demographers commonly call migration, the second to what sociologists and economists would call inter- and intraprofessional mobility. The two, of course, frequently coincide in the reproduction of the labor force for specific zones and types of capitalist production. For materialist demography, the analysis of labor migration as part of the dynamic of the reproduction of the labor force suggests a way to reintegrate migration and "natural" increase—fertility (births) minus mortality (deaths)—into a single demographic theory.

The Exclusion of Materialism in Historical Demography

Historical demography is just beginning to discover historical materialism. This fact is more than happenstance. Historical demography, a generation after its birth, remains essentially a set of methods for the reconstitution of families for the measurement of some demographic events: births, deaths, and marriages. These methods are, in and of themselves, the result of a unique, but single type of data: the Roman Catholic and Anglican parish registers, or their equivalents (Mormon records or Japanese temple lists, for example). This definition of historical demography in terms of sources is self-consciously explicit:

> Demography ... is the most abstract of the social sciences, because it only studies man [sic] in terms of numbers and lengths of time. ... The originality of historical demography is to work with sources which were not created by historical demography or for it. ... Our work ... is to see how from these sources—which were not created with a scientific pur-

pose in mind—one can construct good statistics [Dupâquier in Sauvy, 1982: 44-45].

What is striking to the social scientist in general and, more specifically, to the materialist social scientist, is the absence of a reason for tabulating demographic events. Orthodox historical demography does not have a substantive objective; it is hardly surprising, therefore, that historical demography has not generated a set of complementary or competing *problématiques*.

The dual constraint of rigorous data requirements for the application of contemporary demographic methods to historical statistics and of a narrow set of data sources has retarded the search for alternative methods and sources for the historical study of population. Yet the potential in historical demography for innovation is great, if new methods can be invented (see Cordell and Gregory, 1980). In fact, materialist analysis must incorporate demographic production and reproduction into its historical method if social relations of production are to be fully explored, and feminist analysis must provide a framework for the study of the entire demographic regime.

A MATERIALIST APPROACH

Marx on Population

Materialist analysis in demography begins with Chapter 25 of *Capital* (Marx, 1954: I) with its important insights for demographic analysis—in particular, that each historic mode of production has its own law of population. First, in the capitalist mode of production, neither the absolute nor the proportional decrease or increase in the working population renders capital insufficient; nor does its decrease render capital overabundant. On the contrary, it is the expansion and contraction of capital that produces, alternatively, the relative lack or overabundance of labor. Second, in the process of accumulation, the proportional decrease in the amount of capital allocated to the costs of wages and salaries and the training of labor (variable capital) leads to a decrease in relative demand for labor. A *relative surplus population* is thus created since part of the workers are no longer necessary. It is called relative because it does not originate from an increase in population that is greater than available resources (as Malthus argues), but originates in the increase in the fraction of capital allocated to machines, technology, and infrastructure (constant capital) in the accelerating increase in total capital. This is what Marx calls the law of population specific to the capitalist mode of production. Third, this relative surplus population contributes to the growth of the industrial army of reserve, that is, the reservoir of labor always and necessarily available for capital's use. Hence, capital controls both the supply and the demand for labor.

Marx identified three types of relative surplus population: (1) *floating*, workers who can be and are replaced by other categories of workers or by machines; (2) *latent,* nonwage laborers in agriculture, who either will eventually have to sell their labor to capital due to the deterioration of their material conditions, or who are ready to leave once the opportunities arise; (3) *stagnant,* those who survive in extreme conditions, with irregular employment and with minimal wages, characterized by extreme poverty.

In our view, these concepts are not necessarily the best place to start. First, the basic concept of "reserve army" refers almost exclusively to capitalist relations of production; it says nothing about others.

If we look at the components of the reserve army, some originate in other spheres of production, or as some might say, in other modes of production (see *Canadian Journal of African Studies, 1985*). Such is the case with latent and stagnant relative surplus population. In the latent form, for instance, production is imbedded in domestic social relations. These relations of production and reproduction, and the division of labor, must be examined in order to understand the significance of the family for demographic behavior. The same can be said for the stagnant form, where domestic relations of production are perpetuated or re-created (e.g., in urban shanty towns) to ensure survival. Finally, in all three forms there is significant labor involved in the production of human beings. Focusing exclusively on the law of relative surplus population neglects domestic labor, the role of women, and the formation of the family. With the help of feminist materialism, demography can more fully comprehend this hidden force of capitalism.

The second fundamental limitation of Marx's law of surplus population is linked to the first. He says nothing about the specific demographic phenomena that contribute to relative surplus population: the procreation of human beings (fertility and nuptiality), their survival or nonsurvival (mortality), and their mobility (migration). Materialist demographic theory must therefore do two things: work its way back from an aggregate formulation (the concept of relative surplus population) to a dynamic analysis of each demographic component and then integrate demographic production and reproduction into the larger social processes of production and reproduction.

Demography and Total Social Production

Total social production is the production of both the means of subsistence and of human beings. Engels's ([1884] 1948: 5-6) famous quotation is a useful starting point:

> The determining factor in history is . . . the production and reproduction of immediate life. . . . On the other hand, the production of the means of subsistence, of food, clothing, and shelter and the tools requisite therefore; on the other, the production of human beings themselves, the production of the species.

It is probably accurate to argue that Marxism has dealt essentially with the first type of production. It has concentrated on the confrontation of capital and labor in the arena of accumulation and of production of the means of subsistence. The origin of capital and the capitalist class, the laws of capital accumulation and their effects on the working classes, and the reproduction of capitalist relations of production have been the privileged objects of analysis. The origin of the labor force and the laws of production and reproduction of human beings have been much less studied. It is on this subject that we would like to concentrate, drawing on recent contributions from feminism and economic anthropology. First we offer a series of ten theoretical propositions.

(1) In order for social organization to function, conditions that make possible the continued production of both the means of subsistence and of human beings in sufficient quantity and quality must be met: This is what we call *social reproduction*.

(2) The production of human beings is an integral part of total social reproduction. While on the surface, the production of human beings may appear to be the aggregate of isolated acts of individual couples, in reality, it is a socially determined form of production.

(3) As with any type of production, the production of human beings requires *labor*. Thus, total labor implies both labor to produce the means of subsistence and labor to produce human beings. A key process in the production of human beings is the division of labor.

(4) A fundamental social necessity is that the labor force must produce both the means of subsistence and human beings: Thus the production and reproduction of the labor force is one of the conditions for total social reproduction.

(5) Another of these conditions is that there must be control of production, of the division of labor and of values and norms. The

crucial questions become who controls, how this control is exercised, and, conversely, how control is resisted?

(6) The reproduction of the labor force implies three elements: (a) the replacement of older workers, to respond to new demands and to offset deaths or emigration; (b) the maintenance of the existing labor force in good health, which requires food, shelter, sleep, and so on; and (c) a system of social security for unemployed, older, disabled, sick, and other nonworking members of the population. For a given social formation the renewal process may involve both the production of new human beings (procreation) and the recruitment of human beings produced "elsewhere" (immigration).

(7) Each of the above elements requires labor and access to means of subsistence: There are specific costs related to replacement, maintenance, and renewal. Thus, demography must also ask what group or groups absorb these costs, in terms of both labor and access to means of subsistence.

(8) It is the family as an institution that represents the main locus of production and reproduction of the labor force. It is responsible for replacement, maintenance, and renewal of the labor force. Within the family, the sexual division of labor is crucial; it is women who have performed most domestic work related to the production and reproduction of the labor force. Generational specialization also needs to be analysed. The costs mentioned above are shared on an unequal basis, most frequently passed on to women and offspring as "unpaid" family labor. Thus the *power structure* within the family conditions and reproduces this division of labor. The extent to which these responsibilities and costs are shared with other social institutions depends on specific historic conditions.

(9) The conditions for the production of the labor force are maintained and reproduced not only by power relationships—including force and repression—but also by *ideology* and *values*. Dominant groups control the institutions that create and reproduce the ideology that justifies the existing division of labor and of power (religion, schools, mass media, and so on) and the institutions that enforce consensus and compliance (legal system, army, police, and so on); dominated groups in resisting these ideologies frequently create their own. In each historical circumstance, the specific ideological mechanisms must be identified.

(10) Finally, and perhaps most fundamentally, we need to identify the competition and conflict between dominant groups for the control of the labor force, as well as the conflict between dominated and dominant groups. These concrete and historical struggles for the use

of labor are the source of change in the production and reproduction of the labor force, for the production and reproduction of a demographic regime specific to a particular historical period in a particular social formation.

These propositions can be demonstrated only by looking at different strategies for the production and reproduction of labor. What are the dominant social relations in the specific social formation being studied? The social relations of production must be defined: are they capitalist, feudal, or slave? What is the dominant form of production and what are the other forms of production? What are the specific mechanisms of articulation between or among these forms?

STRATEGIES FOR THE PRODUCTION AND REPRODUCTION OF LABOR IN AFRICA

Households

Identified by various terms, the production and reproduction of labor in the household is the major demographic process of the so-called domestic mode of production. While this domestic mode of production is an abstract model of precapitalist African societies, and was conditioned by the colonial experience, the principles of the household demographic regime are worth examination (see also Gregory and Piché, 1981, 1982).

Agriculture, cattle-raising, and crafts were dominant subsistence activities in the domestic mode of production. Productivity had to be sufficient to maintain and reproduce the household, and to permit the repetition of agricultural and livestock cycles. Land was a "means of labor," and access to it was determined by social relations based on family or clan membership.

Production and reproduction occurred within the household or family unit. Production and consumption took place primarily within a larger domestic group. Each family had access to land—to pass from generation to generation—as long as it was being used. The survival and success of the household depended on its labor: The more people of working ages, the greater the production.

The dynamics of the domestic mode of production must be analyzed both in terms of relations of production and relations of reproduction. Given the small size of the productive units, and given mortality, accidents, and sickness, the capacity to survive was dependent on the capacity to renew and recruit productive members. This was precisely the function of the broader reproductive system.

Extended families established alliances in order to assure reciprocity in the exchange of women between lineages. Women not only guaranteed the procreation of household labor by their fertility; their domestic activities also contributed significantly to the daily production and reproduction of the household's labor. The exchange of women was essential in order to maintain a relative equilibrium between the sexes, as well as between economically active and inactive fractions of the household. Polygyny was a frequent strategy of wealthier households to meet labor requirements (see O'Brien, Chapter 11, this volume).

Male elders in these societies in large measure asserted authority over the reproduction of the household by controlling matrimonial relations: the exchange of women and the determination of when and whom their sons and nephews should marry. This patriarchal gerontocracy not only determined the relations of production and reproduction of the human species but also controlled the use of household labor for agricultural, cattle, and crafts production, and the reproduction of labor power on a day-to-day basis.

Demographic behavior generated high fertility, in the face of high mortality, in order to supply sufficient labor power and to permit the reproduction of the next generation. Marital migration, primarily virilocal, permitted the exchange of women between families and lineages.

Clientage and Slavery

But the reproduction of labor is not only realized through strategies endogenous to the household. Just as individuals enter and leave populations through immigration and emigration, so may they enter and leave the village or household labor force. In precapitalist African societies such mobility manifested itself in various ways, the most prominent being clientage and slavery.

Relationships of clientage have taken several forms in Africa (Miers and Kopytoff, 1977: Introduction). The first might be called "pawning," whereby an individual (or her or his relatives) asked to be taken into a group in payment of a debt. In principle this relationship was a temporary one that would come to an end after a specified period of labor or the payment of the debt by the person's family. In fact, "pawns" often were integrated as subordinate members of their patron's families, or larger social groups.

Second, blood-partnership relations also reproduced labor outside of marriage and procreative reproduction. Symbolized by the ritual exchange of blood and reinforced by supernatural sanctions, such ties bound individuals and, very often, the two larger units of which they were a part. These bonds sometimes created reciprocal sets of obligations, in warfare, trade and work. In other cases, blood-partnerships were made between victor and vanquished at the conclusion of hostilities (Cordell, 1979).

A final example of clientage that transformed labor from one African society to another is the tie established between "first settlers," who held rights over the use of land, and later arrivals who sought access to it. In order to gain access to productive land, later arrivals often had to accept a subordinate position. Such relationships were most common where land was limited (Horton, 1972-1974).

Slavery was an additional way in which precapitalist African societies reproduced labor (see Chapter 3, Klein). To be sure, slavery took many forms and was but part of a larger category of dependent relations extending to marriage. While individuals and groups exercised some choice in establishing their client relationship with a patron, slaves and captives were the victims of political and military aggression. Violence, frequently perpetuated by organized states, subjugated less powerful states, groups, and social classes.

Slave raiding was a central feature of the political economy of many pre-twentieth-century African states. Yet slave raiding for long-distance trade was a mechanism that also reproduced labor for social formations outside of Africa (see Manning, Chapter 2, in this volume). Slaves were an important commodity in the trans-Saharan trade for a thousand years (Austen, 1979). The Atlantic slave trade greatly intensified and reoriented this demand for African labor (Curtin, 1969).

For African societies themselves, slave raiding also contributed to the internal transfer of labor through forced migration. Not all captured slaves were exchanged. Those that were retained—women as well as men—contributed directly to the labor force of the capturing society, and were integrated as agricultural laborers, herders, craftspeople, domestic servants, and soldiers (Robertson and Klein, 1983). Important, too, was the integration of female slaves as concubines and wives, providing labor and producing future labor through procreation. It is not surprising that the terms *domestic slavery, household slavery,* and *lineage slavery* have been used to describe African captivity (Rey, 1975), for captivity was a way of merging a slave strategy of labor production and reproduction with the household strategy.

Capitalist Strategies for
the Production and Reproduction of Labor

Abolition of the slave trade and slavery (Meirs, Kopytoff, and Roberts, in press) was the result of both conflicts *internal* to Africa and the *external* expansion of European powers. The imposition of capitalist social relations posed new problems for the reproduction of labor. The most important challenge for colonial capitalism was the recruitment of wage labor (Arrighi, 1973). Where labor was organized, produced and reproduced according to the logic of precapitalist social relations there was no need to sell labor to capitalist enterprises. At the risk of oversimplifying, we can identify two stages in the strategies of capitalist labor recruitment. The first was based on forced mobility; the second, which grew out of the first, was the creation of a reserve army.

Forced Mobility (see Gregory and Piché, 1981). Following the very early expeditions of exploration that successfully recruited limited voluntary labor from African societies for short periods, colonialism was obliged to force Africans into selling part of their labor. As many chapters in this book dramatically illustrate, the role of the colonial administration was crucial: Without force, Africans would have undoubtedly resisted wage employment with greater success. Three specific strategies turned African populations into effective instruments of labor. The first strategy was the institution of a per capita head tax. Payment of this tax was eventually required in European currencies, and tax rates were rapidly escalated. Since, by definition, wage employment did not exist in the noncapitalist sphere, households were forced to send migrants to seek employment in the places where European capital hired unskilled labor (see chapters 7, 8, 9, 10, 14 and 15). A second way in which labor was extracted from the noncapitalist sphere was through the "blood tax" of military conscription (Echenberg, 1975, and Chapter 6, in this volume). Those recruits not needed as soldiers were frequently used as laborers for public and even private needs. A third strategy was the explicit use of forced labor. The obligation of village chiefs to provide young laborers for the construction and maintenance of colonial buildings, ports, railroads and roads dates from the beginning of the colonial period (Cordell and Gregory, 1982; many essays in this volume). These forms of forced mobility produced the significant secondary effect of "flight" (Asiwaju 1976; Echenberg, Chapter 6, in this volume).

Reserve Army. Strategies of forced labor mobility opened the way for the creation of a reserve army readily available for wage employment without the necessity of institutionalized force. This reserve army was created through the progressive erosion of the autonomy of precapitalist societies and the imposition of a capitalist logic of development (Dupré, 1982). Institutionally induced mobility was no longer necessary, and was replaced by structurally induced mobility.

Colonial labor policies and the need for a cash income sapped precapitalist social formations of their viability (Amin, 1974a and b). This process took several forms: decrease in craft production due to the absence of part of the labor force during the off-season (Rey, 1975); loss of labor for the family production unit; development of a market for manufactured goods; development of commercial agriculture; and declining food production. Furthermore, the noncapitalist sphere became organically linked to, and dominated by, the logic of capitalist development. Selling labor for wages, in one form or another, became a necessity for rural households; yet household production remained vital. More and more African peasant families had to combine household production, cash cropping and migrant income to survive. This type of capitalist development has been characterized by Meillassoux (1975b) and Rey (1976) as the assymetrical articulation of two modes of production, the dominant capitalist mode and the dominated domestic mode.

Thus a reserve army was created that contributed to the reproduction of labor for capitalism. Yet, this should not lead us to a simplistic conclusion. Forced mobility was a policy that reproduced cheap labor for capitalism. Attempts to resist forced labor and tax policies usually provoked violent repression. But what ever the *costs* to capital and the state, forced labor was necessary early in the colonial period; the later creation of a reserve army provided an alternative source of cheap labor. If capitalists and colonial administrators abandoned forced labor, it was because of the resistance and the struggles of Africans, a resistance that rendered repression costly.

While the specific forms of this reserve army varied, two historical periods may be distinguished (see Chapter 9, Cordell). In the first, given the need for cash income and the deterioration of agriculture, a growing portion of agricultural producers are marginalized on the edge of peasant production. But, given limited access to wage employment and low wages, this labor force circulates between capitalist and noncapitalist employment (Wolpe, 1972, 1979).

The second is marked by the creation of an urban floating surplus population. This appears with the progressive proletarianization of labor and the creation of an urban lumpen-proletariat (see Lututala, Chapter 10; Proctor, Chapter 16). Part of this labor force is composed of wage earners who are underemployed and unemployed (temporarily and permanently), including in-migrants. At the individual level, there is circulation among capitalist employment, unemployment, and noncapitalist activities. At the aggregate level, there is a relative surplus population readily available for wage employment,

HISTORICAL MATERIALIST DEMOGRAPHY AS A METHOD FOR THE STUDY OF CONTINUITY AND DISCONTINUITY: THE DEMOGRAPHIC REGIME

The four strategies for the production and reproduction of labor that we have described are not exclusive and are not restricted to particular historical situations.[1] Historical materialist demography leads us to specific questions about the social conditions for the addition and subtraction of labor for production and reproduction. In Africa these additions and subtractions are the combined result of domestic, slave, patron-client, and capitalist social relations.

Let us begin with *births*. Domestic relations of production and reproduction continue to condition human fertility in Africa, even if capitalist social relations are now dominant in most (all?) African social formations. Likewise, *nuptial* practices continue to be significantly influenced by the patriarchal gerontocracy, where the male elders of different families (or lineages) contract reciprocal marriage agreements for the younger generation. Births add to the future labor force in response to the dual pressure for procreation described earlier: provision of labor for the capitalist and the domestic spheres. At earlier moments in the histories of African societies, the materialist logic of procreation was determined by the labor needs of the domestic unit of production and reproduction. At the same time the biological offspring of slave populations (or of slave concubines) and of client populations were further procreative additions to the labor force (see Chapter 2, Manning; Chapter 3, Klein).

If we refer back to our earlier definition of demography, historical materialist demography raises several questions about African fertility and nuptiality. What is the role of the family, in both earlier and contemporary periods: not only in terms of its productive and reproductive capacity, but also as the locus for the sexual division of labor and for sex-role stereotyping, as essential parts of female specialization as procreative and reproductive agents? In addition to the stimulus generated by labor-intensive production, which groups of people define the high fertility (and low celibacy) norms; which groups and institutions enforce them? When fertility behavior and performance changes, as among the urban elite in contemporary Africa, what is behind the change? And what are the explanations for continued resistence by a larger fraction of Africans to fertility reduction?

Immigration is the second of the demographic parameters adding to the production and reproduction of the labor force. In contemporary Africa, migration is perhaps the most dynamic factor in the demographic regime. The circulation of labor from the domestic sphere to the capitalist sphere (and frequently, back again) is a fundamental element in the growth and contraction of the wage labor force, and in the industrial army of reserve (see in particular the chapters in parts 3 and 5 of this volume). At previous epochs in African history, migration also played a crucial productive and reproductive role, including the forced migration of slaves. But in the past, as well as at present, the most basic form of migration is marital mobility. Predominantly feminine, due to virilocal marriage among most African patriarchial societies, nuptial migration not only assures the possibility of exogenous procreative unions, but also provides the essential adult female labor for sex-specific tasks of production and reproduction.

Obviously, questions of power and inequality are crucial to an analysis of migration. In addition to the power of the patriarchal gerontocracy, there is the more recent power of capital in its efforts to free labor from precapitalist productive relations, and recapture it—most often through migration—for the capitalist sphere. To do this capital resorted to violence and force—using the army and the police—and manipulated racist ideologies. These tactics continue today, and profoundly shape the conflicts in South Africa (see Chapter 16, Proctor).

The dialectical dynamic of migration as part of the demographic regime is, of course, reflected in the fact that for every immigration flow there is a stream of *emigration* (see Manning, Chapter 2; Gregory and Mandala, Chapter 14, for very different examples). But the net effect of these additions and subtractions is rarely zero. Even in the case of reciprocal marriage alliances between families and lineages, the exchange of women may well be unequal, depending on the relative social position of the groups involved. In the case of dominated social groups (slaves, captives, clients, pawns), the net effect of marital exchange with dominant groups is undoubtedly negative. Africa, as a whole, obviously suffered substantial quantitative and qualitative losses to her labor force during the 1000 years of trans-Saharan and the 300 years of trans-Atlantic slave trade (see Manning). Likewise, despite the high rate of return migration to peasant agriculture from capitalist spheres of production (cities, mines, plantation agriculture) in the colonial and independence eras, the noncapitalist sphere is the net loser in this unequal exchange.

After births and immigration, as additions to the labor force, and after emigration as a subtraction from the labor force, we come to the fourth and final parameter in the demographic regime: *death*. For conventional demography, the biological component of death is predominant, and most demographic models are based on the regularity of changes (if they occur) in the age and sex structure of morbidity and mortality.

Historical materialism must go beyond the limits of these biologically based constraints to demographic analysis (see Becker, Diouf, and Mbodj, Chapter 5). Of fundamental importance in understanding the subtractions to the labor force that occur through mortality (and we would add morbidity) is the social context of health and illness (see Cordell, Gregory, and Piché, in press). In contemporary Africa, inequality in terms of access to good health is flagrant. So-called modern health services, good and adequate food, clean water, safe and comfortable housing, and a host of other factors in the social environment, are not equally accessible. The poor and the unemployed, and frequently the rural population, are exposed to greater risks of ill-health and death. In earlier epochs, the potential risks were also unequally distributed (see chapters 9 by Cordell, and 12 and 13 by Turshen and Dawson). Perhaps most dramatic was high mortality among populations subjected to slavery; death was frequent during raids, transport, and enslavement. Death was also frequent during colonially induced famines (see Chapters 7, Gervais, and 13, Dawson). It would also be pertinent for the oral historian to analyse the attitudes and practices of Africans concerning the health of women and children (see Turshen, Chapter 12), of the physically and mentally handicapped, the injured, and the aged.

These four parameters constitute the *demographic regime,* defined dynamically as interrelated strategies for the reproduction of labor. They are part of a unified process. Demographic strategies are devised at the household level and embedded in intrahousehold power structures; they are the result of conflictual as well as cooperative relationships between men and women, old and young (see Chapter 14, Gregory and Mandala). They are also class-specific in the sense that the concrete conditions in which they take place are determined by the positions of households within the production process (see O'Brien, Chapter 11). In brief, the demographic regime of a society is the sum of dialectical class-specific demographic strategies developed within contradictory as well as cooperative sex and age specific domestic units.

We have outlined how the demographic paradigm can be transformed by the methods of historical and feminist materialism. We need to develop this theoretical framework, and to suggest additional questions about specific moments in African history. We also need additional empirical studies, conceived and executed from an historical perspective of feminist and materialist demography. Finally, we need to invent new methods (see the conclusion of Chapter 5). Marx and Engels, and our contemporary materialist and feminist colleagues, have given us a few guidelines. Both for African studies and for demography it is time to create the rest.

NOTE

1. For the time being, we argue that a "mode of production" is an abstract model, the varieties of which are characterized by only one type of social relations of production and reproduction (e.g., slave, feudal, capitalist, see Gregory and Piché, 1985; Cordell, 1985b). In concrete historical situations a "social formation" is characterized by different types of social relations articulated in a dynamic and sometimes contradictory fashion. Thus, in contemporary Africa, one could identify peripheral capitalist social formations, where capitalist social relations are *determinant* but not necessarily *predominant* quantitatively; domestic (or familial or household) social relations persist in larger spheres of production and reproduction.

PART I

PRELUDE TO COLONIALISM: SEQUELS OF SLAVERY

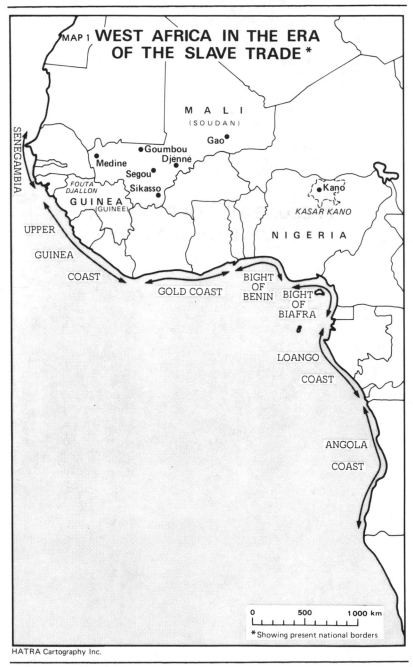

MAP 1 **WEST AFRICA IN THE ERA OF THE SLAVE TRADE ***

M A L I
(SOUDAN)

SENEGAMBIA

Gao

• Goumbou
Djénné
• Medine
Ségou •
FOUTA DJALLON
Sikasso
G U I N E A
(GUINEE)

• Kano
KASAR KANO

UPPER

N I G E R I A

GUINEA

COAST

GOLD COAST

BIGHT OF BENIN

BIGHT OF BIAFRA

LOANGO

COAST

ANGOLA

COAST

0   500   1 000 km

*Showing present national borders

HATRA Cartography Inc.

Map 1   West Africa in the Era of the Slave Trade

2

LOCAL VERSUS REGIONAL IMPACT OF SLAVE EXPORTS ON AFRICA

PATRICK MANNING

MATERIALIST ANALYSIS IN THE HISTORY OF AFRICAN SLAVERY

Years ago, Philip Curtin noted that the volume of slave exports from the African coast fluctuated sharply, presumably in response to changing local political conditions. Yet Curtin is perhaps best known for his 1969 study of the aggregate volume of the Atlantic slave trade that shows—in contrast to the local fluctuations—a remarkably smooth overall pattern of expansion, peak (in the late eighteenth century), and contraction. Some time later, Kopytoff and Miers (1977) assembled a volume of studies of the institutions of African "slavery" (the quotes are theirs) aimed at showing the uniqueness and variability of unfree states; yet the editors were forced to title and to organize their volume in terms of an approach to slavery that treats it as one institution, albeit a most variable one. These dilemmas, posed implicitly by writers who do not label themselves historical materialists, highlight the potential benefits of a materialist approach to African slavery, in the sense that such an approach is aimed in part at resolving the apparent contradiction between the boundless variability of individual events and the evolution of broad historical patterns. It thus seems appropriate to begin with a comment on materialist contributions to the study of African slavery.

Although there are Marxian writers on African slavery, it is not possible to isolate a specifically materialist literature on the subject.

Author's Note: I wish to thank John Thõrnton, Victor Piché, and E. Ann McDougall for comments on an earlier version of this chapter and David Eltis for allowing me to see figures from his forthcoming book.

So much research on the subject has been restricted to establishing basic facts—the need to establish the structure of African slavery seems logically to precede the ability to discern the contradictions within them—that a great deal is shared among authors following and opposing historical materialism.

How will we know materialist analysis of African slavery when we see it? Presumably identification depends more on content than on the label attached by the author, so I propose four criteria for identifying a materialist approach: It is first of all comprehensive. By *comprehensive*, I mean geographical breadth, a multidisciplinary analysis of relations among the several spheres of human activity and analysis over a substantial period of time. It requires analyzing slavery as an institution interacting with other institutions. Second, materalist analysis focuses on the study of *contradictions* within the system, however defined, and on the changes brought about by those contradictions. Third, it gives great weight to the *material conditions* of life—hence the economics of slavery—but also requires a sensitive and nuanced analysis of the interaction among material, social, and ideological conditions. Fourth, a materialist approach is *critical*—not necessarily in the sense of being negative but in the dual sense of expressing moral judgment on willful perpetrators of social oppression, and, more important, of giving close attention to those factors that produce social change, whether for good or for ill. A materialist approach focuses on discontinuity, contradiction, and interaction rather than on continuity, harmony, and social inertia. One need not be a materialist to focus on breadth of analysis, on contradictions, on the passage of time, and on a critical approach, but it is only the materialist framework that in principle calls for all of these ingredients.

Two great projects are linked in the materialist analysis of African slavery: the elucidation of contradiction and change in slavery itself and the linking of slavery to capitalist development. But the overall picture in each of these areas is still too dim to allow a full-scale materialist interpretation. Such a comprehensive picture will require linking the rise and fall in the volume of slave trade, the changing economic role of slavery in the New World, changing prices and values of slaves, the demographic impact of slavery in Africa, and changing institutions of African slavery. Nor does this overall picture arise naturally out of the assembly of smaller studies. For instance, the analysis of social contradictions entailed in African slavery has been based on data from the nineteenth century, but the conditions of slavery in the eighteenth century were quite different. Forty years ago,

Williams (1944) criticized capitalism from the vantage point of West Indian slavery, but the argument has yet to be generalized to account fully for the African role in the rise of capitalism.

At this stage of the enterprise, very little of the work on African slavery can be called materialist if one insists that it meet more than one of these criteria; on the other hand, much or perhaps most of the recent work on African slavery could be called materialist if meeting one of the four criteria is sufficient.

Another method for identifying materialist contributions to studies of slavery is to identify alternative approaches. Two fairly standard alternatives may be posed. The first may be labeled *neoclassical.* It is most easily discussed in terms of general equilibrium economics: It focuses on a self-regulating market and, while it recognizes the intense conflict between buyer and seller, it emphasizes the harmonious resolution of their differences. Bean's work (1975; Thomas and Bean, 1974) is representative of this outlook. The second alternative may be labeled *institutionalist.* It is most easily discussed in terms of social anthropology: It focuses on the uniqueness of social institutions and on the power of social structures to transform economic relations. The transhistorical synthesis of Patterson (1983) fits into this category, as docs the more specific analysis of Kopytoff (1979). And yet the work of such major contributors to the literature as Eltis (1977), Curtin (1969, 1975), and Miller (1975) is not easily lumped into any of these three categories.

Perhaps the key contribution of a materialist outlook, at present, is its critical approach. Many contributors to the literature on African slavery still manifest a remarkable tendency to minimize the damage inflicted on Africa by the slave trade, and to allow for African consequences of slave trade only in the moral and ideological spheres. This, in a world which still undervalues the morality and the thought of Africans, can lead to a dangerous underestimation of the impact of the world economic system on African life. Surely all agree on the remarkable ability of African societies to resist, survive, and adapt in the face of the pressures of slave trade—the Livingstonian image of African society being laid waste by slave trade is now abandoned in most cases (but see Inikori, 1982, and Mahadi and Inikori in this volume). Yet the emphasis writers give to the emerging factual picture is crucial. Ony may choose to minimize the impact of slavery on Africa—thus emphasizing the continent's isolation—or to explore the limits of the impact, thereby emphasizing the links between Africa and the wider world.

REGIONAL LEVELS OF DEMOGRAPHIC DRAIN:
A SIMULATION APPROACH

Analysis of the demographic impact of the slave trade may occur on three levels. The continental level, the whole of the African continent or some large portion of it, is useful for intercontinental comparisons and the assessment of broad trends in the Atlantic economy. The regional level, focusing on the comparison of regions such as Angola, the Bight of Benin, and Senegambia, is appropriate for distinguishing slave-trade regions from each other (see Map 1). But as these regions are still larger than most modern African nations, there remains ample scope for local analysis, aimed at discerning the great variety of local experience. This section estimates the regional demographic impact; the next goes on to consider implications at the local level.

A number of authors have assessed the regional and local demographic impact of slave exports, including Anstey (1975: 79-82) for Angola, Loango, and the Bight of Biafra; Patterson (1978: 80) for Gabon; Northrup (1978: 81-82) for the Bight of Biafra; Manning (1982: 32-34) for the Bight of Benin; and Thornton (1981) for each of the regions from Senegambia to Angola. Some of these are analyses of regions in isolation (e.g., Patterson and Manning); others are related to an assessment of the continental impact of slavery. Thus the analyses of Anstey and Northrup are linked to the assumptions of Fage (1969), who concluded that slave exports halted but did not reverse population growth in West Africa.

Similarly, my approach derives from my simulation modeling of the continental impact of slave exports (see Manning, 1985; Manning and Griffiths, 1985, for a description of the technique and a justification of the levels of parameters). This simulation projects, for each ratio of annual slave exports to estimated regional population, an African population structure and growth rate. Results on the continental level suggest that the population of the Western Coast of Africa (that area from which the Atlantic slave trade claimed its victims) declined by 10 to 30 percent between 1760 and 1850. The task here is to tailor that continental analysis to the regional level.

The numbers of slave exports by region from 1700 to 1850 are now known within tolerable confidence limits; they are summarized conveniently by Lovejoy (1982) and Eltis (forthcoming). But since the simulation analysis requires a ratio of the flow of slave exports to the stock of African regional population, it is necessary to project populations of the African slave-trade regions over time. We begin by con-

structing high and low estimates of the 1850 population for Gold
Coast, Bight of Biafra, and the other countries. These were calculated
by accepting official estimates for the populations in 1930 and projecting them back according to growth rates based on known African and
European rates of the time: (1) at an annual growth rate of 0.5 percent
to get a high estimate of the 1850 population, and (2) at an annual
growth rate of 1.0 percent to get a low estimate of the 1850
population.

For each region, and beginning with both high and low estimates of
the 1850 population, the procedure was to work backward in time by
comparing each decennial rate of slave exports with the estimated
population at the end of the decade, and to draw from that ratio the
consequences for the regional growth rate and population structure:
growth rate and sex ratio were calculated as functions of the export
ratio. For ease of calculation, these projected consequences assumed,
for each region, export slave proportions of 37 percent female and 20
percent children (the global average), a regional birth rate of 42 per
1000, and a regional death rate of 37 per 1000 (figures drawn from
eighteenth-century Angolan data, Thornton, 1980), yielding an intrinsic growth rate of 5 per 1000, and a life expectancy at birth of 27.5
years. The high and low estimates were then calculated for the beginning of the decade, using the estimated growth rate; the procedure was
then repeated for the previous decade, using the level of slave exports
for that decade, and so on.

Figures 2.1 through 2.7 show the results of these calculations.
Before discussing them, I should note that they could be revised in
several ways. The projected consequences of any given ratio of slave
exports to regional population could be adjusted for the composition
of the slave export population appropriate to that region, rather than
the overall average. In the case of Angola, for instance, where the proportion of adult female exports was relatively low, this would make
the consequences of a given level of slave exports appear less severe
than the results shown. A similar result might appear for the Bight of
Biafra if the assumed level of mortality upon enslavement were reduced because kipnapping—the region's leading mode of
enslavement—involved less carnage than war. And we will *always* be
able to argue about the geographic scope and population size of the
region from which slaves were drawn.

Figures 2.1 through 2.7 show, for each region, the level of Atlantic
slave exports by decade (solid line) and the high and low estimates of
regional population as influenced by slave exports (dotted lines). The
graphs have two interesting properties, one artificial and one intrinsic.

First, they have been scaled so that, when the line representing slave exports lies below the lines representing population, the regional population continues to grow, albeit often at a reduced rate. When the line representing slave exports lies above the lines representing population, however, the drain is sufficient to cause regional population to decline. The second property is inherent in the logic of retrojecting populations exporting known numbers of slaves: The high and low estimates of regional population get relatively and absolutely closer to each other as one goes back in time. This is because a given number of slave exports might cause a small population to decline but allow a large population to grow: The two estimates of population are necessarily closer together at the earlier time than at the later time.[1] This logical property of population projections is such as to warrant some hope that African population levels in past centuries may one day be known with a certain confidence. With that, we turn to a region-by-region discussion of the results.

For Senegambia, estimates are based on the assumption that the regional population was that within the confines of modern Senegal and Gambia. On that assumption, the region experienced modest population decline for five decades during the eighteenth century and two decades during the nineteenth century. On the other hand, the slave-exporting region could reasonably be interpreted to include the area of modern Mali, which would roughly double the regional population. At the same time, Senegambia thus redefined was the only region exporting significant numbers of slaves both to the Atlantic and across the Sahara. Austen (1979) estimated Moroccan slave imports (which came almost entirely from this region) at 2500 per year in the eighteenth century and 3300 in the nineteenth century, or somewhat more than the volume of Atlantic slave exports. This serves to reinforce the impression that Senegambia, while not seriously depopulated, did not experience population growth in the eighteenth and early nineteenth centuries. A further point, suggested for a later period by the analysis of Klein (chapter 3 in this volume) is that slaves may have moved among Senegambia and neighboring regions in significant numbers.

I have followed Lovejoy (1982) in suppressing the Windward Coast region of Curtin's analysis by including Liberia, Sierra Leone, Guinea, and Guinea-Bissau in the Upper Guinea coast, and by joining Ivory Coast to the Gold Coast. Slave exports from the Upper Guinea coast, thus defined, were sufficient to reduce regional population in the 1760s and 1770s and from the 1810s to the 1830s, and to halt growth in the three intervening decades.

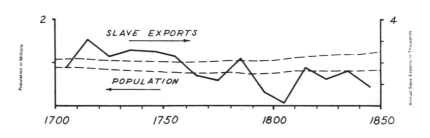

Figure 2.1   Senegambia

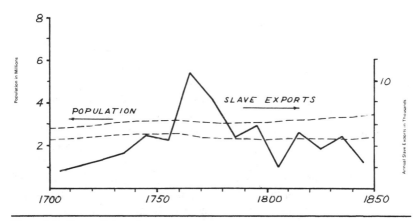

Figure 2.2   Upper Guinea Coast

For Gold Coast, the decades following the rise of Asante included enough slave exports to bring about a decline of from 8 percent to 18 percent in regional population; the late-eighteenth-century peak in slave exports brought further decline. The virtual halt of slave exports in the nineteenth century permitted population to grow again.

For the Bight of Benin, population declined almost without interruption from 1700 to 1850. This is the most serious long-term population drain projected for any African region. It shows a more serious decline in the Bight of Benin population than that projected in Manning (1982: 340-343) for three reasons: The impact of a given ratio of slave exports to regional population is assumed to be more serious than before, now that simulation results can replace guesswork; the

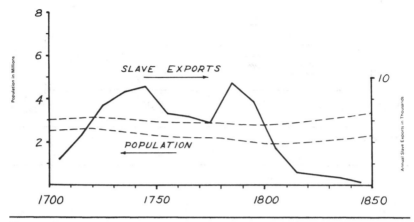

Figure 2.3 Gold Coast

volume of nineteenth-century slave exports is now assumed to have been higher; and the Hausa are now left out of the population from which exported slaves are assumed to have been drawn.

For the last four decades of the eighteenth century, slave exports from the Bight of Biafra were sufficient to cause population decline; slave exports prevented population growth during several additional decades.

Most analyses of the volume of the Atlantic slave trade treat West Central Africa—including the coast from Gabon in the north to Benguela in the south—as one great slave trade region. Reasons for this have included the ambiguity of ships' logs reporting voyages to the area, the tendency of slaves from one hinterland area—Kongo—to be delivered both north to Loango and south to Luanda, and the cultural and linguistic similarity of slaves drawn from the region. Significant exceptions to this tendency are found in the more regionally specific work of Birmingham (1966), Miller (1975), Martin (1972), and Eltis (1977). Because West Central Africa is so large an area for the regional analysis undertaken here, I have drawn on the work of these scholars to distinguish two regions: the Loango coast and Angola. I have accepted Miller's estimates for exports from Angola, and subtracted them from Lovejoy's totals (1982: 485, 490) for West Central Africa to derive estimates for Loango for the years up to 1810; I have relied on Eltis (forthcoming) for later years.

Since the slave-export estimates for Loango are calculated as a residual, they surely exaggerate the erratic movements of regional

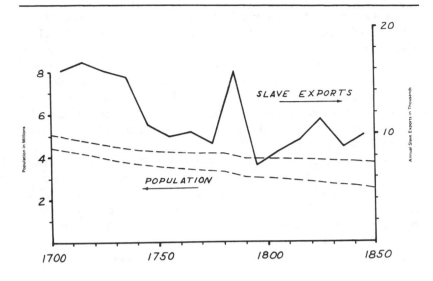

Figure 2.4 Bight of Benin

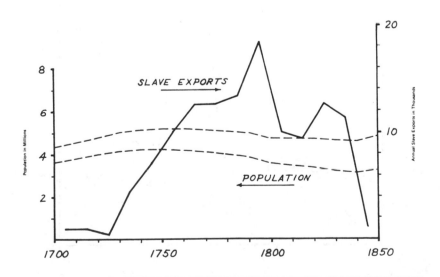

Figure 2.5 Bight of Biafra

totals. Comparing these figures with Martin's qualitative description (1972: 78-92), one is not surprised to see a peak in exports in the 1780s and 1790s, but one is not prepared for such a high level of exports, and one expects a still higher level in the 1760s and 1770s. But even if the slave-export totals were adjusted to conform to Martin's description, the demographic conclusions would be similar: population growth in the early eighteenth century, stagnation in the middle part of the century, very sharp decline at the end of the century, and continued decline until 1850.

The portrayal of Angolan population (Figure 2.7) suggests steady increase in the volume of slave exports, which halted population growth in the mideighteenth century and overcame it from the 1790s through the 1840s. The results indicate a population, which, devastated in midnineteenth century, did not return to its eighteenth-century level until the turn of the twentieth century.

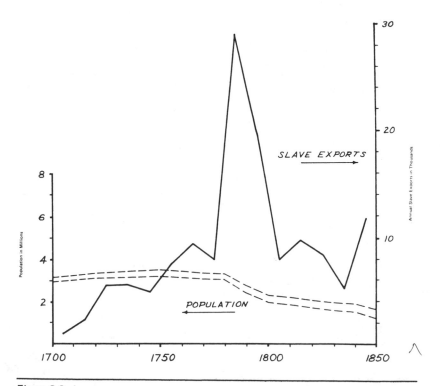

Figure 2.6 Loango

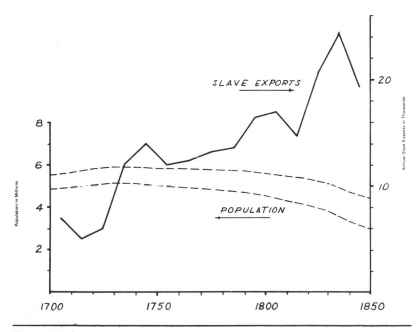

Figure 2.7   Angola

These results are summarized in Table 2.1, which displays the incidence of projected population decline by region and by decade including, in the final column, Western Africa as a whole (the sum of all regions). The table shows that the negative demographic impact of slave exports was most general in the era from 1760 to 1840, and that it was more regionally specific in earlier and later times.

LOCAL VERSUS REGIONAL IMPACT OF SLAVE EXPORTS

The simulation model, in addition to projecting growth rates of African regional population, projects the ratio of males to females in that population. For those numerous cases where slave exports were just sufficient to halt population growth, the ratio of adult men to women was roughly 0.85: 15 percent fewer men than women. For cases where enough slaves were exported to bring about substantial population decline, as in the Bight of Benin for most of the period from 1700 to 1850, and in the Bight of Biafra in the late eighteenth century, the number of adult men exceeded women by 20 to 25 per-

TABLE 2.1
Decades in Which Population Declines Are Projected
for African Regions

Decade	Senegambia	Upper Guinea	Gold Coast	Bight Benin	Bight Biafra	Loango	Angola	West Afri
1700s				X				
1710s				X				
1720s	X			X				
1730s			X	X				
1740s			X	X			X	
1750s			X	X		X		
1760s		X	X	X	X	X		XX
1770s		X		X	X	X	X	XX
1780s			X	X	X	X	X	XX
1790s			X		X	X	X	XX
1800s			X	X	X	X	X	XX
1810s	X	X		X		X	X	XX
1820s				X	X	X	X	XX
1830s	X	X		X	X	X	X	XX
1840s				X		X	X	XX

cent. In the most extreme projection, Loango in the 1780s, the number of adult men would have been roughly half the number of women. (As a rule of thumb, the proportionate surplus of women over men—0.33 for Loango and 0.14 for the Bight of Benin—may be taken as a lower bound to the proportion of slaves in each regional population.)

Just as the population drain from slave exports was uneven within each of the African regions, so also was the variation in the sex ratio. As I have argued elsewhere, males and females were captured in roughly equal numbers, so that the sex ratio remained relatively even among heavily raided peoples; those areas that collected slaves rather than lose them served to concentrate female slaves (Manning, 1985). Thus the Bight of Benin might have been divided into two equal segments, one with an even sex ratio and one with a ratio of 67 (67 males per 100 females), with an overall sex ratio of 80. This sort of reasoning gives additional confirmation to the census of Angola for the years 1777 and 1778 reported by Thornton, in which the sex ratio was roughly 50: this could correspond either to the very extreme conditions of the Loango region as a whole for the brief period of the 1780s, or it could correspond to the conditions for the slave-collecting half of a larger region for which the sex ratio was 67, as in Angola for a number of decades.

For Gold Coast and the Bights of Benin and Biafra, one may offer assertions as to the local foci of depopulation and surpluses of women. Gold Coast had exported few slaves until the late seventeenth century, when the volume of slave exports rose along with the rise of Akwamu. The rise of Asante after 1710 is associated, on one hand, with a centralization of power in the Akan area, the replacement of Akwamu and Denkyera with Asante power, and the end to fratricidal war in the Akan heartland; and, on the other hand, with a rise in the level of slave exports to a quantity sufficient to reduce regional population during the mid-eighteenth century. Udry, in unpublished work in progress, argues that many of the slaves exported at this time came from the Guang-speaking areas on the northern frontier of Asante. The slaves known as Coromantee, Akan slaves who led the Jamaican revolts of midcentury, were therefore drawn from this area.

Population decline was far more serious in the Bight of Benin, and began three decades before Danhomè made its conquest to the coast between 1724 and 1727. While Danhomè and Asante were in some senses analogous, Danhomè was forced to accept Oyo as its overlord in the 1730s and remained within reach of hostile neighbors until the midnineteenth century. A survey of New World slave populations originating in the Bight of Benin shows that the coastal Aja peoples provided virtually all slaves exported from the region from the late seventeenth to the mid-eighteenth century (Manning, 1982: 30). This result is consistent with the political narrative of the region summarized, for instance, by Akinjogbin (1967). Perhaps the population of Danhomè grew while that of its neighbors declined; but since Danhomè was involved in many wars and did not win them all, it is equally likely that the kingdom itself suffered population decline.

In the nineteenth century, Yoruba became the dominant group among the region's slave exports, in large part because of the wars associated with the collapse of Oyo. Population of the Yoruba-speaking areas of the Bight of Benin declined in the nineteenth century, though the depopulation was less severe than that for the Aja-speaking areas in the eighteenth century.

The timing of the rise of the Aro clan and its oracle to prominence in slave exports remains unsettled. Northrup has argued that those Igbo slaves whose origins can be traced came from all over Igbo country, which would imply that the late-eighteenth-century decline in population was shared by all regions. On the other hand, the earlier importance of Ibibio slave exports, along with the fact that Aro and other Igbo clans moved into areas previously occupied by Ibibio, might be taken as evidence that the eighteenth-century trade led to substantial Ibibio population decline (Northrup, 1978).

The projection of severe decline in the populations of the Loango and Angola regions in the late eighteenth and nineteenth centuries echoes Vansina's impression (1966; 180-207). Available descriptions indicate that few slaves came from the immediate hinterland of the Loango coast. One major source was the Kongo heartland, south of the river; the other was the middle reaches of the Congo River, where the Bobangi acted as the main intermediaries and transporters (Harms, 1981). The late-eighteenth-century population decline may be somewhat exaggerated, to the degree that slaves were drawn from the area of modern Angola, the population of which I have placed in the Angola region. But on the assumption that the combined levels of export for Loango and Angola are correct, the decline in population must have been in one segment or the other.

In Angola, for which the hinterland is taken to include all of modern Angola as well as Shaba, the results show a population large enough to withstand depopulation until the export of slaves grew to its level of 1750. This gives support to an interpretation of the demographic history of Angola that Miller (1983) has termed the "ring of fire." That is, slave exports in the sixteenth and seventeenth century may have been sufficient to cause decline in the population of the relatively restricted areas—Kongo, Imbangala, the Kwanza Valley—from which they were drawn, but cannot have caused decline in the population of the region as a whole; this view might be elaborated to include both an interior area where slave trade had not yet reached and a coastal area where population had stabilized. In this context, Miller's argument that drought and epidemics were the major factors limiting the size of population may be accepted. But for the end of the eighteenth century and for much of the nineteenth century, the fire seems to have extended its influence to the whole region, and its population declined.

SOCIOLOGICAL THEORY AND DEMOGRAPHIC HISTORY

The overall impression is one of great physical mobility in Western Africa, a large proportion of the population in dependent positions, unequal sex ratios, and decreasing total population for a century. Some of the analytical assertions made by scholars working on African slavery receive new meaning in this context. Thus, Harms's (1983a) presentation of the Bobangi view of social life as a zero-sum game appears as an optimistic outlook in the context of a declining regional population. Lovejoy's (1983) interpretation of ethnic groups as flexible occupational groups rather than as inherited destiny might be expanded to account for the many slaves who made involuntary changes in ethnic (and occupational) category. W. MacGaffey (1983) has defined the lineage mode of production as a conceptualization of a basically bilateral kinship system influenced by slave trade; he might have emphasized that the social system was influenced by particularly intensive slave trade which resulted in a severe shortage of men. Meillassoux's (1983a) reluctance to admit to the existence of a slave mode of production in Africa—in the sense of an organic relation of exploitation linking the free peasant sector to the sector of aristocrats and their slaves—might be justified by the reasoning that the demographic turmoil of the continent prevented the coalescence of a coherent social order. The debate about the relative importance of production and reproduction to the value of female slaves will take new turns once it becomes clear where population was declining and where it was growing (Robertson and Klein, 1983).

The resolution of these and other questions on African slavery can only be achieved through closer attention to the continental and Atlantic contours of the phenomenon. In particular, the great variations in the price of slaves—crudely, a sharp increase at the beginning of the eighteenth century and a decline in the nineteenth century—are of crucial importance. For instance, it may be that differences in time and in the price of slaves may help to resolve the Terray-Dumett controversy over the use of slaves in Akan gold mining (Terray, 1975; Dumett, 1979). Even at this early stage of analysis, however, the history of African slavery provides some general lessons for the analysis of African demographic and economic history. First, migration was of fundamental demographic importance. Hence the demands of the problem exceed the limits of analytical techniques based on closed populations and the conventional theory of demographic transition (see Chapter 1 of this volume). Second, the history of African slavery provides a reminder that there exists no clear precontact baseline in African demographic or economic history. One way to evoke the succession of African transitions and intercontinental links is to note the temporal coincidences of the eighteenth-century African slave trade with the European peak of mercantile capital; of nineteenth-century expansion of African slavery with the European rise of industrial capital; and of twentieth-century African labor systems with the world dominance of finance capital.

NOTE

1. For two populations P and R at time $t = 2$, the ratio of which is $P/R = a$, and the growth rates of which are each reduced through equal annual numbers of emigrants $E(t)$, it can be shown in general that the ratio of the two populations in an earlier time $t = 1$ will be less than a.

3

THE DEMOGRAPHY OF SLAVERY IN WESTERN SOUDAN
The Late Nineteenth Century

MARTIN A. KLEIN

Moses Finley (1968) has written that there have been only five slave societies: ancient Greece and Rome, Brazil, the West Indies, and the United States. For Finley, such a society is one in which slavery has displaced other forms of dependent labor, and thus, presumably, is the major source of production. Keith Hopkins (1978: 99) takes a look at the demography of these societies and notes that they tended to run from 30 to 40 percent slave.[1] Neither lists any African society as a slave society, though some African societies were as much as two-thirds servile and fit without any doubt the definitions given by Hopkins and Finley.[2]

This chapter will examine the demography of the Western Soudan (see Map 1), where slave societies, or, as I prefer to call them, slave modes of production, existed. The chapter will focus on two former French colonies, the Soudan (briefly known as Haut-Sénégal-Niger and now Mali) and Guinea. It will, first, seek to demonstrate the magnitude of slavery in the region. Second, it will argue that slavery became central to the operation of such societies, and that such numbers could exist only where slavery had replaced other forms of labor. Third, it will look at the problems of reproduction, which became crucial wherever slave labor became important.

HOW MANY SLAVES?

There are two major sources of information about slavery in French West Africa. The first was a study of slavery made in Soudan in 1894, when only a small part of the colony had been conquered. The second was a much larger study made across French West Africa in 1904. Both are preserved in Series K of the Senegalese national archives in Dakar (ANS). In addition, there are local studies and censuses. There are major problems in using colonial data. Administrators were ill-informed about the societies they ruled and lacked the personnel to do a really efficient job of data collection. Furthermore, slavery was a touchy question. Africans had good reason not to report fully their slave holdings for they feared the French reaction. Similarly, administrators were often nervous about potential unrest and as a group were very hostile to any action against slavery. Many administrators in both 1894 and 1904 refused to estimate the slave population; others simply "eyeballed" it.

Nevertheless, these are the data we have. Furthermore, there are some patterns and ways of checking some of them. One problem is simply taking the 1904 estimate and producing a global estimate. I have used the following method. First, where I have absolute numbers but no percentages, I use 1904 or 1905 population figures to produce a percentage. Second, where I have only percentages, I use the reverse process to estimate the number of slaves. Third, for those *cercles* (districts) where I have no figures, I have produced estimates by analogy to similar cercles and by analysis of their ethnic mix, political situation and geographic position. Table 3.1 sums up the results for Haut-Sénégal-Niger (earlier the French Soudan).

Some of the patterns here are striking. The figures for the desert and desert-side cercles are all high except Gao, which is suspiciously low. We would probably get similarly high figures from savannah states such as Ségou, which was listed at 54 percent in 1894, and from Sikasso; in both areas, however, the conquest had led to either the confiscation or freeing of large numbers of slaves. By contrast, in southern parts of the Soudan we find a belt of societies that were egalitarian and often acephalous stretching from upper Guinea almost to Nigeria. These societies were more densely populated than many of their northern neighbors and were regularly raided for slaves, but they were not major exploiters of slave labor. The major slave users in the area were largely intrusive groups of Juula or Fulbe.

Thus what we have for the Soudan is an estimate of about 700,000 slaves, making up about 18 percent of the total population. This is clearly too low. First, certain cercles are obviously underreported. Gao was inhabited largely by Tuareg and Songhai, both major slave-holding groups (Olivier de Sardan, 1973, and 1975). Medine was a commercial cercle, which was a center of the slave trade to lower

TABLE 3.1
Slave Population, Haut-Séngal-Niger

Cercles	Slaves	Estimated Slave Population	Total Population	Slave Percentage
Bafoulabe	15,000		59,805	26
Bamako		61,999	177,149	35
Bamba		13,604	34,012	40
Bandiagara	20,000		197,870	10
Bobo-Dioulasso		46,000	236,000	20
Bougouni	3,340		95,592	4
Diebougou	—	—	—	—
Djenne	15,981		69,635	23
Dori	41,500		88,475	47
Dounzou	8,000		51,415	16
Gao	8,000		46,011	17
Goumbou	24,000		66,947	36
Kayes	30,000		71,421	42
Kita	27,500		56,624	49
Koury		33,639	224,266	15
Koutiala	22,300		223,403	10
Lobi	8,000		188,900	4
Medine	650		4,931	13
Niafunke		23,838	59,597	40
Nioro	45,688		114,228	40
Ouagadougou		147,790	1,477,982	10
Raz el Ma	1,600		1,952	82
Satadougou	1,500		34,194	4
Segou	25,150		140,610	18
Sikasso	50,000		164,410	30
Sokolo	13,300		34,770	38
Timbuctou		13,579	22,232	60
Total	361,509	340,449	3,942,431	18

SOURCES: ANS, K 18 and 19; ANM, 5 D 51; census data, 1905-1913.

Senegal. Second, there clearly had been a lot of slave movement and liberation incidental to the conquest. The most massive emancipations were to come after 1905, but the French often freed slaves of hostile rulers, and slave flight was frequent even before the exodus that began in 1906.

Third and perhaps most important, a major check on this early data can be found in social surveys by modern scholars. Meillassoux (1975a: 222) did a survey in 1965 of the town of Goumbou. It did not cover the whole cercle, but for the town itself, it showed that 24 percent of the population was of slave descent. The slave exodus from Goumbou after 1906 was very large. The 24 percent figure is therefore quite high and casts doubt on the 36 percent for the earlier period. The most striking data, however, are from the Fulbe of the inner delta of the Niger. While among other ethnic groups, the French stopped counting slaves by 1908, the agricultural slaves or *rimaibe* of the Fulbe were seen as virtually a distinct ethnic group and were therefore regularly counted. In 1952, Charpentier did a *mémoire* on the sub-division of Djenné that suggested that Fulbe areas were as much as 70 to 80 percent rimaibé. A decade later, Jean Gallais (1967) reported 42,592 rimaibé out of a Fulbe-speaking population of 85,502. That figures out to 49 percent of the Fulbe-speakers. Only a few years later, a government demographic survey of the area controlled by the Office du Niger reported the rimaibé as 53.6 percent of the 111,575 Fulbe-speakers in the area. The rimaibé had not fled the delta in massive numbers, but they were certainly more likely to leave than the Fulbe and their mortality rate is even today marginally higher (Hill, Randall, and Sullivan, 1982). This confirms that at an earlier date, the rimaibé obviously accounted for a substantial majority of the population.

For the adjacent colony of Guinea (Table 3.2), the 1904 reports are more complete, and the estimate of the slave population is higher. Less reasoning by analogy is necessary. The result is a global estimate of almost 35 percent. However, some districts are inexplicably low. We can understand low figures for the forest zone of the northeast (Beyla and Kissidougou), but not for cercles such as Río Nuñez on the coast and Ditinn in the Futa Jallon. My skepticism is reinforced by a letter written less than a year later by Noirot, the chief admin-istrator of Guinea (ANS 22 G 19). Noirot's figures showed slaves slightly under 27 percent of the total population, largely because he operated with a higher total population; unfortunately, he does not present all of his figures. More importantly, he is skeptical of his data. For the Malinke cercles of the upper Niger, he suggests raising the figure by 5 percent. For the Futa Jallon and the Soussou cercles of the coast, he argues that slaves were at least as numerous as the free.

Noirot's estimates were confirmed by the work of two later scholars. In 1940, Vieillard estimated the free-slave ratio at about 2 to 1 in the lower Futa and about even in the central Futa cercles. A few years later, Richard-Molard (1951: 85-93, 104) estimated the descen-dants of slaves at about 40 percent of the total population, but he ad-mitted that his method may have undercounted. He had done two sur-veys, which produced figures of 36 percent for Labe and 29 percent for the outlying area of Koubya. His method, however, was simply to use as the freed slave population the population of the *rounds,* or slave villages. However, a small but probably significant group of

TABLE 3.2
Slave Population, Guinea

Cercles	Slaves	Estimated Slave Population	Total Population	Slave Percentage
Beyla	25,000		70,124	35.7
Boussourah	800		7,380	10.8
Dinguiraye	10,900		30,074	36.2
Ditinn	15,000		135,954	11.0
Dubreka		38,315	76,630	50.0
Faranah	3,600		39,092	9.2
Friguiabe	34,000		68,000	50.0
Kade	13,000		20,000	65.0
Kankan	10,000		57,000	17.5
Kissidougou		1,989	39,786	5.0
Koin		28,373	56,746	50.0
Kouroussa	31,700		34,430	92.1
Labe	60,000		187,315	32.0
Medina Kouta	13,100		26,133	50.1
Mellacoree	25,000		75,000	33.3
Ouassou	4,300		13,000	33.1
Rio Nunez	5,680		51,767	11.0
Rio Pongo	75,000		115,000	65.2
Siguiri	12,000		45,856	26.2
Timbis	20,000		117,546	17.0
Timbo	30,000		84,189	35.6
Touba	8,000		17,620	45.4
Yambering	24,920		49,839	50.0
Total	422,000	68,677	1,418,481	34.6

SOURCES: ANS K 20; ANS 22 G 18, "Tableau Recapitulatif du Recensement," 1904.

slaves lived in the Fulbe settlements—wives, concubines, and trusted retainers. Furthermore, quite a large group fled the Futa during the first decades of the century. Undoubtedly, the figure for the Futa Jallon at the moment of conquest was as Noirot suggested, over 50 percent.

Slave flight means that the percentage of freed slaves in any district is lower than the percentage of slaves before the French conquest. We cannot come up with precise figures for any period. We can, however, suggest that for the Soudan, slaves made up between a quarter and a third of the total population, and that a large part of the colony was marked by slave percentages of at least 40 and sometimes over 50 percent. For Guinea, the slaves probably made up between a third and a half of the population.

THE CONCEPT OF SLAVE SOCIETY

The question is what all of this means. What is the importance of the fact that 40 or 50 percent of a society is servile? When Finley and Hopkins talk of the rarity of slave societies, they are underlining a basic distinction in the roles that slavery fulfills in different societies. Slavery exists in a wide range of human societies. Finley (1968) distinguishes between slave and slave-owning societies. In the latter, slavery existed, but had not displaced other forms of dependant labor. In these societies, it became a way for the wealthy and powerful to get desired services, but these services were not central to the functioning of the society. Where other ways of recruiting labor were more efficient, the development of slavery was limited. Prisoners of war could be put to work in mines or on public works where they suffered high mortality, or slaves could, as in China, be a major source of concubines and servants, but in neither case is the reproduction of the slave population a central concern to the society. Martin Wilbur has written that he chose to study slavery in China hoping to better understand the condition of the lower classes, but realized with time that he was learning more about the ruling group (Wilbur, 1943: 243; Mendelsohn, 1949). This obviously changed at the point where a large mass of slaves became the major source of labor. The society then found itself with two new problems: first, controlling that mass, and, second, reproducing it.

The existence of slavery made possible the evolution of a slave mode of production in those areas where labor was scarce or where for political reasons it was difficult to extract surpluses from free people. In ancient Greece, it was Solon's prohibition of debt slavery that created a labor shortage (Finley, 1980). In Brazil and the West Indies, land was freely available, but could be exploited only if labor could be imported. In Africa, land was available and therefore, had little value. As Africa began to supply slaves for other areas, its marketing networks expanded and so too did the use of slaves within Africa (Lovejoy, 1983). With the decline of the slave trade in the nineteenth century and the increase in various commodity trades, slaves were increasingly directed to work within Africa.

The process was economic. In slave-using societies, most slaves were purchased. The purchase was not necessarily for productive purposes. A rich man might want the services of a concubine, a servant, or an artisan. What is important is that the system had to be productive enough for him to afford such luxuries, and the system in such societies increasingly depended on slave labor. Pollet and Winter

(1971) argue that the Soninke slave generally earned the cost of his purchase in less than three years. What marks the slave society is that slavery is no longer a marginal institution. Slave labor produces almost all the surplus, which supports the elite, facilitates elaboration of the state, and is exchanged for needed imports. What was important about slave modes of production was that slave labor was the basis of production, and if slaves did not make most of what was produced, they created most of the surplus needed for trade and for the feeding of the elite. Furthermore, in the slave mode of production there was a sharp distinction between those who worked and those who did not. In societies with low slave populations, masters often worked alongside their slaves (Klein and Lovejoy, 1979: 195). In those with high populations, they supervised.

Slave societies do not exist in isolation. They are often expanding, although their growth is frequently constrained by the difficulty of acquiring labor. Furthermore, this hunger for labor is fed by two other practices. First, slave societies manumit a significant number of slaves or in some way absorb them into the free population. This is probably a crucial variable in motivating slaves to work within the system. It also tends to isolate the newly enslaved, always more likely to resist or rebel. Second, slaves rarely reproduce themselves. There are significant exceptions, such as the United States, where growth of slave population was considerable (Curtin, 1969). Nevertheless, low fertility rates were the norm, the labor supply tended to shrink, and slave owners were driven by a hunger for labor. Slave societies generally did not produce their own slaves and thus relied on more warlike societies to provide them (Meillassoux, 1978). The growth of slave-based production thus encouraged other societies to specialize in producing slaves. Like the capitalist mode of production, the slave mode thus created its unique form of dependency.

SLAVE REPRODUCTION

One of the central problems for any slave society was persuading slaves to consent to their own exploitation (Lovejoy, 1981). Two practices were often crucial. The first was manumission, previously mentioned. The second was the ability of slaves or their offspring to improve their status. In Africa, there was usually a distinction between first-generation slaves, those taken or bought during their own lifetimes, and those "born in the house." The key difference was that first-generation slaves could be sold, but there were also significant differences in the way they were treated. Those born in the house had more autonomy and often lived separately. They were more likely to receive positions of trust. Many Sudanic peoples have different terms for the second group: *woroso* or *woloso* among Mande-speakers, *rimaibé* among the Fulbe, *harratin* among the Moors, and *bella* or *buzu* among the Tuareg. Some writers do not see those born in the house as slaves. The *harratin* and *bella* are often defined as freed slaves and, in fact, they have greater autonomy than the *woloso* because they are more likely to be left alone large parts of the year. Derman (1973) and Richard-Molard (1951) call the rimaibé serfs. For Meillassoux (1983c), there are two crucial variables. First-generation slaves were reproduced through capture and purchase and generally came from outside the society. Equally important, they could be sold, while those born in the house could not. He, therefore, sees only the former as slaves. I prefer to see the two as part of a larger whole both because the second emerged from the former and because they served the same function. Both provided labor, though on somewhat different terms. I also see both groups as powerless, though slave collectivities could on occasion assert themselves against masters (Patterson 1983).

It is crucial in understanding slave reproduction that many slaves were not being reproduced, the newly enslaved because they ran away, trusted slaves because they were manumitted. This does not, however, fully describe the problem of reproduction; it seems more important that the remaining slaves rarely reproduced themselves. The data in Table 3.3 are somewhat ambiguous, perhaps because they are least reliable on the question of children. Children are never defined, though they probably included all those not yet sexually mature. If we discount those *cercles* with inexplicable data, children account for between 29 and 40 percent of the total slave population. This is not high, particularly given that the final years of the slave trade within Africa focused on children. If these statistics are correct, children represent only 83 percent of the number of adult women. Equally striking is a census from Beledugu that indicated that 37 percent of the free population was made up of children, but only 23 percent of the slaves. Furthermore, data from other parts of Africa suggest that low slave fertility was common (Meillassoux, 1983b, 1983c).

The birthrate was low even though about 60 percent of the adult slaves at the turn of the century were women. Furthermore, the distribution was such that almost all females of reproductive age were attached to males—a few of the pretty ones as concubines and the rest as

TABLE 3.3

Numbers of Men, Women and Children: Select Cercles
in Senegal, Guinea, and Haut-Sénégal-Niger

Cercles	Male		Female		Children		Total
	N	%	N	%	N	%	
Bafoulabe	4,825	32	6,540	44	3,455	23	15,000
Bandiagara	2,356	36	3,161	48	1,108	17	6,625
Bougouni	1,700	51	1,640	49			3,340
Buriya	2,000	25	2,500	31	3,500	44	8,000
Dinguiraye	3,114	29	4,388	40	3,415	31	10,917
Djenne	3,961	25	7,981	50	4,039	25	15,981
Dori	15,300	38	24,565	62			39,865
Dounzou	3,000	38	3,800	48	1,200	15	8,000
Kade	5,000	38	6,000	46	2,000	15	13,000
Kaedi	10,000	28	8,000	22	18,000	50	36,000
Kolen	1,250	25	1,750	35	2,000	40	5,000
Kouroussa	3,600	33	4,200	38	3,200	29	11,000
Koutiala	4,050	42	4,020	41	1,630	17	9,700
Lobi	2,000	25	4,000	50	2,000	25	8,000
Louga	2,696	30	3,629	41	2,615	29	8,940
Maasi	1,200	24	1,800	36	2,000	40	5,000
Matam	3,831	19	6,161	31	10,008	50	20,000
Medina Kuta	5,389	41	5,437	42	2,276	17	13,102
Medine	125	19	400	62	125	19	650
Podor	6,234	33	10,166	55	2,209	12	18,609
Raz el Ma	440	28	500	31	600	38	1,600
Satadougou	545	36	380	25	575	38	1,500
Segou	9,172	36	8,805	35	7,184	29	25,150
Siguiri	4,097	34	3,480	27	4,410	37	11,987
Sokolo	6,152	46	4,002	30	3,198	24	13,300
Sumpi	2,036	34	2,031	34	1,918	32	5,985
Tenkogo	2,000	13	4,000	27	9,000	60	15,000
Timbi-Medina	1,300	17	4,000	53	2,200	29	7,500
Timbi-Tunni	1,500	22	4,000	58	1,400	20	6,900
Tivouane	2,951	25	4,236	36	4,447	38	11,634
Touba	2,400	30	2,720	34	2,880	36	8,000
Yatenga	2,573	37	2,436	35	1,994	38	7,003

SOURCE: ANS, K 18 to 20.

the spouses of warrior or agricultural slaves. We do not know how
they avoided having large families, whether it was contraception,
abortion, infanticide, or simply sexual abstinence.

In order to understand this point better, we must examine the position of the female slave. In Africa, female slaves have almost always
been preferred to males, and have generally attracted higher prices
(Robertson and Klein, 1983). It has been assumed that this difference

in price was explained by the value of women as reproducers, but in a recent article, Meillassoux (1983c) argued that the major reason was that women could be more fully exploited as workers because they performed a wider range of tasks. In a response, I accepted the thrust of Meillassoux's argument but insisted that it was an incomplete explanation. The key fact seemed to be that once allowed to farm for themselves, male slaves usually owed their masters twice as much grain as female slaves. Clearly, men could produce more grain, or at least, that is what the slave masters believed. Several other factors clearly had to be considered. First, women were more easily integrated and less likely to resist or escape, particularly once they had children. Second, they were useful both in integrating and rewarding men. In a female-surplus society, extra women could be used in many ways. The more attractive became concubines. Captive women were also the most important booty offered to slave soldiers. Given the contempt the warriors had for labor, it was probably their wives that fed them. Male slaves were generally also given wives, and it was not impossible for a hard-working male slave to accumulate enough money to pay the rather low brideprice for a second wife. Last, though reproduction has been exaggerated as an explanation of higher prices paid for women, it was probably not irrelevant. Here we must examine the conditions of reproduction within the slave ménage (Klein 1983a, 1983b).

Slaves did not marry. They did, however, form long-term regular unions. They just did not have the rights in each other and in their progeny that married people normally had. They sometimes lived in the master's compound, but more likely, those who had long been part of the community or were born into it, lived apart, often in their own villages. Those who lived separately frequently worked their own plots of land in exchange for a fixed obligation. That fixed obligation varied from society to society, but for a man was generally close to what was needed to feed an adult male for a year; for a female it was half of that (Meillassoux, 1975a: 249-250; Pollet and Winter, 1971: 239). That left little room for maneuver. Given the conditions of hoe agriculture, the best that a hard-working male could produce was about enough grain for three adults. That assumed good health and usually good rains. This meant that the slave menage could not afford many nonproductive hands. The young, the old, and the sick threatened survival.

Normally, family members have mutual obligations. Parents assume that older children are going to work alongside them and when they get old, are going to take care of them. In Soudanic slavery, the children belonged to the mother's owner. They were left with the mother until their adult teeth came in, at which time the master had the right to claim them. Thus the slave menage bore the cost of reproduction. It fed the child while he or she was not productive but could count neither on the child's labor once old enough to work nor on support in old age. Masters had successfully passed the cost of reproduction to the slaves, but in doing so, limited any incentive the slaves may have had to procreate. It was more rational for a slave menage either to buy a slave of its own or to invest in a second and younger wife (Roberts, 1981: 186).

When emancipation came, the slave family asserted itself. Slaves frequently migrated in family units. Masters often used force to try to keep control of children (Klein and Roberts, 1981). Conversely, freed slaves often spent years trying to find and get back their children. The slave family had no legal identity, but it had a de facto existence. The problem from the slave's point of view was that he or she could count on nothing.[3] There were norms that protected the slaves. They were supposed to be fed when they worked on the master's lands and they were supposed to be helped in times of disaster, but several of the more perceptive reports in 1904 make clear that this protection was not guaranteed. The slaves had no sanctions to bring to bear against the master, no impartial court to which they could appeal.

CONCLUSION

A society in which one-third to one-half of the population is enslaved clearly has sharp class distinctions. It is a society in which a small part of the population lives off the labor of others. The reports on West African slavery show a sharp distinction between societies with only 10 percent or less of the population in slavery and those with over a third. In the former, slavery was incidental to the operation of the society. People bought slaves, but masters worked alongside them. These societies are marked by progressive integration. These are the societies described by most of the authors in Miers and Kopytoff (1977). For the other societies, there were two pervasive concerns. One was control over the mass of slaves. The second was reproduction, which in effect meant access to more slaves. The process was a circular one. Where there was a large mass of slaves, it probably meant both that integration into the larger society had been slowed and that the society was acquiring more slaves. The more slaves there were, the more important they were. Slaves were, within the slave mode of production, the major capital investment, the major form of wealth, and the basis of both elite privilege and state power.

NOTES

1. The only example Hopkins gives of the Caribbean is Cuba, which was 30 percent slave in 1861. The British sugar islands, however, were more heavily servile, the ratio of slave to free rising to about 7 to 1 on Jamaica in 1713 (Dunn, 1972: 312). This, however, was unusual. On the mainland, only South Carolina had a black majority (Wood, 1974).

2. The highest percentages tended to be around juula cities, near the centers of various slave-using states, and near the desert-side trading towns. (See ANS, K 18, Kankan; K 19, Sikasso and Bobo-Dioulasso; K 21, Kong; see also Meillassoux, 1975a.)

3. This point was made by two of the more insightful administrators in 1904. See the report on Bamako, ANS K 19 and Mellacoree, ANS K18.

4

POPULATION AND CAPITALIST DEVELOPMENT IN PRECOLONIAL WEST AFRICA
Kasar Kano in the Nineteenth Century

ABDULLAHI MAHADI
J. E. INIKORI

Population expansion, by raising the ratio of cultivators to land and by forcing people into previously unsettled or sparsely settled regions, stimulates the division of labor and the growth of trade, and intensifies class differentiation and institutional change in the direction of capitalist relations of production (Inikori, 1984). To a large extent this was what happened in Western Europe during the Middle Ages (Hopkins, 1973: 77). However, left to itself, population growth would reach a point where efforts to maintain an equilibrium between population and resources would limit further growth and inhibit capitalist transformation. There should be in existence an external commodity trade of a significant magnitude (Inikori, 1984: 7). In this regard, two similar historical cases readily come to mind: England in the sixteenth century and *Kasar* Kano, located in present-day northern Nigeria, in the nineteenth. Whereas England realized full capitalist transformation largely because of the existence of external commodity trade of a significant magnitude, *Kasar* Kano was not able to attain full transformation primarily because of a limited market for external trade, occasioned mainly by underpopulation in the entire West African region.

This chapter examines in some detail the effects of population growth in precapitalist *Kasar* Kano, where demographic expansion was sustained from the seventeenth to the nineteenth century (see Map 1). The essay argues that where population growth was maintained over a long period in agricultural regions of precapitalist West Africa where there was surplus land, the effects were parallel to those in other major regions of the world during similar periods. Demonstration of this fact should enable historians to appreciate the adverse consequence of underpopulation in vast areas of West Africa between 1600 and 1870. We argue that this underpopulation severely limited the opportunity for *Kasar* Kano to trade with its African neighbors, near and far. Because of this limited trade, the process of capitalist transformation propelled by sustained population growth could not be completed before the British conquest.

UNDERPOPULATION IN WEST AFRICA

The population of precolonial West Africa was small in relation to its size (Hopkins, 1973: 15; Mason, 1969; Hammam, 1983: 19). Population distribution in West Africa in the nineteenth century is brought to light by the reports of Europeans who traveled extensively in the region throughout the century (among others, Bovill, 1964: vol. 1; Clapperton, 1966; Barth, 1965). These reports were based on eyewitness and conscious observations and covered all of West Africa. Descriptions included patterns of settlements and population distribution. And it is clear that a substantial part of the region was either uninhabited or only sparsely populated (Clapperton, 1966: 17-102, passim; Monteil, 1895: 310-313).

Three major explanations have been suggested for underpopulation in precolonial West Africa. Some writers have tended to see the problem largely in terms of geographical factors, ranging from climatic problems such as droughts in the Savanna and Sahel to those of light or poor soils (Mason, 1969: 562; Lovejoy, 1983: 69-70; Hopkins, 1973: 13, 15). Epidemics in the form of smallpox, malaria, meningitis, and other plagues have also been identified as major causes of depopulation (Hopkins, 1973: 17). The third major reason for underpopulation in precolonial West Africa is historical.

These three sets of reasons are important, but not equally so. It is true that people died by the thousands during prolonged droughts (Lovejoy, 1983: 70). Droughts also had long-term effects on population growth, because it took years for food and livestock production to recover. The extended dry spells associated with ecological problems have profoundly affected the growth and density of the population. The role played by drought in fostering epidemics by lowering the resistance of the population was considerable. But the low level of population growth and density cannot be attributed solely to bio-geographical factors.

Historical factors seem to stand out clearly as a major explanation for the low level of population in West Africa. The most relevant historical factor was slave-raiding and the slave trade. Of the several dimensions of the impact of the trade on the size of the population of West Africa, only the physical removal of people to North Africa, the Middle East, India, and the Americas has been given adequate attention. Even here, only the numbers of slaves who actually left Africa have been cited. Successive scholars have shown that much remains to be done to arrive at satisfactory figures for the number of people lost to West Africa in the era of the slave trade. As research has proceeded, figures have been revised upward, an indication that existing estimates of the volume of the trade, particularly the trans-Atlantic trade, must be considered conservative (Inikori, 1984: 34). Similarly, the figures quoted for slaves carried to North Africa should also be regarded as minima (Lovejoy, 1983: 21; Hopkins, 1973: 83). This should also apply to estimates of people killed in raiding and transit.

Equally important for a reconsideration are the cumulative effects of slave raiding and the slave trade on West Africa in the nineteenth century. The centuries-old preference for women, children, and eunuchs in the trans-Saharan trade must have had long-term effects (Lovejoy, 1983: 16). The predominance of young men in the Atlantic trade also removed a virile segment of the population. There were also psychological and related problems that impeded population growth. The trauma of recurrent slave raids, the accompanying scorched-earth tactics, and the inability of people to produce enough food as a result of insecurity limited population expansion. Hence the impact of slave raiding and slave trading on the population must not just be seen in terms of the number of people removed from the region. The side effects were also very important. But even regarding exports, it would be wrong to suggest that the number was too low to have affected economic activity in West Africa (Hopkins, 1973: 121). Certain parts of West Africa, notably some of the coastal states and *Kasar* Kano, which had relatively large and dense populations because they could protect themselves from large-scale losses and retain imported slaves, experienced economic expansion in the nineteenth century. The leading area was Kano, and it is relevant to emphasize that population was a major factor in this development.

POPULATION EXPANSION IN KASAR KANO

Evidence of high population density in *Kasar* Kano in the nineteenth century is copious. Reports of the European travelers (noted earlier) who passed through *Kasar* Kano are consistent on the population densities of the region.[1] Travelers also tried to estimate the population of *Birnin* Kano (Kano city, the capital of the emirate). According to these estimations, the population of the *Birnin* rose from about 30,000 to 40,000 inhabitants in the early 1820s to about 60,000 in the middle of the century. By the 1800s, the population was estimated at 60,000 to 80,000. And by the last decade of the century the number was put at about 100,000 (Mahadi, 1983: 1). The significance of these figures does not lie in their accuracy; they were largely impressionistic. But that travelers cared to make these estimates shows the strong impression that the population of *Kasar* Kano made. Even more significant, however, is the increase in population of the Birni shown by these figures; and the growth of the Birni population reflects the parallel demographic expansion of *Kasar* Kano generally.

Imam Imoru, a renowned Islamic scholar of the late nineteenth and early twentieth centuries, reported that Kano "is a highly populated land." He also emphasized the transformation of environment (Imoru, 1973: 44, 144). The size of the population of Kano in the nineteenth century is also reflected in British estimates and censuses in the early 1900s. Estimates of Northern Nigeria ranged from 20 million people in 1900 to 10 million in 1921 and gave Kano about 35 percent of the total (Meek, 1925: 170-173). It was officially acknowledged, however, that the 10 million figure for 1921 was too low: "Many people were no doubt omitted from the count [of 1921], either unintentionally, or deliberately with the view to the concealment (as they thought) of their taxable capacity" (Meek, 1925: 171). It may also be relevant to point out that colonial fiscal, agricultural, industrial, and commercial policies had undermined Kano's economy, leading a sizable number of people to move to mining centers, notably on the Jos Plateau, and areas of construction activity.

In spite of this, the population density in *Kasar* Kano remained the highest in northern Nigeria in the early twentieth century. While the average density for the whole of Northern Nigeria stood at about 39 persons per square mile, that of Kano Province, in spite of its being diluted by the relatively sparsely populated *Kasar* Katsina, had an average of 116.7 persons per square mile (Imoru, 1973: 144; Meek, 1925: 173).

Although Kano's population increased remarkably in the nineteenth century, it was not evenly distributed. The central region and areas around political and administrative centers had high concentrations. But a substantial part of other areas was relatively sparsely populated. These were important agricultural regions. This pattern of population distribution was important for specialization between agricultural and industrial producers. Demographic expansion had taken a long time, dating from the seventeenth and eighteenth centuries in particular. It was partly the result of efforts of the successive rulers to procure labor for agriculture and other forms of production. It also stemmed from immigration, especially in the period of economic expansion in the eighteenth century.

The early rulers of Kano appear to have had a clear-cut policy. They encouraged the large-scale importation of slaves from the Bauchi region, the Gongola, Benue and Niger valleys, Zazzau, and elsewhere. This policy was consistently pursued from the fourteenth to the nineteenth centuries. The numbers of people were large. In the second half of the fifteenth century, for example, an official is reported to have settled 21,000 captives in 21 settlements in about seven years, excluding those settled in *Birnin* Kano and elsewhere. In the first half of the seventeenth century, another state official vigorously pursued a similar policy. In order to enable the settled captives to multiply, equal proportions of male and female captives were settled in the slave villages and agricultural estates (Anonymous, 1928: 106-107, 110, 118).

The precise role played by such captives in the economy of Kano is not clear, but their contribution to agricultural production over the centuries stimulated population growth. Accompanying economic expansion made Kano a leading region of West Africa by 1700 (Mahadi, 1982: vol. 2, 444-741). More and more people moved into *Kasar* Kano from different parts of the Sudan and beyond, leading to the establishment of numerous settlements and increases in the urban population (Mahadi, 1982: vol. 2: 224-265). These developments stimulated still greater economic expansion, leading to further population growth in a cycle that attained its peak after 1850.

There were several reasons for the phenomenal population growth in the nineteenth century. First, the Jihad wars of the early nineteenth century and Rabeh's invasion of the Chad Basin toward the end of the century sparked large movements of people. The peaceful atmosphere in Kano inevitably attracted refugees from near and far (Mahadi, 1983: 2-49). Large-scale immigration was further enhanced by the economic opportunities for immigrants. Large-scale immigration of skilled Nupe into Kano during this period, for example, was caused in part by the civil war in the Nupe Emirate in the early part of the century; economic opportunities in Kano, especially in the textile industry, also attracted them (Clapperton, 1966: 95, 128; Bovill, 1964:

654). Employment opportunities also stimulated the institution of *cin rani,* the seasonal migration of large numbers of people from the countryside and other emirates into Kano during the dry season. Part of the "floating population" of *Birnin* Kano that Monteil (1895: 281-282) put at 2 million people annually may have consisted largely of these *yan cin rani* as well as *almajirai* (pupils) and *dalibai* (students) who tended to settle permanently in Kano. The tendency to settle was encouraged by the low cost of living, along with the difficult living conditions in some neighboring states such as Borno (Barth, 1965: vol. 1, 551-612; Monteil, 1895: 307-308).

Unlike other parts of West Africa, Kano not only succeeded in protecting its population from slave raiding and the slave trade, but also imported large numbers of captives to meet its labor requirements.[2] They were relocated mainly on the agricultural and industrial estates, although some were settled in towns and worked in household industries. Some who were sufficiently assimilated earned cash for their masters through wage labor. But whether on large agricultural establishments or in towns, the owners encouraged the integration of their slaves into the mainstream of Kano society. This was important not only for the economy but also for slave reproduction.

The factors discussed above favored the natural growth of the Kano population in the nineteenth century. Political stability, adequate security, ample employment opportunity, a low cost of living, and tantalizing economic opportunity encouraged people to settle and raise children. Increased sedentarization among the Fulani, the establishment of numerous *ribats* (fortresses) by the government, and the increased adherence to Islamic laws and principles promoted the practice of *purdah,* perhaps another important element in urbanization and population growth. The self-serving and prevailing interpretation of the Quran concerning the proper number of wives, as well as the encouragement given to produce as many children as possible, probably contributed to population increase. In addition to the low cost of living, the lack of sufficient markets for Kano products (which limited the opportunity for productive investment) tended to encourage many people to invest in marriages, which led to population growth.

By the second half of the nineteenth century the greater population density brought major structural and institutional changes, or the intensification of changes that had begun earlier. It should be pointed out at this stage, however, that population was not the only catalyst of change. Political changes, both in Kano and in the central Sudan, also paved the way for economic alterations. But there is no doubt that population was the most important single factor in economic and social developments of the period.

The remarkable growth of the nonagricultural population—the ruling class and their followers, those engaged in industrial production, and traders—in the nineteenth century increased demand for foodstuffs. There was also increasing demand for raw materials, notably cotton, indigo, and skins for the expanding industrial establishments. The members of the ruling class also needed extra income to maintain their expensive lifestyle. These changes brought an increased demand for land. In the central region land shortages provoked radical changes in the land tenure system by 1800. Practices that had hitherto shackled agricultural enterprises were simply violated by the ruling class. The jihads of the early nineteenth century made this process easier because they upset the status quo and produced an almost entirely new set of rulers who reordered political, economic, and social relations. Allocation of offices accompanied by allocation of land generated crises that took time to resolve (Mahadi, 1982: vol. 2: 387-394). The traders (*attajirai*) took advantage of the situation to assert control of large parcels of land and/or acquire new ones, usually at the expense of the peasantry.

By the middle of the century, a new pattern of ownership had emerged. Members of the ruling class, including the attajirai, came to own large tracts ranging in size from 350 to 1053 acres (Mahadi, 1982: vol. 1, 461). Leading attajirai, including Tuaregs, Arabs, and other North Africans appear to have owned even larger parcels. Some were so large that one "needed a horse to cover the length and breadth in a day" (Mahadi, 1982: vol. 1, 463). The need for a lot of land was partly due to the fact that mixed farming integrating large-scale livestock-raising became a dominant form of production. The amount of land required and the number of people involved in its acquisition—including many princesses, queen mothers, and other female officials—resulted in acute shortages, especially in the central Kano region and near other important urban centers. Many people also lost land, and those peasants who retained some plots found them uneconomical to work. Land increasingly acquired market value and private property became pronounced. Consequent to this development was the emergence of a landless class. The government adopted a number of measures to solve the land problem. Peasants were encouraged to move into sparsely inhabited parts of Kano. Incentives, such as tax relief and provision of free seeds by government, were introduced. Many people did indeed move. Others, however, refused, and those who were forcibly evicted often drifted back to their former lands.

Many who clung to their small parcels took part-time employment on the large agricultural estates as cultivators or as herders; others worked in the fast-expanding industrial sector. Still others entered into the service of merchants.

All these changes intensified changes in relations of production. More and more people offered their labor for wages both on a part-time and permanent basis. The increasing development of the division of labor and the growth of per capita income provided the necessary conditions for the expansion of industry as a specialized or semi-specialized sector, separate in some cases from agriculture. The expansion of the industrial sector provided more employment opportunities, thus encouraging population growth, which was important for the labor supply and the growth of the domestic market.

As the century advanced, the degree of specialization between and within economic sectors increased remarkably. Aided by climatic and biogeographical factors, outlying parts of Kano specialized in the production of various types of agricultural commodities. But the most remarkable degree of specialization took place within the industrial sector, particularly within the textile industry for which Kano became famous. There was, for instance, increasing specialization between the cotton and *tsamiya* (silkworm) textile industries. Within the cotton textile industry, there was considerable specialization between producers of goods for export and for local consumption, between cloth beaters and dyers. Larger scale enhanced product specialization, increasing the utilization of labor. In all sectors, economy of scale was becoming more the rule than the exception (Shea, 1974/1977: 55-61).

The people of Kano were keenly aware of the advantages of large-scale production. They also realized the significance of constant innovation. Modifications in the dyeing and beating stages of textile production were significant in determining final cost: a dyed and beaten cloth could cost twice as much as an undyed and unbeaten piece (Shea, 1974/1977). To lower the unit cost and therefore increase profit, producers constantly reorganized their operations to permit more efficient use of labor, improve training for workers, reduce capital expenditure, and eliminate unnecessary transport charges. To maximize profit, by-products of the various industrial establishments were effectively used in different forms in other sectors of the economy, including the building industry (Shea, 1974/1977).

Increase in demand for goods, and availability of relatively cheap labor and capital, made it possible to increase output, sometimes dramatically. The growth of demand for dyed textiles in the savanna, sahel, and central Saharan regions, for example, encouraged Kano producers to raise output through increased use of the *laso* pit instead of large clay pots. By the end of the nineteenth century, these dye-pits, each having a capacity of from 400 to 1,000 gallons of water, probably numbered over 50,000 (Shea, 1974/1977). The growth of this industry reflects attempts to take advantage of large-scale production to achieve lower unit cost. Through increased coordination and specialization, producers also attempted to lower unit costs by increasing total output. The export-oriented dyeing centers were large, often having more than 300 dye pits worked by 100 dyers. This reduced the rate of redundancy among dyers and made it possible to lend and rent dye pits. As in the textile industry, other sectors of the economy also underwent quantitative and qualitative changes on more or less similar scales, depending on the extent of product demand.

New practices made slave ownership more profitable. Slaves were numerous in Kano; estimates of ratios of slaves to free people range from 32 to 1 to 1 to 1. They either were assimilated into free households—so as to enable them to participate actively in all economic activities—or were given freedom to engage in economic activities like any free person. Much of the money they earned was handed over to their masters. Other institutions and policies evolved to extract as much money as possible from slaves. These included *murgu* and *fansar Kai* (self-redemption). Murgu involved taxing slaves who engaged in occupations of their choice. Such taxes, fixed according to the profitability of the occupation, could be paid daily, weekly, or monthly. Generally such taxes were high, especially in the case of those engaged in profitable occupations. Fansar kai involved payment of a substantial amount of money to purchase one's freedom. This took a long time. Even after a slave had purchased his or her freedom, exploitation continued because ex-owners represented their freed slaves. This practice sometimes extended to the next generation as well (Imoru, 1973: 230, 232). Hence slaves not only provided regular revenue to their owners, they also supplemented free wage labor. To raise adequate funds for either murgu or fansar kai, slaves had to sell their labor to all bidders, often cheaply (Robinson, 1980: 132).

THE LIMITS OF EXPANSION

Kano's major problems during this period were the lack of adequate export markets, and, to a lesser extent, limited supplies of raw materials. Attempts to find markets led to the transport of goods over long distances—to North and Central Africa, the Middle East and Europe—because West Africa could not absorb Kano's production.

The problem of market demand had internal and external dimensions. Within Kano, the prevailing social structure gave rise to an extremely uneven distribution of income, which limited the size and growth of the domestic market. The per capita income of the slave and nonslave rural population was very low. Had incomes risen markedly, the proportion spent on foodstuffs would have declined, while that spent on manufactures, such as textile goods, would have grown. But this did not occur, and the domestic market for industrial goods remained small. Wealthier people spent more on manufactures, but they were too few to induce producers to increase their output (Hopkins, 1973: 57-58).

Producers attempted to solve the problem by extending their trading network to distant regions. But underpopulation in vast areas of Africa (including West Africa) severely limited the development of markets and commodity production in regions that could have become major trading partners. The widespread low ratio of population to cultivable land in these areas, together with the historical processes that produced this demographic situation, created economies focused on subsistence production and characterized by an extremely limited division of labor. Consequently, Kano's external trade in Africa tended to concentrate on luxury goods intended to meet the needs of relatively high income groups because only they could afford the high prices. Because prevailing conditions prevented the development of a mass external market for Kano's manufactured goods in Africa, the multiplier effects of long-distance commerce were limited. West Africa was made up of several regional economies that were not closely linked. Although transport charges per ton per mile were no more expensive than in other parts of the world, they were higher per consumer.

The situation was further worsened by the security problems posed by slave raiders and traders. A remarkable part of West Africa's population, notably in the southern Chad basin, central Nigeria (especially the Bauchi mountains and Jos Plateau), and Adamawa highlands, was isolated from the rest of West Africa. Their inhabitants were condemned to cope with a very harsh environment that limited them to subsistence production. Such people could hardly be expected to consume Kano manufactured goods (Barth, 1965: vol. 1, 511). But even people living on the plains, whose fertile agricultural lands were suitable for the production of raw materials that could have been exchanged for Kano goods, suffered from widespread insecurity. In addition to the wars that left settlements in ruins, organized raiding and kidnapping greatly affected the level of production (Clapperton, 1966: 33, 61-62, 64; Monteil, 1895: 248). Nor were merchants safe. Traders, in spite of the security measures they took, were often attacked by highway robbers who usually sold their victims into slavery (Robinson, 1980: 130-131). This sometimes forced merchants to take indirect routes, thus not only raising transportation costs but also delaying the return. Such trips, indeed most long-distance journeys, were made only once a year, so that stocks accumulated in Kano. This tied down capital. Some of the goods produced in Kano, for example, had to be exported to North Africa or the northern parts of the Sahara and reexported back to the Western Sudan for disposal (Barth, 1965: vol. 1, 511). This must have inflated prices enormously.

Matters were not helped by the existence of numerous states/polities in West Africa, each with customs barriers. Traders had to pay tolls and taxes, which were sometimes very high in relation to the value of the goods. When a trader added the value of taxes to the goods for sale, prices increased substantially. High taxes, tribute, and other demands, such as labor, reduced income and purchasing power.

Equally important was the nature of society. The number of slaves or servile groups in the societies of West Africa was very large, to the extent that they formed a majority in many of the states of West Africa (see Klein, Chapter 3, in this volume). In the area of Futa Jallon, slaves constituted two-thirds of the total population; in the middle Niger valley, the population in the immediate vicinity of towns was 70 to 80 percent slave; two-thirds of the population of Oyo were slaves. The situation in the Central Sudan and the Chad basin was the same (Lovejoy, 1983: 114-115, 120, 184-185, 191-192, 195). This limited the development of mass markets for Kano products. From an economic point of view, the main disadvantage of slavery was not that it was inefficient, but that it limited market expansion by decreasing the purchasing power of the mass of the population (Hopkins, 1973: 25).

CONCLUSION

Population, both in terms of size and composition, was critical in preventing the growth of markets in precolonial West Africa. Low population densities encouraged extensive cultivation, favored dispersed settlement, and promoted local self-sufficiency. Kano was able to attain the level of development it did largely because of the relatively high concentration of population in the emirate and its neighbors. These emirates supplied Kano with a substantial part of its raw materials; they were also important markets for Kano's industrial goods.

Population was not solely responsible for all the significant economic developments that took place in Kano in the nineteenth century. Other factors at work were important, including the existence of skilled labor and favorable government policies. But these factors were related to the concentration of population in Kano. Large numbers of state officials executed government policies. They, and other members of the ruling class, in Kano and neighboring emirates constituted an important market for Kano textiles and leather goods. And this demand brought technological innovation in the dyeing, cloth-beating, tanning, and leather-working industries.

All these factors failed to generate the steam necessary to propel capitalist development. Had a more extensive and growing external market for industrial products existed with adequate external sources of relatively cheap raw materials, Kano's transformation would have been completed before 1900. The historical misfortune of Kano is that they did not exist, thus limiting the level of capitalist development. This, in turn, made the potential Lancashire of Africa vulnerable to colonial manipulation toward the end of the century.

NOTES

1. According to Monteil, for example, "All lands within more than one hundred kilometres around the town [of Kano], are under cultivation in order to be able to feed the immense fixed and floating population."

2. In the early part of the nineteenth century, many captives were taken in several parts of Kano by the jihadists. But it would appear that many or most of them were resettled on large agricultural estates within *Kasar* Kano (Bovill, 1964: 638-639).

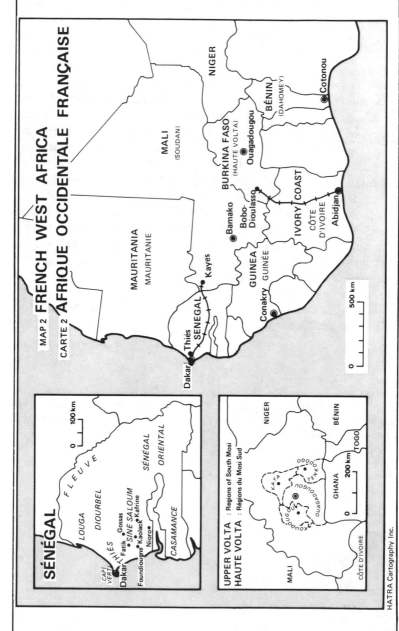

HATRA Cartography Inc.

Map 2 Senegal and the Sine-Saloum Region

PART II

**WEST AFRICA: THE DEMOGRAPHIC EFFECTS
OF FRENCH COLONIAL POLICIES**

5

L'EVOLUTION DEMOGRAPHIQUE REGIONALE DU SENEGAL ET DU BASSIN ARACHIDIER (SINE-SALOUM) AU VINGTIEME SIECLE, 1904-1976

CHARLES BECKER
MAMADOU DIOUF
MOHAMED MBODJ

Jusqu'à une époque très récente, une des principales lacunes de l'histoire de l'Afrique subsaharienne a été l'oubli des données relatives à la population, aux étapes de sa mise en place, et aux dynamiques qui ont assuré à cette vaste région sa configuration humaine actuelle. Symptomatiques sont les paragraphes succincts et très pauvres qui se trouvent dans la synthèse *Histoire générale de la population mondiale* (Reinhard et al., 1968), qui semble conclure implicitement à l'impossibilité d'une démographie historique africaine et à l'absence insurmontable des sources.

Certes, une exploitation des registres paroissiaux a été réalisée pour Palmarin, localité de la Petite-Côte, qui a apporté des résultats importants (Lacombe, 1970). Mais, cette enquête démographique rétrospective représente une tentative isolée avec les limites spatiales et temporelles.

De même, un travail important de collecte et d'exploitation des données relatives au Sénégal (voir carte 2) entre 1930 et 1965 a été mené par Metge (1966a et b), avec une analyse détaillée de la constitution du tissu urbain à partir du dernier quart du XIXe siècle jusqu'à l'année 1965. Il représente un point de départ nécessaire, qui complète considérablement la thèse de Verrière (1965) sur la population du Sénégal où figurent des renseignements historiques pour le XXe siècle.

A l'exception de ces travaux, et de quelques notes rapides, l'histoire de la population a été très peu explorée, surtout pour les périodes précédant le XXe siècle. Quand elle a été abordée, c'est à l'intérieur d'études où les problèmes de population ne sont évoqués que d'une manière incidente, comme dans la synthèse de Curtin (1975). La contribution la plus remarquable est celle d'un géographe, Pelissier (1966) qui introduit tous ses chapitres sur les civilisations agraires sénégalaises en décrivant les étapes de l'implantation des ensembles humains, à l'aide des données alors disponibles et des résultats d'enquêtes personnelles.

Si les lacunes les plus importantes se situent au niveau des populations rurales, on dispose de recensements assez détaillés pour les villes de Saint-Louis ou de Gorée dès le milieu du XVIIIe siècle. Ces documents ont été souvent utilisés, rarement cités, alors qu'ils mériteraient d'être dépouillés systématiquement. Cependant, on ne sait pas toujours les conditions dans lesquelles les données ont été collectées, ce qui rend leur utilisation très délicate. Mais, en général, les premiers recensements d'une région coïncident assez souvent avec la mise sous tutelle coloniale: c'est ainsi qu'en 1865, on a un recensement de la zone du Cap-Vert et en 1891, les premiers recensements sur l'intérieur, qui sont parfois très précis. En 1895 et 1904, il y aura des recensements sur tout le territoire colonial, correspondant à de nouvelles organisations administratives. Avec le XXe siècle, ils deviennent plus intéressants, plus détaillés, plus systématiques à l'échelle du pays. Leur régularité permet d'essayer de tracer l'évolution de la population sénégalaise, en particulier pour le Sine-Saloum.

L'EVOLUTION CONTRASTEE DES REGIONS SENEGALAISES

Au cours de la période coloniale, les "recensements" administratifs, réalisés surtout à des fins fiscales, ont été affinés progressivement, mais il ne semble pas qu' on ait pu éviter une réelle sousestimation des habitants. L'exploitation des documents administratifs, assez mal conservés, sous forme d'archives incomplètes ou de récapitulations générales, est possible, mais leur utilisation à des buts démographiques ne peut être réalisée que dans certains cas et sur certains sujets. Le plus fréquemment, les données se limitent à des chiffres globaux, répartis imparfaitement selon le sexe et l'âge, les appartenances religieuses, plus rarement selon le statut social (libres, nobles, captifs) et le niveau d'instruction. Alors que des recensements plus précis sont effectués sur la population européenne, les comptages de la population sénégalaise sont faits avec un soin très inégal. Ainsi a-t-on des années ou les autorités ont insisté sur les opérations d'inscription sur les rôles (1904, 1931, 1942), et aussi des moments où l'on surveille tel ou tel mouvement de population (par exemple les migrations saisonnières, ou les migrations en général).

Cependant, ce n'est qu'à la fin de l'époque coloniale que la place des données démographiques sera reconnue, avec la réorganisation des services statistiques qui effectuent une série de recensements urbains dont celui de Dakar en 1955, ceux de Diourbel, Ziguinchor en 1951, de Thiès, Saint-Louis en 1954. De même, est menée une enquête régionale sur la Moyenne-Vallée du Sénégal en 1957 (Enquête Misoes), ainsi que des études moins strictement démographiques lors de la préparation du premier plan de développement entre 1958 et 1960.

Mais la véritable première enquête démographique sera effectuée en 1960-1961: sondage au 1/20 en zone urbaine, et fraction sondée variable selon la strate rurale. Les résultats sont publiés en grande partie par Verrière (1965) et utilisés par Metge (1966a et b). A partir de l'indépendance, diverses études régionales seront entreprises, surtout dans le Sine-Saloum (enquête à passages annuels, à partir de la fin 1962, par l'Orstom), mais aussi dans l'arrondissement de Khombolé et à Pikine. En 1970-1971, une nouvelle enquête nationale par sondage concerne un échantillon de 150.000 personnes, réparti en 2 strates, sur tout le pays, 3 passages successifs étant faits à 6 mois d' intervalle; cette enquête n'a été que partiellement dépouillée, mais a permis de mieux apprécier la sous-estimation antérieure. Ce n'est qu'en avril 1976 qu'a lieu le premier recensement général de la population, dont les résultats manifestent un accroissement très important de la population; il semble que la croissance très rapide enregistrée s'explique en grande partie par une sous-estimation des effectifs lors des enquêtes précédentes, mais aussi par un taux d'accroissement beaucoup plus fort que celui qui était appliqué pour les projections démographiques.

On doit remarquer qu'à partir de 1970, les chiffres retenus par les comptages administratifs (Ministères de l'Intérieur, et du Plan et Aménagement du Territoire) tendent à se rapprocher de ceux obtenus lors des opérations proprement démographiques (recensement, estimations). Ainsi, le total de la population de droit au 1er Janvier 1984 était estimé à 6.306.759 par le Bureau National du Recensement (BNR) et à 6.471.261 par l'Intérieur. Il est sûr que les comptages administratifs ont été améliorés, mais le renversement observé—avec une supériorité des chiffres obtenus par comptage administratif sur ceux obtenus avec les techniques démographiques—est étonnant et demanderait une critique approfondie des méthodes de collecte des données.

Le rapide survol des données rassemblées permet de constater à peu près un quintuplement de la population sénégalaise (coefficient 4,74) entre 1904 et 1976. La superficie n'ayant pas changé (196.722 km², on retrouve la même multiplication pour la densité moyenne qui passe de 5,4 h/km² à 25,8 h/km². A l'intérieur de ces données, on peut déjà noter que la population africaine a été multipliée par 4,6 entre 1904 et 1976, la population non-africaine par 40, mais surtout que la population rurale a été multipliée par 2, 5, tandis que la population urbaine l'était par 17.

Cependant, il faut tout de suite remarquer des nuances régionales importantes. En effet, à l'intérieur du cadre d'ensemble retracé ci-dessus, avec ses principales étapes, on constate des différences accusées selon les subdivisions du Sénégal. Ces variations peuvent être analysées au niveau des circonscriptions actuelles, telles les régions et les départements. Ainsi, on observe plusieurs faits à la lecture du tableau 5.1, qui donne pour tous les départements et régions, les chiffres de population de 1904, 1958 et 1976, ainsi que les taux d'accroissement. (Pour la Casamance et le Cap-Vert les chiffres de 1904 et 1958 sont inexistants ou inadéquats pour une comparaison entre les départements.)

(1) Une répartition assez équilibrée dans les régions, avec le Sénégal Oriental moins peuplé et le Cap-Vert encore peu occupé, au début du siècle. A ce moment, les régions de Thiès, du Fleuve, et de Louga étaient les régions les plus peuplées (19, 17, et 16 pourcent de la population du Sénégal) et renfermaient plus de la moitié de celle-ci.

(2) En 1958, à la fin de l'époque coloniale, les proportions sont très différentes, et soulignent la grande mobilité durant le demi-siècle écoulé. Le Sine-Saloum est devenu la première région (22 pourcent de la population) avant la Casamance (18 pourcent), et Thiès (14 pourcent). Les parts du Fleuve et de Louga ont beaucoup diminué (12 et 9 pourcent), celle de Diourbel un peu moins, mais le Cap-Vert atteint déjà près de 11 pourcent.

(3) Au recensement de 1976, la croissance du Cap-Vert est le fait marquant (18 pourcent de la population) mais le Sine-Saloum qui ne compte plus que 20 pourcent du total reste plus peuplé. Le déclin relatif du Fleuve (10 pourcent), de Louga (9 pourcent), de Thiès (14 pourcent), mais aussi de la Casamance et du Sénégal Oriental est à mettre en relation avec le développement du Cap-Vert où se concentrent les activitiés économiques et les personnes.

(4) Cette évolution est confirmée dans une large mesure par les estimations de la Direction de la Statistique et les chiffres du Ministère de l'Intérieur

TABLEAU 5.1

Population des Departements et des Régions: 1904-1976

Département	Région	Population Totale			Accroissement Annuel (%)		
		1904	1958	1976	1904-1958	1958-1976	1904-1976
Dagana		58000	79000	203000	0,58	5,70	1,76
Poder		71000	84000	139000	0,31	2,98	0,94
Matam		68000	104000	169000	0,80	2,90	1,27
	Fleuve	197000	267000	511000	0,58	3,90	1,33
Louga		71000	76000	170000	0,13	4,86	1,20
Kébemer		75000	77000	154000	0,05	4,10	1,00
Linguère		30000	45000	95000	0,75	4,25	1,57
	Louga	176000	198000	419000	0,23	4,50	1,20
Bakel		28000	42000	86000	0,77	4,30	1,58
Kédougou		23000	40000	62000	1,05	2,60	1,40
Tambakounda		28000	55000	127000	1,28	5,00	2,07
	S. Oriental	79000	137000	275000	1,04	4,20	1,77
Tivaouane		125000	102000	229000	-0,37	4,90	0,84
Thiès		47000	112000	256000	1,65	5,00	2,37
Mbour		44000	101000	186000	1,58	3,60	2,97
	Thiès	216000	315000	671000	0,70	4,50	1,58
Bambey		73000	75000	155000	0,05	4,37	1,04
Diourbel		40000	63000	144000	0,87	5,00	1,79
Mbaké		14000	45000	122000	2,22	6,00	3,06
	Diourbel	127000	183000	421000	0,70	5,00	1,68
Fatik		69000	105000	170000	0,80	2,98	1,27
Kaolak		14000	108000	217000	3,90	4,20	3,85
Foundiougne		12000	50000	104000	2,70	4,40	3,06
Gossas		8000	80000	133000	4,40	3,00	3,94
Kafrine		25000	103000	239000	2,70	5,00	3,16
Nioro		26000	58000	134000	1,50	5,00	2,27
	Sine-Saloum	154000	504000	997000	2,20	4,10	2,60
	Cap-Vert	45000	249000	892000	3,28	7,80	4,24
	Casamance	140000	414000	700000	2,00	3,00	2,27
Total du Sénégal		1134000	2267000	4888000	1,30	4,60	2,05

SOURCES: 1904—Archives du Sénégal 22 G 19, METGE (1966a; 287); 1930—Archives du Sénégal D 597; 1958, 1962, 1970—Répertoire des villages de 1958, 1964 et 1972; 1976—Recersement National du Sénégal, avril 1976.

au début de 1984. Le Cap-Vert serait alors devenu la première région du Sénégal. Le déclin relatif du Fleuve, de Thiès, du Sine-Saloum, du Sénégal Oriental et de la Casamance se serait porsquivi, alors que Diourbel aurait connu une légère croissance.

Le tableau 5.2 résume cette évolution régionale qui traduit des changements à une grande échelle, mais masque un peu—comme on le constatera pour le cas des Départements du Sine-Saloum—de nettes disparités sous-régionales.

(5) L'examen des taux d'accroissement départementaux montre que les moyennes nationales ne sont pas atteintes par les Départements du Nord et du Nord-Ouest entre 1904 et 1976 (Dagana, Podor, et Matam, Louga, Kébémer, et Linguère, Tivaouane, Bambey, et Diourbel, Fatick, mais aussi pour Bakel et Kédougou à l'extrême Est. Pour ces Départements, on a en général une moyenne fort inférieure entre 1904 et 1958, alors qu'entre 1958 et 1976, la croissance de centres urbains dans certains départements cache le dépeuplement des zones rurales (par exemple, Saint-Louis et Richard-Toll dans Dagana, Louga, Tivavouane, Diourbel, et Tambacounda.

(6) Entre 1904 et 1976, les taux les plus forts s'observent dans tous les Départements du Sine-Saloum, à l'exception de celui de Fatick, en Casamance, dans le Département de Mbaké où le croissance de Touba et Mbaké est impressionnante, et bien sûr dans le Cap-Vert même où la population a été multipliée par 20).

Malgré les problèmes qui se posent à propos de la valeur des chiffres de population aux diverses dates, et donc au sujet des taux et des

TABLEAU 5.2
Pourcentages des Régions dans la Population Sénégalaise
en 1904, 1958, 1976, et 1984

Région	1904	1958	1976	1984[a] Intérieur	1984[a] Statistique
Fleuve	17,37	11,78	10,46	8,57	9,71
Louga	15,52	8,74	8,57	10,10	7,82
Sénégal Oriental	6,97	6,04	5,63	5,63	5,63
Thiès	19,05	13,90	13,73	13,23	13,29
Diourbel	11,20	8,07	8,62	9,38	7,94
Sine/Saloum	13,58	22,23	20,40	20,08	19,79
Cap-Vert	3,97	10,98	18,26	20,53	21,89
Casamance	12,84	18,26	14,33	12,48	13,93
	100,00	100,00	100,00	100,00	100,00

a. Population totale.

pourcentages avancés, il est assuré qu'ils traduisent assez fidèlement une évolution globale. Ils soulignent en particulier les faits de plusieurs centres urbains secondaires; le déclin des régions du Nord qui a été caractéristique de l'époque coloniale; les transferts importants de population vers le Saloum pendant la même période, alors que la Casamance connaissait aussi un accroissement notable. Au cours des 20 dernières années, la mobilité en direction des zones rurales a relativement diminué tandis que les flux s'orientaient davantage vers les villes, surtout vers Dakar-Pikine; ici les forts accroissements enregistrés manifestent une véritable "explosion démographique" et également une relative amélioration des techniques de recensement.

Il ressort donc que les régions et les départements qui les composent ont connu une évolution très différenciée durant les 85 dernières années. Les phénomènes globaux qu'on a mis en évidence peuvent autoriser à délimiter des secteurs où les densités et la répartition de la population ont changé notablement, des zones pourvoyeuses ou réceptrices de migrants, et servent à placer dans un contexte général des changements locaux dont l'analyse minutieuse reste à faire dans la plupart des cas.

LE BASSIN ARACHIDIER (SINE-SALOUM) DE 1904 à 1976

La région arachidière offre, avec le Cap-Vert, l'exemple le plus frappant d'une étude de la dynamique du peuplement. Alors qu'il s'agit au Cap-Vert d'une croissance urbaine accélérée, dans le cas du Sine-Saloum l'accroissement concerne la population rurale et urbaine avec des courants migratoires importants depuis le début du 20e siècle. Le Sine-Saloum offre plusieurs avantages, aussi bien sociologiques, historiques, économiques que proprement démographiques. Historiquement, l'entité administrative actuelle[1] est la réunion de deux royaumes de même origine (le Sine et la Saloum) et d'une partie des petits royaumes du Badibou et du Niom. Ce cercle puis cette région n'a pratiquement pas évolué dans ses limites entre 1904 et 1984. Mais, si le Sine a l'avantage d'être très homogène d'un point de vue ethnique, par contre, le Saloum a un peuplement très diversifié. Le Sine-Saloum est devenu le coeur du Bassin Arachidier et la zone agricole la plus importante du Sénégal. Sa capitale, Kaolack, est le deuxième centre commercial, et elle est restée du milieu des années 1920 au début des années 1950 le deuxième port de l'Afrique occidentale française (AOF) après Dakar, en même temps qu'elle assumait une importante fonction industrielle. Jusque dans les années 1980, cette région a été la plus peuplée de Sénégal, alliant une très forte population rurale et le réseau urbain le plus dense après le Cap-Vert. Son importance est aussi reflétée par la quantité de la documentation: bien que lacunaire, elle est souvent plus intéressante que pour la plupart des autres régions.

Dans ses grandes lignes, le Sine-Saloum a évolué dans le même sens que l'ensemble national, mais à un rythme plus rapide. Ainsi, a-t-il multiplié, entre 1904 et 1976, sa population totale par 6,5 alors que le Sénégal ne la multipliait que par 4,3. La population urbaine était multipliée par 32 (Sénégal: 17) et enfin la population rurale par 5,7 (Sénégal: 2,5). Il se place derrière le Cap-Vert pour le développement de la population urbaine, mais confirme sa place de première région agricole depuis la première guerre mondiale. L'accroissement annuel se décompose en trois périodes contrastées : 2,4 pourcent pour 1904-1930, 2,1 pour 1930-1958 et 3,9 pour 1958-1976. Ces taux font apparaître la période de 1930-1958 comme moins privilégiée, aussi bien pour les villes que pour les campagnes. (Pour les chiffres absolus, voir le tableau 5.3; pour les taux voir le tableau 5.4.)

Dans le réseau urbain, Kaolack représente 66 pourcent de toute la population urbanisée à partir de 1930, alors qu'en 1904, ce rapport n'était que de 30 pourcent. Ce développement est conforme au rôle économique de la ville: première exportatrice d'arachide, deuxième port et deuxième centre commercial de l'AOF. Sur le plan agricole, cette période correspond aussi à celle de la plus grande expansion de l'arachide.

On constate une liaison entre le développement de la culture arachidière et les mouvements de population dans le Sine-Saloum. Cela nous conduit à affiner l'analyse et à comparer, à l'intérieur de la région, l'évolution des effectifs humains et celle de la production arachidière. Nous constatons alors que la progression de l'arachide est autant due à un développement spatial croissant qu'à une augmentation continue des spéculateurs. En effet, si le Sine-Saloum ne représente que 14 pourcent du territoire national, il constitue 31 pourcent des terres cultivables, alors que sa population n'est que de 13,6 (1904), 22,2 (1958), et 20,4 pourcent (1976) de l'ensemble national. Cette disponibilité théorique est mise à profit par l'arachide qui occupe de plus en plus de terres: 13,7 pourcent de la surface cultivable en moyenne en 1923-1927, 22,6 en 1935-1940 et 41,4 pourcent en 1965-1976 (pour le Sénégal, 14,4, 18,3 et 30,2 pourcent respectivement). Ainsi, la croissance annuelle moyenne de la production arachidière est très importante: 4,7 pourcent entre 1904 et 1976 (3,5 pourcent pour le Sénégal). Elle procède de plusieurs facteurs: le croît

TABLEAU 5.3
Population des Arrondissements du Sine-Saloum de 1904 à 1976

Arrondissement Ville	Département	1904	1930	1958	1962	1970	1976
Diakhao		22435		34491	35306	31698	35980
Fimela		5405		15505	17473	21660	25480
Niakhar		23407	88222	26104	26929	29611	32218
Tataguine		16064		24495	27688	30947	66794
Fatik		1322	2147	4650	7198	13037	9998
	Fatik	68633	90369	105245	114594	126953	170470
Diédieng		4833	27337	18593	22375	23574	37300
Gandiaye		4115	13775	18571	20578	21795	31972
Ndofane		3642	(ensemble)	25459	25722	25706	43080
Kaolack		1506	12479	45222	69560	97924	104154
	Kaolack	14096	53591	107845	138235	168999	216506
Kolobane		2242		23314	30055	26938	48490
Kahone		5316	34901	23266	25357	18692	32643
Ouadiour		515		23923	26866	17188	33631
Guinguinéo		44		5333	6634	8643	10948
Gossas		—	2572	4611	4515	7590	7365
	Gossas	8117	37473	80447	93427	79051	133077

Djilor	3144 ⎫		17520	18454	19286	32793
Niodior	2521 ⎬	38011	6719	8914	11595	14346
Toubakouta	4919 ⎭		22161	25026	24030	48514
Sokone	170		1932	3966	6224	5698
Foundiougne	993	1576	1657	1623	2181	2669
Foundiougne	11747	39587	49989	57983	63316	104020
Médina Sabakh	7671	5729	15129	17766	18985	34246
Paoskoto	9361	8129	23398	30293	29618	49527
Wak Ngouna	7751	15313	16364	21329	29826	41933
Nioro	750	–	2769	2769	5841	7757
Nioro Du Rip	25533	29171	57660	72157	84270	133463
Birkelane	5874	7931	33679	43360	39444	60436
Kounguel	6026	11384	22470	27480	32810	57833
Malem Hodar	4510	9801	31580	36449	46365	71947
Nganda	8006	5117	12769	22968	18981	38143
Kafrine	226	–	2280	2280	7000	10924
Kafrine	24642	34233	102778	132537	144600	239282
Total (-villes)	147757	265650	435510	510188	518749	837305
Villes	5000	18774	68454	98745	148440	159513
Total general	152757	284424	503964	608933	667189	996818

SOURCES: Voir tableau 5.1.

TABLEAU 5.4
Arrondissements et Départements du Sine-Saloum:
Taux d'Accroissement de la Population entre 1904 et 1976

Arrondissement Ville	Département	Période			
		1904-1930	1930-1958	1958-1976	1904-1976
Diakhao		1,10	0,05	0,22	0,65
Fimela				2,80	2,18
Niakhar				1,16	0,45
Tataguine				5,74	2,00
				2,64	1,21
Fatik	Fatik	1,87	2,80	4,30	2,85
	Fatik	1,07	0,50	2,70	1,27
Diédieng		4,60	1,70	3,98	2,88
Ndofane				2,96	3,49
				3,29	3,10
Gandiaye		4,76	1,08	3,06	2,89
Kaolack	Kaolack	8,47	4,70	4,79	6,38
		5,27	2,50	3,96	3,85
Kolobane		5,79	2,54	4,15	4,36
Kahone				1,89	2,55
Ouadiour				1,93	5,98
				2,75	3,76
Guinguineo		—	2,10	4,07	7,96
Gossas		—		2,65	—
Gossas	Gossas	6,06	2,77	2,82	3,96

Djilor	} 5,03	} 0,71	3,54	3,30 }
Niodior			4,32	2,44 } 3,10
Toubakouta			4,45	3,23 }
Sokone	—	—	6,19	4,99
Foundiougne	1,80	0,17	2,68	1,37
Foundiougne	4,78	0,83	4,15 } 4,10	3,08
Médina Sabakh	1,01	3,50	4,63	2,10
Paoskoto	0,00 } 0,64	3,85 } 2,28	4,26	2,34
Wak Ngouna	2,66	0,24	5,36 } 4,71	2,37 } 2,28
Nioro	—	—	5,89	3,30
Nioro du Rip	0,50	2,47	4,76	2,32
Birkelane	1,16	5,30	3,29	3,29
Koungueul	2,48 } 1,30	2,50 } 3,90	5,38	3,19
Malem Hodar	3,03	4,30	4,69 } 4,66	3,92 } 3,15
Nganda	-0,02	3,30	6,27	2,19
Kafrine	—	—	9,10	5,53
Kafrine	1,28	4,00	4,81	3,21
Total (— Villes)	2,29	1,78	3,69	2,44
Villes	5,20	4,73	2,05	4,93
Total general	2,40	2,06	3,87	2,64

SOURCE: Voir tableau 5.1.

démographique naturel, l'apport des quelques 29.800 *Navetaan*—migrants saisonniers—qui, en moyenne, viennent chaque année dans la région entre 1934 et 1957, et qui ne sont pas décomptés dans les chiffres de population (6 pourcent en 1958); le part croissante de l'arachide dans la force de travail du paysan (38 pourcent entre 1904 et 1929, 53 pourcent entre 1930 et 1951, 55 pourcent entre 1952 et 1976); et enfin les meilleurs rendements à l'hectare dans les Départements de Kafrine et Nioro, dus à une meilleure qualité des terres, des précipitations, à une mécanisation plus précoce et à l'utilisation intensive des *Navetaan* qui privilégient ces secteurs.

On peut distinguer trois grandes zones:

(1) *Une première*, occidentale, avec le Sine et le Bas-Saloum: elle est caractérisée par le faiblesse de la progression démographique entre 1930 et 1958. Le Sine, concentré dans le Département de Fatick, présente des taux d'accroissement très faibles par rapport à la région, voire au Sénégal: 1,1 entre 1904-1930, 0,5 entre 1930-1958, et 1,3 entre 1958-1976. L'évolution du Bas-Saloum (Département de Foundiougne) accuse certaines tendances du Sine bien que la croissance entre 1904-1976 y soit bien supérieure à celui du Sine: 4,8 de 1904 à 1930, 0,8 de 1930 à 1958 et 4,2 de 1958 à 1976.

Pour cette zone Ouest, on sait que la part dans la production arachidière régionale a représenté, durant cette période, 35 pourcent en moyenne avant 1938, 25 pourcent entre 1938 et 1954, et seulement 17 pourcent après 1954. Dès lors, il est possible de poser une hypothèse qui postule un lien entre la stagnation, voire la régression de la production, et le moindre accroissement démographique. Cette zone, ayant été occupée la première par l'arachide à la fin du XIXe siècle, a même abrité la première capitale régionale. Jusqu'en 1930, la production arachidière reste notable.

Mais le Sine déjà densément peuplé, commence à alimenter d'importants courants migratoires vers l'Ouest (Diéghem méridional et Dimag) et le Sud-Est (frontières avec le Saloum), tout en occupant une grande partie des franges du Sine même qui étaient dépeuplées à la fin du XIXe siècle. Par contre, on assiste dans le Bas-Saloum à une forte expansion des peuplements originaires de la zone, mais surtout à une arrivée de nombreux migrants venus du Nord du Sénégal, mais aussi de l'Est. Après 1930, le Sine continue à développer les mouvements migratoires et pendant les années 1934-1936, l'Administration tente de canaliser les flux et de les orienter vers l'Est dans le cadre de l'opération "Terres Neuves" (Pelissier, 1966; Dubois, 1975).

On peut avancer comme explication à ce renforcement du courant migratoire, qui devient également sensible dans le Bas-Saloum dès 1930, l'appauvrissement des terres qui voient leur rendement baisser, le relatif surpeuplement du Sine et de certains secteurs du Bas-Saloum (en particulier les Iles), mais aussi le déclin de Foundiougne. En effet, la disparition du port à la fin des années 1920 a entraîné la régression de la ville et freiné le développement des pays voisins. Néanmoins, malgré les départs vers l'Est enregistrés après 1930, le Bas-Saloum voit sa population croître lentement; les réserves de terre y sont restées très importantes et, depuis l'Indépendance, le Département retrouve un certain dynamisme, grâce à une immigration venant du Sine, du Bawol, du Kayor, du Walo, mais aussi de l'Ouest du Rip. Dans cette reprise, il ne faut pas oublier l'influence de la Gambie qui a conservé un système de traits libéral (marché libre), quand le Sénégal l'a supprimé au profit d'un circuit étatisé. Par contre, le Sine voit sa population progresser très modérément après 1958, par accroissement naturel, et fournit de gros contingents de migrants vers les villes et vers tout le Saloum.

(2) *La deuxième zone* à individualiser constitue le centre de la région, avec le Nord-Ouest du Saloum et le centre de ce royaume (Départements de Kaolack et de Gossas). Elle a connu un ralentissement plus modéré à la même période que l'Ouest: 5,3, 2,5 et 3,9 pourcent de croissance annuelle pour les périodes 1904-1930, 1930-1958 et 1958-1976 dans le Département de Kaolack, alors que dans celui de Gossas les taux pour ces périodes étaient 6,1, 3,0 et 2,8. Ici, on remarque également des nuances pour les deux parties, mais les traits majeurs sont la croissance assez forte jusqu'en 1930, avec la conquête souvent pionnière dans les arrondissements de Ouadiour et Kolobane où la maîtrise de l'eau autorise l'habitat sédentaire, puis un ralentissement entre 1930 et 1958 qui est un peu moins net dans le Département de Kaolack, et enfin une reprise assez modérée après 1958, en particulier dans le Département de Gossas.

Ce schéma fait penser, pour la première phase, à la forte pénétration de la colonisation mouride dès le début du siècle jusque vers le milieu des années 1930, mais aussi à l'expansion des vieux terroirs et à une arrivée importante de migrants d'origines diverses. Dans une seconde phase, un blocage se manifeste à partir des années 1930, avec le début d'une inflexion des courants migratoires plus vers l'Est et le Sud: cette modification s'accentuera après l'indépendance, indiquant sinon une saturation des terres, du moins des problèmes importants de gestion agricole. De toute façon, on doit mettre cette évolution en rapport avec celle de la production: alors que le Centre produisait plus de 37 pourcent des arachides du cercle avant 1938, ce pourcentage stagne ensuite quelque peu à 36 pourcent jusqu'en 1955, pour descendre depuis lors à 30 pourcent en moyenne.

Cependant, le schéma d'évolution démographique pour cette zone centrale est à corriger, en tenant compte du rôle tenu par la capitale régionale—Kaolack, situé à la charnière des deux départements—dans la croissance de la région, mais aussi des villes secondaires que sont Guinguinéo et Gossas. En effet, Kaolack a attiré des migrants nombreux originaires en grande partie de la région, représentant un pôle démographique, économique, commercial et administratif. Le déclin démographique relatif des arrondissements ruraux est donc compensé, et masqué en partie, par l'essor urbain.

(3) La situation est radicalement différente dans *la troisième zone* qui comprend l'Est et le Sud-Est du Saloum, c'est-à-dire les départements de Nioro du Rip et de Kafrine. Ici, on enregistre un faible taux d'accroissement demographique entre 1904 et 1930 (0,5 pour Nioro et 1,3 pour Kafrine), puis une forte allure entre 1930 et 1958 (2,5 et 4,0 respectivement), et enfin une décélération moins accusée entre 1958 et 1976 (4,8 et 4,8). Encore une fois, la part prise par ce sous-ensemble dans la production arachidière confirme les données démographiques: alors que ces deux départements ne produisaient avant 1938 que 28 pourcent du total régional en moyenne, ils en font 38 pourcent entre 1938 et 1954, et 51 pourcent après 1954.

L'explication de ces faits démographiques et économiques réside dans un fort courant d'immigration provenant de l'Ouest et du Centre-Nord du Sine-Saloum, les hauts rendements obtenus sur des terres neuves, et la mécanisation plus précoce, dès 1960. Cela est particulièrement valable pour l'Est où l'Administration a tenté d'organiser la migration vers les "Terres Neuves" de Kafrine dans les années 1930; après la 2ème guerre mondiale, ce département sera privilégié par les projets d'intervention. Le résultat est d'ailleurs net, car la seule part de Kafrine dans la production du cercle est de 20 pourcent environ avant 1938 pour monter à 25 pourcent jusqu'en 1948, 31 pourcent jusqu'en 1960, et 35 pourcent a partir de l'indépendance. Cela en fait le département le plus important, en matière agricole, au Sénégal.

Nioro connaît une immigration moins forte mais plus soutenue, alimentée avant tout par le trop-plein venant de Gossas et, au delà, du Bawol et de Kayor. D'autre part, la frontière gambienne n'a pas cessé de jouer un rôle important dans les mouvements de population, surtout dans les périodes de crise et pendant les deux guerres, offrant toujours de multiples opportunités (marchandises, prix, différences de change, etc.). Ce secteur a également attiré beaucoup d'anciens *Navetaan*, installés d'abord dans le Sud du Département de Kaolack, au Laghem, avant de poursuivre vers le Sud. Ainsi, l'Est du Sine-Saloum et, à un degré un peu moindre, le Sud et le Sud-Est apparaissent-ils encore comme des secteurs pionniers dont le dynamisme est certes actuellement ralenti, mais nullement assoupi. Si l'on doit enregistrer la progression du Bassin Arachidier vers le Sud-Est jusqu'aux environs de Tambacounda, entre 1954 et 1980 (Lake et Touré, 1984), les secteurs de Kafrine et Nioro demeurent très actifs, tant dans les dynamiques de peuplement que pour la vitalité économique.

L'analyse générale qui est esquissée ici pour la région du Sine-Saloum demande un approfondissement, avec un passage à des unités démographiques et économiques plus petites, mais les difficultés (absence des sources, problème d'utilisation des données) sont réelles. Cependant, on dispose des éléments nécessaires pour une histoire des villages et des mouvements migratoires à une échelle plus fine.

Une telle histoire permet de proposer une typologie des établissements humains et de mieux distinguer pour chaque secteur, les nuances de l'évolution démographique (poids respectifs du bilan naturel, de l'émigration et de l'immigration dans les petites unités retenues). Grâce à elle, et en utilisant les renseignements fournis dans des ouvrages plus généraux (Pelissier, 1966; Colvin, 1981; David, 1980; Mbodj, 1978, 1981; Metge, 1966; Lake et Touré 1984), il est possible de mieux cerner la diversité des faits de population qui traduit une diversité sociale dans la principale région rurale sénégalaise.

CONCLUSIONS

Cet article a voulu montrer qu'il est possible d'étudier l'évolution historique de la population sénégalaise, surtout au XXeme siècle où les documents écrits sont plus nombreux. Il est certain qu'il a laissé de côté un certain nombre de thèmes tels que la répartition par sexe, le poids de la jeunesse, l'étude de la fécondité, de l'espérance de vie, etc. En outre, le XXème siècle ne représente que l'étape contemporaine d'une évolution multiséculaire. En réalité, il est parfaitement possible de remonter beaucoup plus haut dans le temps, de partir de la mise en place des peuplements et de décrire les principaux moments de l'histoire de la population. Car les sources qui le permettent existent, mais restent souvent à rechercher et à exploiter.

Tout d'abord, il faudrait explorer la mine de renseignements que recèlent les 16.900 monuments, composant les 1.987 sites de la zone mégalithique qui se trouve comprise sur les seules vallées du Saloum et de la Gambie. Dans cette zone protohistorique, en utilisant la méthode de comparaison des semis des sites, on constate que le rapport sites actuels-sites protohistoriques est de 3.326/1.987, soit 1,67 seulement; dans plusieurs secteurs, les sites anciens sont en proportion très nettement supérieure. Ici comme dans les autres zones protohistoriques, les techniques de l'archéologie démographique pourraient permettre une stimulante recherche. En effet, les nombreuses inhumations associées à des monuments funéraires ou à des sites, devraient fournir des idées assez précises sur les stocks de population, les répartitions par âge et par sexe et l'espérance de vie.

En second lieu, la Côte Occidentale de l'Afrique, et plus particulièrement la Côte Sénégalaise, a été particulièrement marquée à partir du XVIe siècle par les relations de voyages européennes qui ont été rarement exploitées jusqu'à présent par la démographie historique. Ainsi, leur recensement et leur exploitation sont-ils un travail prioritaire. De même, à partir du XVIe siècle, l'importance de la présence française au Sénégal se traduit par une relative abondance de registres paroissiaux, d'actes privés de type notarial, de notes et de bulletins officiels, mais également par l'existence d'abondantes sources d'archives où l'on peut rencontrer des notations démographiques incidentes, parfois très intéressantes, surtout à propos des mouvements de population et des phénomènes qui ont affecté les phénomènes démographiques (traite des esclaves, crises de subsistance et crises climatiques, migrations et conquêtes, guerres). Evidemment, la zone côtière est privilégiée dans ce domaine, mais une extrapolation pourrait être tentée à partir de l'exploitation de ces documents bien conservés en général. Cependant, les sources se dégradent d'année en année, et leur conservation exige dès lors une action rapide.

En dernier lieu, il faut citer une source qui a été très négligée et peut être très utile lorsqu'elle est manipulée avec précautions: la tradition orale. L'un des points pour lesquels sa fiabilité a été la plus éprouvée est la généalogie dont l'intérêt est évident. On sait qu'elle a été à la base d'études particulièrement précises sur trois siècles d'évolution de populations africaines (Charentré et al., 1972) ou amérindiennes (Chapman et Jacquard, 1972).

En somme, l'importance des sources disponibles traduit un très grand potentiel dans le domaine de l'histoire démographique du Sénégal. Il faut garder à l'esprit le contexte de chaque série de données, quitte à affecter à chacune un coefficient de confiance. L'analyse et l'interprétation des séries pourraient être complétées ou recoupées par des enquêtes de terrain de type pluridisciplinaire (archéologie, linguistique, tradition orale, anthropologie, etc.). Dans certains cas, l'utilisation de techniques courantes en Occident serait envisagée, telle que le reconstitution des familles. Ces differentes méthodes de collecte et d'exploitation des sources seront combinées selon les objectifs visés. Nous en proposons quelques-unes qui nous paraissent prioritaires.

Au premier rang de ces objectifs, on peut citer la mise en place du peuplement et sa diversité régionale, puis l'évolution des effectifs en fonction des facteurs politiques, humains, économiques, écologiques. Ensuite, on pourrait aborder l'étude de la mortalité, ainsi que celle de la fécondité. Il est certain que l'établissement d'une hiérarchie ne signifie pas qu'on néglige d'autres thèmes importants et parfois imbriqués fortement avec les précédents : migrations, phénomènes urbains, etc. Mais nous avons à l'esprit certaines considérations vis-à-vis de l'histoire qui expliquent ces propositions.

Il s'agit d'abord d'une meilleure connaissance de la population actuelle, afin d'opérer une politique économique qui tienne mieux compte de ceux qui sont les premiers concernés. La population des années 1980 se déploie sur trois ou quatre générations, et celle des années 1990 à venir est déjà constituée pour l'essentiel. Par exemple, son taux de croissance actuel ou son espérance de vie doit être maîtrisé au mieux sur toute son histoire, c'est-à-dire sur trois ou quatre générations pour pouvoir être correctement utilisé dans un plan de développement. Dans un pays socialiste, l'enjeu démographique est primordial, or l'option officielle du Sénégal est le socialisme.

Ensuite, l'histoire de l'Afrique ne peut rester en dehors ou à la traîne de ce grand mouvement d'histoire économique et sociale qui conditionne la pratique scientifique contemporaine. L'une des possibilités qu'offre justement l'élaboration d'une démographie historique sénégalaise est de servir éventuellement de base à des modèles démographiques africains. Ces modèles doivent vérifier ou infirmer un certain nombre d'hypothèses qui se contredisent et qui se prétendent toutes scientifiques. Cette possibilité est surtout valable pour des régions similaires à la Sénégambie, mais pour lesquelles les lacunes documentaires et archéologiques sont relativement importantes. La construction de modèles éviterait des généralisations qui peuvent être fécondes en tant que synthèses, mais qui sont plus sûrement abusives comme démarches scientifiques.

Ces considérations restent à l'état potentiel tant que des équipes pluridisciplinaires ne pourront les assumer dans la cadre de programmes appropriés, au sein de structures qui sont encore à mettre en place. Tant il est vrai que les universités francophones n'appréhendent souvent les études de population qu'en termes de démométrie. Cette vision réductrice a des conséquences affligeantes, telles que ignorance totale des étudiants en sciences sociales dans cette discipline qui appartient indiscutablement à son rayon d'action, le manque de profondeur socio-historique des analyses démographiques en Afrique, masqué par un recours nomriliste au quantitatif à qui on confère de fait un statut de véracité absolue, et enfin le confiscation de ses méthodes par des professionnels dépendant des appareils de décision gouvernementaux qu'on ne peut même pas interroger sur le bienfondé des démarches et des conclusions.

C'est pourquoi, nous avons l'intention de mettre sur pied une équipe dakaroise, dont le premier objectif serait de donner à la démographie historique la place qui lui revient dans l'activité scientifique locale. Outre des études régionales qui sont en cours de réalisation, le groupe voudrait engager une réflexion sur les méthodes de cette discipline, et sur son statut à l'intérieur d'une anthropologie générale. Une des premières matérialisations sera la mise en chantier d'un ouvrage collectif sur l'histoire de la population sénégalaise depuis les origines.

NOTE

1. Depuis le Juillet 1984, le région du Sine-Saloum a été scindée en deux: la région de Kaolack et celle de Fatick. Ces nouvelles régions sont regroupées dans la présente étude.

6

"FAIRE DU NEGRE"
Military Aspects of Population Planning
in French West Africa, 1920-1940

MYRON ECHENBERG

      The military would seem an unlikely subject for inclusion in a book on historical demography. For one thing, African military service in French West Africa (see Map 2) was entirely confined to single young males, affecting population reproduction only indirectly, and in ways for which current research does not permit exploration. Nor can it yet be demonstrated that military service had a significant impact on mortality rates for the population as a whole. However, in the area of migration, the third great demographic variable, military recruitment and employment of Africans had direct demographic implications. This chapter explores two demographic aspects of French military policy in West Africa in the interwar years. First, it examines the tentative, quasiscientific efforts of French planners in the early 1920s to measure the size of the cohort of males in their twentieth year in the West African colonies. Second, it explains how military recruitment policy affected overall migration.

DEMOGRAPHIC IMAGINATION AND NUMERICAL REALITY

    Military statistics for West Africa come from the Military Series, Série D, in the *Archives de l'Afrique occidentale française, Archives*

Author's Note: I wish to thank McGill University for sabbatical leave in 1983, enabling me to conduct part of the research for this project. Participants in the workshop in the Département de démographie at the Université de Montréal in 1984 offered comments on an earlier draft.

nationales du Senegal (ANS), Dakar. This series offers surprisingly detailed data for a part of the world where good demographic statistics are even today difficult to obtain. The primary reason for this was the Army's need to measure and evaluate the size of its annual intake of recruits. Each mobile draft board kept careful records and passed these on first to the colony capital and then to the federation capital in Dakar. The statistics formed the essential part of obligatory annual reports at the colony and federation level. The entire collection was prepared annually under the signature of the *Général Commandant Supérieur* (GCS) of the French Colonial Army in West Africa. In addition, chief medical officers frequently wrote annual medical reports on what was termed the physical quality of the year's recruits. While some reports are missing and presumed lost, most of them can be found in the ANS.

Unfortunately, little detail has been provided about methods used to prepare civil lists of recruits. Comments inter alia by commanding officers and the data themselves indicate that most regions followed instructions, although some consistently used shoddy techniques. Thus Guinea and Senegal were said to provide trustworthy records, while those from Niger, Mauritania, and parts of Ivory Coast were decidedly less so (ANS, 4D70/81: General Freydenberg, Annual Report on Recruitment for 1932, Dakar, 15 Septenber 1932). With regard to the *bons absents,* a category extremely damaging to French authorities, the figures remained dramatically high (see Figures 6.1 and 6.2; this term was military shorthand for *bon pour le service militaire mais absent* that is, the men were presumed to be physically fit for service but had "dodged" their draft board summons). Deliberate manipulation probably would have involved efforts to reduce the size of the lists (the numbers of absentees), which would make local authorities look good. On the other hand, local officials disliked the draft and were anxious to show its unpopularity with their African subjects. They thus used it to explain severe labor shortages, which in turn excused shortfalls in economic growth. It is therefore tempting to assume that for these mixed motives local officials chose to keep accurate lists.

French military assumptions about the size and potential of the West African population under their control date from the beginnings of their rule. As an ambitious colonel in 1910, Charles Mangin propounded the view in *La Force Noire* that Black Africa was an inexhaustible reservoir of men ideally suited for military service. Accustomed to thinking of manpower rather than technology as a critical measure of military strength, Mangin and his supporters hoped to counterpose France's colonial populations against the more rapid population growth of Germany. How could France with a stagnant or even declining birth rate hope to win back the lost provinces in a future war against a Germany, which already had a larger population, and a higher birth rate? For Mangin West Africa provided the desperate answer. He estimated that the region alone could easily furnish 10,000 volunteers a year, and that the potential far exceeded that figure (Mangin, 1910: 276).

The reality was far different. French West Africa was in fact thinly populated, notwithstanding a few densely peopled regions such as the Mossi plateau, the Bambara belt south of the Niger, and the Futa Jalon mountains around Labé in Guinea. Early censuses were extremely crude guesses rather than systematic enumerations, but the published figures set the overall population at 10 million or less (France, 1922). Even more significant, French civilian administrators were already aware of a labor shortage. The peoples of West Africa, plagued by the political disorder accompanying the wars of French conquest and by the dislocations of the slave trade in the latter half of the nineteenth century, needed their labor to maintain subsistence food production in the household economy. Yet the growing appetite of the market economy introduced by the French regime, especially with its large labor requisitions for the building of infrastructure, made for labor shortage, not surplus. Thus Governor-General William Ponty, while sharing with Mangin a belief in the military potential of West Africans to serve France, tempered the military demands for labor. Mangin's minimum target of 10,000 soldiers a year became the maximum so as not to ruin the economic development of the colony (ANS, 5D37/89: Ponty to Minister of Colonies, 23 September 1909).

Mangin's grandiose schemes for a Black Army had been given life in 1909 when instructions from Paris to Dakar called for the recruitment of 8000 *Tirailleurs Sénégalais,* or Senegalese Rifles (ANS, 5D 37/89: contained in Ponty to Minister of Colonies, 23 September 1909). This represented a fourfold increase from roughly 2000 soldiers a year. The additional men would have come forward easily, Mangin assumed, because most West Africans were "martial peoples," and many soldiers of the recently conquered African states would welcome the opportunity to continue as professional soldiers (Mangin, 1910: 285). The enlistments were to be voluntary, and the attraction was a bonus premium for signing up. This sum might attract not only free men but perhaps also recently freed slaves. Presumably, if the premium were transferred directly to the former master, a young male slave might earn his freedom by joining the French Colonial army (Roberts and Klein, 1981).

By 1912, however, it had become obvious that the colony was having difficulty supplying even 5000 volunteers. Ponty then initiated a system of partial conscription, a step that led to the militarization of French West Africa with the coming of the World War I (Lassalle-Séré, 1929: 97-100).

Marc Michel's definitive *L'Appel à l'Afrique* (Michel, 1982; see also D'Almeida-Topor, 1973) shows that in five years of war, West Africa furnished 161,361 men, including the massive "Diagne" levy of 63,000 in 1918. Using 1921 census data to measure recruitment against total population, Michel finds that Senegal was the colony that paid the highest price in soldiers since the burden of military service was not apportioned evenly (Michel, 1982: 405-408). Casualties for Black Africans ran at approximately 185 per thousand or 30,000 killed in action. These very substantial rates compare closely to the overall mortality rates of the French Army of around 260 per thousand, 1.3 million dead among the 5 million French citizens and subjects in uniform.

Despite this heavy tax in lives, militarists like Mangin, now a general and war hero, clung to obsessions about militarization of the colonies. Mangin argued in his war memoirs that the West African contribution of over 160,000 men was insufficient because colonial officials deliberately held men back (Mangin, 1920). He claimed rather preposterously that had the politicians and colonial administrators given him a free hand in recruiting, he would have raised a Black Army of a quarter million, even a half million troops.

Tragically, instead of being dismissed as a crank, Mangin was actually placed in a position in the years after 1918 where his extreme notions could affect policy. Part of the reason lay in the persistence of French demographic fears. The war had bled France of over two million men who would not only no longer join the labor market but who would not play their part in population reproduction. As early as 1920, generals such as Gassouin were warning of the "hollow" cohorts, a dearth of young Frenchmen for the universal military conscription in the years from 1934 to 1938 (ANS, 4D 143/100: General Gassouin Report, Dakar, 8 June 1920). The perceived need then was for an expanded colonial contribution in peacetime to replace missing French citizens.

In 1920 an interministerial commission was formed to study the demographic implications of continued and expanded conscription in West Africa. Mangin was made the chairman, representing the interests of the Minister of Defence. Officials of lower prestige from the Ministry of Colonies attempted to curb what they held to be excessive demands of the military. They represented the views of the colonial administration and of business interests who wished to keep a labor reserve in French West Africa. To resolve the potential impasse the commission authorized what may have been the first "quasi-demographic" surveys of a segment of the French West African population.

The French military, impatient to fill its depleted ranks with colonial troops after 1918, did not wait for the results of the inquiry before expanding peacetime conscription. General Gassouin, then commander-in-chief for French Colonial Forces in West Africa, announced a standing army of 55,000 Senegalese Rifles for 1920 and projected a force of 110,000 by 1925 (ANS, 4D 143/100: General Gassouin Report, 8 June 1920). To meet this target an annual levy of 18,000 men would be required initially, rising to 25,000 by 1925. (In contrast, it will be recalled that the largest prewar levy had been 8000 for 1912.)

The interministerial commission ultimately produced a set of preliminary findings in January 1922 (ANS, 1922 Preliminary Report) and a more definitive report in July 1923 based upon a survey and partial census (ANS, 1923 Final Report). The reports reveal the underlying demographic assumptions of French planners. The commission identified five variables it felt necessary to measure or estimate.

The Overall Population. The commission began with earlier crude censuses that were little more than estimates: 10,758,000 people as of 1906, increasing to 11,878,000 by 1916, and finally 12,494,000 by 1922. No formal census was taken and the commission did not evaluate the quality of the data (ANS, 1923 Final Report). It might be reasonably assumed that the 1906 figure was a crude guess, the 1916 a slightly more refined one, and the 1922 estimate a somewhat more accurate one.

The "Recruitable" Population. Various assumptions reduced the size of the population subject to military recruitment. Nomadic peoples were declared unsuitable for formal military duty in the Senegalese Rifles, and their numbers deducted. The French included Moor, Tuareg, and most Pular speakers as nomadic. In addition, areas of recent dissidence such as the lower Casamance in Senegal were exempted from the draft, while peoples inhabiting the lower Ivory Coast were delared to be "too feeble and unwarlike" to provide anything but a tiny number of soldiers. These largely subjective assumptions about which elements of the population were useful militarily reduced the net population as of 1922 to 10,638,000, almost 2 million less than the estimated overall population (ANS, 1923 Final Report).

The Male Population. The preliminary report of January 1922 recognized the absence of data to estimate sex ratios in the West African population. The commission report attempted an extrapolation, nevertheless, and produced the very low ratio of 72.4 males per 100 females based upon fragmentary ratios from the war period (an estimate from Guinée for 1917 varying from 71.2 to 83.2, and one for Haut-Sénégal et Niger at 69.2). But migration of males as part of the growing industrial army of reserve labor in West Africa was already a reality by the 1920s as thousands of young males and somewhat fewer females left French West Africa to work on the plantations of the British West African colonies (Amin, 1974b: 74-77). Given the already high rate of migration, it is entirely possible that demographic surveys would have revealed actual sex ratios as low as these or even lower, if what is being measured is the number of males present in a community at the time of the survey. But the commissioners were entirely silent on this issue and instead offered the figures on sex ratios as absolutes.

The commission's final report in 1923 offered different figures, this time based upon a survey of 5000 people in each colony, selected as being "as typical as possible" (see Table 6.1).

With sex ratios ranging from a low in Senegal of 84.8 to a high in Niger of 100.0, the commission opted to use the mean of 92.3. But the decision was not actually based upon the partial data collected in West Africa. Having noted that the sex ratio of males in France was 92.7, the commissioners felt satisfied that their new estimate was reasonable.

Males in their Twentieth Year. The preliminary report of 1922 took the entirely perfunctory step of accepting French demographic find-ings in their estimate of males in the military cohort. In France, however, males in their twenty-first year rather than in their twentieth year did military service. Not bothering to make this correction, the commissioners used the French male cohort coefficient for the twenty-first year of .015 (that is, 1.5 percent of the total French population), as the norm for West Africans in their twentieth year.

The final report did try to correct this absurdity by incorporating results from the 1922-1923 West African survey. For the first time the commissioners admitted to the dilemma they faced in analyzing the

TABLE 6.1
Sex Ratios Based on the Survey of 1922-1923
by Colony and by Region and Ethnic Group
for Haute-Volta

Colony	Ratio	Haute-Volta by Region and Ethnic Group	Ratio
Sénégal	84.1	Ouagadougou, Mossi	100.0
Soudan	91.6	Kaya, Mossi	91.2
Guinée	93.1	Bobo-Dioulasso, Bobo	96.1
Niger	—	Dédougou, Bobo	100.0
Dahomey	92.3		
Côte d' Ivoire	91.2		
Mauritanie[a]	98.8		

SOURCE: ANS (1923 Final Report).
a. Black Africans only.

uneven data. In Soudan and Upper Volta, for example, officials simply averaged the coefficient as 10 percent of all males between the ages of 19 and 28, while in Niger local commandants took 2.2 percent of the total male population. Others made errors of arithmetic or logic. In one *cercle*, for example, of 213 males between 19 and 28, it was claimed that no less than 154 were 19 years old. Despairing of accurate coefficients based upon such shoddy work, the commissioners fell back on European data once again. This time they at least bothered to find coefficients for males in their twentieth year. Noting the figure of .0163 for France and .0164 for Germany, the commissioners opted for the French figure for West Africa. Was the German number included to show the logic of a comparative figure or the legitimacy of choosing the French one? We cannot know.

Males Physically Fit for Military Service. Last but not least was the variable of physical fitness. The war years were held to be unreliable statistically because of the haphazard recruitment methods (Michel, 1982). Instead the final report used percentages of men declared unfit for military service as determined by the annual military recruitment of 1921. These ran at 722 per thousand for French West Africa as a whole. Guinea, held to be the model colony for reliable military statistics, had a rejection rate of 800 per thousand, with some regions such as Futa Jalon running as high as 936 per thousand. The Guinea rate of 800 per thousand was used for the colony as a whole.

When the computation based upon all the variables was made, it produced the following estimated annual military cohort: 10,638,000 population $\times$ .48 male coefficient $\times$ .0163 males in their twentieth year $\times$ .20 physical fitness ratio = 16,646 as the maximum annual cohort. The final report of the commission concluded therefore that a range of from 12,000 to 14,000 soldiers a year was a reasonable burden to apply to West African population (ANS, 1923 Final Report).

However suspect the methods and the data, this result proved a triumph for the civilians over the military. Colonial officials and business interests had agreed that Mangin and Gassouin's projected army of 80,000 or more would be a disaster. Now the interministerial commission was setting a moderate annual levy, which meant a standing army of roughly 55,000 Senegalese Rifles, exactly the figure civilian Governors Ponty and, after him, Clozet had suggested.

This essentially political decision confirmed an underlying reality of French policy. Colonial governments did not have demographic policies, they had labor policies. The pseudoscientific element of the demographic survey conducted by the interministerial commission was a shoddy exercise that in the end produced a result consistent with what the conflicting competitors for West African labor needed. The sham nature of the demography was self-evident. Not only were the methods slipshod, but no effort was made to determine the size for example of a cohort of young females of child-bearing age, or even to suggest that fertility was a key variable in any attempt to estimate the current and especially the future demographic potential of West African society. The commissioners were never able to estimate accurately two major characteristics of the population, the age/sex structure or even more fundamentally, the overall size. By measuring only young males, the most mobile group and the one that most immediately interested them, they were dooming their efforts to failure. It is ironic nonetheless that this early demographic exercise should ignore women so completely in its attempt to estimate the population of West Africa.

The Conscription Law of 1919, which preceded the creation of the interministerial commission by one year, had ushered in a system of universal male conscription that remained in place for the entire interwar period (Echenberg, 1975: 182-185; Davis, 1934: 179-182). The system was in practice similar to the lottery technique used under Napoleon III in France. In each *cercle,* a list of eligible males was drawn up, initially with the help of the African canton chiefs, but after 1926 by the *commandant de cercle* using actual census lists, systematically maintained in most cercles for males only. A mobile draft board toured the countryside to examine males in their twentieth year. A medical review eliminated those who were unfit. Lots were then drawn to determine the first portion of the cohort as it was called, those who would serve a three-year tour of duty in the Senegalese Rifles. The remainder passed into the second portion, which was in theory an inactive reserve, to be called up in case of partial or total mobilization.

AFRICAN RESISTANCE TO MILITARY RECRUITMENT

To describe conscription in this fashion is to imply that Africans were docile victims of a system that callously exploited them without so much as even indirect consultation. This was not the case. In fact, Africans resisted and modified conscription in numerous effective ways, ranging from substitutions, to self-mutilation, to flight from the recruiter, by far the most important method. So extensive and systematic was avoidance of military service through absenteeism and flight that it became a significant motive in the patterns of regional migration that emerged in the interwar era. Migration as resistance to the military recruiter mainly involved the flight of individuals in their twentieth year, but refugees often included older and younger brothers and other kin, who feared being taken as hostages or substitutes. Proximity to colonial frontiers was also an important consideration. Among the Agni of eastern Ivory Coast, for example, entire villages picked up and moved across to British Gold Coast as a result of French recruitment demands during World War I (British military recruitment was a modest affair; see Thomas, 1975). These *bons absents,* as the French labeled the absentees, usually far outnumbered those actually drafted. The general average of *bons absents* for French West Africa between 1923 and 1946 was just under 20 percent of all men listed on the census lists, that is, roughly 180 per thousand in the age cohort. In absolute numbers, this amounted to 36,000 men out of 196,000 on average per annum for the interwar period.

Such rates as these merit some elaboration for they testify to a remarkable phenomenon, the ability of Africans to resist recruitment effectively by dodging their draft board call-ups. Figures 6.1 and 6.2 show mean percentage rates of absenteeism as well as fluctuating rates in each colony.

Not all of these absentees can be said to have been draft resisters exclusively, let alone emigrants. To take the last point first, some might indeed have been hidden inside the community, though this entailed great risk. As the civilian administration was quick to point out in apology for these high rates, some bons absents were seasonal

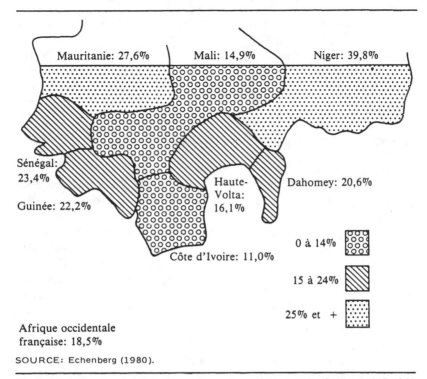

Mauritanie: 27,6%   Mali: 14,9%   Niger: 39,8%

Sénégal:
23,4%

Guinée: 22,2%

Haute-
Volta:
16,1%

Dahomey: 20,6%

Côte d'Ivoire: 11,0%

0 à 14%

15 à 24%

25% et +

Afrique occidentale
française: 18,5%

SOURCE: Echenberg (1980).

**Figure 6.1 Absentees by Colony as a Percentage of Men on Draft Lists, 1923-1946
(means by year)**

migrants, *navétanes* in the peanut fields of Senegal, for example, who happened to be away from their homes during the annual military levy (ANS, 1923 Final Report). Others may have been Dyula long-distance traders or Fulbe herdsmen temporarily earning their livelihood elsewhere. The governor of Guinee went so far as to claim that the population of his colony was so mobile that fully 10 percent of its people could be away from their homes at any given time (cited in ANS, 1923 Final Report).

While there was a grain of truth to some of these qualifications, they basically represent efforts of administrators to explain away damaging evidence of their misrule. The *navétane* migration, for example, took place during the planting, cultivating, and harvesting months from May to October (David, 1980). Conscription, on the other hand, was deliberately timed to occur in the *hivernage* months from January to April, before navetane workers from Soudan, Guinea, or Upper Volta set out in their annual migration. On the other hand, migrant laborers

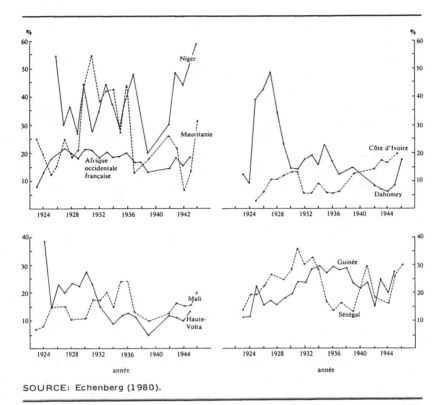

SOURCE: Echenberg (1980).

Figure 6.2 Percentage of Absentees per 100 Men on Draft Lists by Colony, 1926-1946

from the savanna who sought work in the cocoa plantations of the Gold Coast were absent during the hivernage months, because cocoa, a forest product, had a cycle different from that of peanuts and the food crops of the savanna.

Migrants from savanna to forest and coast were pulled by prospects of better wages as well as pushed by French tax collectors and recruiters. Military recruitment was not the only factor that prompted men to leave their homes either temporarily or permanently. But, given that the army called up physically able young men in their twentieth year who for the same reason were sought for agricultural and plantation labor elsewhere, it seems clear that avoidance of conscription constituted an important reason for a young man to absent himself in the years of highest vulnerability. While the *bon absent* living in the Gold Coast may have had mixed motives for having left

French West Africa, he certainly had a compelling reason not to return.

Some absent men may not have fled across colonial frontiers. A certain number temporarily settled in other parts of French West Africa where they were not known by the administration and where they could be protected from the recruiter (ANS, 4D 42/28: General Benoit, Report on recruitment for 1929, Dakar, 12 July 1929). Others, perhaps less well connected, ran a considerable risk in showing up in a new district, especially during the recruitment season. Substitution was a common practice in many regions (ANS, 4D 70/81: General Freydenberg, Report on recruitment for 1932, Dakar, 15 September 1932). Local notables either hired a substitute or used force to coerce unprotected young men to present themselves. In this way, the district or village could not only make good its quota but also reduce the overall number of bons absents.

Absentees risked sanctions and penalties to themselves and others. Theoretically, they and their families, their villages or their chiefs, could all be held to be in violation of the Conscription Law of 1919, which imposed prison sentences for obstructing the draft. This might have been a powerful constraint against flight but the penalties were in fact rarely imposed. In early years, few questions were asked as long as French West Africa as a whole met its quotas. By the mid 1920s, both the military and civilian officials had worked out a compromise: submit those bons absents captured to a medical examination; if they proved fit for military duty they were either inducted immediately or detained for incorporation later in the year. These *bons absents récupérés*, as they were called, numbered approximately 2000 men per annum by the 1930s; they were taken off the top of the federation quota, reducing the actual draft of the cohort from 12,000 to 10,000. It was hoped that this method would deter evaders on the grounds that if men reported as required, the lottery system might mean that they would not be required to serve. As Figure 6.2 indicates, this system did not deter flight and the numbers of bons absents remained high in the 1930s. (It should be noted that in selected colonies, and especially in Soudan in the 1930s and 1940s, the second portion of the draft was no bargain. It meant work in labor brigades on the Office du Niger and other large projects under deplorable conditions; see Echenberg, 1980: 441.)

Another form of military migration involved displacement for three years or more, followed by eventual repatriation to French West Africa. Elsewhere I have examined the difficulties in estimating the rate of return of African soldiers overseas (Echenberg, 1980: 449-450).

Much depended, for example, on whether the soldiers faced combat and the local disease environment. I have suggested that for every 10,715 men absorbed annually into the Army in the period from 1920 to 1938, 44 per thousand or 475 would die, another 110 per thousand or 1200 would re-enlist, while 840 per thousand would return to West Africa. Of this group most might return to their ancestral villages, but an indeterminate number might settle in larger provincial towns and cities. This pattern clearly held true for career soldiers and veterans who preferred the Western amenities of larger centers. The capital of Dakar, for example, was a powerful magnet. By the 1950s it counted four times the number of Army veterans among its population as it had furnished soldiers in the preceding decade (Echenberg, 1980: 447).

CONCLUSION

As it was with French colonial ideology in general, so it was with demography. Policy planners insisted on seeing French West Africa through their own ideological blinders. Their assumptions about the French demographic situation conditioned analysis of the colonies. Yet French military recruitment laid bare two aspects of West African reality that also had an impact on policy. The first was the internal conflict among competing colonial and metropolitan interests for control of African labor. Though never entirely resolved, in the sphere of military recruitment it can be said that the colonial and business interests won out over the metropolitan military ones. The second reality was the very effective resistance of Africans to military recruitment when geography and other circumstances permitted. The phenomenon of the military absentee, the bon absent, suggests that Africans successfully resisted military service when alternative forms of disposing of their labor proved more advantageous.

It is difficult to assess the impact of the military system on the demographic variables of mortality and fertility. Returning soldiers were agents in the spread of communicable diseases, as were all migrants. Because they were the group that traveled overseas in greatest numbers, some investigation of their impact on the health of West African society is merited. For the present, what can be said is that infectious pulmonary diseases such as tuberculosis and pneumonia rather than venereal disease represented the far greater threat to the health of serving soldiers, and presumably of returning ones (France, 1925-1942). In those areas of West Africa where rates of tuberculosis increased dramatically, it would be interesting to determine whether this could be linked to a time when soldiers were returning in large numbers. As for venereal disease, a potentially significant variable not only for mortality but also for fertility, it is not possible to separate soldiers from others among the sexually active migrant workers. Suffice to say that further research needs to be done to determine, for example, whether soldiers may not have been agents responsible for the introduction of new strains of infectious venereal disease.

Although indirect, the impact of military service and migration on West African fertility can be suggested. The removal of large numbers of the physically most able males for periods of three years and more from their village communities must have affected such variables of family life as the age of marriage, and the rate of polygyny, while the value of brideprice was often altered by the returning soldier, especially if he had a large and steady military pension. These variables were dramatically altered by the overall patterns of labor migration, as Piché and Gregory have so ably demonstrated (see the Introduction to this volume, with Cordell, as well as Gregory and Piché, 1981). What should be noted here is that soldiers, and those who fled to avoid becoming soldiers, were also migrants on a large and systematic scale. Along with migrant workers, soldiers also helped change the course of West African demographic history in the interwar years.

7

CREATING HUNGER
Labor and Agricultural Policies in
Southern Mosi, 1919-1940

RAYMOND GERVAIS

It was the fate of one of the most well-structured
kingdoms of the West African Sahel (Delobsom, 1932; Kabore, 1966;
Izard, 1970; among many others) to become the "labor reservoir" for
French West Africa (henceforth AOF, for *Afrique Occidentale Française*—see Map 2) (Cordell and Gregory, 1982; Coulibaly, 1978). The
first explorers and their early administrative successors (Beauminy,
1918-1919) foresaw a "logical" division of functions: Let the richer
coastal colonies acquire the labor they badly need and their prosperity
would eventually reach their poorer Sahelian neighbors.

The development efforts of Hesling, the first *lieutenant-gouverneur*
of Upper Volta, brought the colony to the verge of bankruptcy due to
the extremely harsh fiscal policy of colonial self-sufficiency. The colonial administration was living in a dream world and did not grasp the
reality of the agricultural process.

In this chapter, I will analyze the effects of labor policies on
agriculture and the reproduction of labor. I contend that not only did
"labor exports"—labor migration—have negative effects on
economic development, but they also endangered the demographic
regime. Food and people became rarer. Competition between the colo-

Author's Note: This chapter is a brief presentation of arguments and data
from a thesis in preparation at the Université de Paris VII under the direction
of C. Coquery-Vidrovitch. The data were gathered in Paris, Dakar, Bamako,
Abidjan, and Ouagadougou with funds from the FCAC (Québec) and the
CRSH/SSHRC (Ottawa). Both institutions are sincerely thanked.

TABLE 7.1
Population, Density, and Percentage Mosi:
Southern Mosi, 1923-1939

Year	Kaya	Koudougou	Ouagadougou	Tenkodogo
1923				
Population	202,427	342,600	536,111	230,484
Density	13.7	27.4	15.9	23.0
1939				
Population	267,829	350,320	544,626	200,885
Density	18.1	28.0	16.1	20.0
1926				
Population	249,148	331,366	580,210	250,187
Percentage Mosi	82.4	71.5	74.4	41.5
1934				
Population	262,437	348,073	494,641	187,270
Percentage Mosi	82.0	75.0	79.0	56.1

SOURCES: Annual Political Reports: Upper Volta, 1925-1926 in ANF-SOM, A.P. 1248; Ivory Coast, 1934, 1939 in ANS, 2G 34/7 and 2G 39/3.

nial system and domestic agricultural production units for labor was structurally unequal. It precipitated the demise of previous agricultural work processes without offering any alternatives but bare survival.

COLONIAL LABOR POLICY IN THE MOSI REGION

I have included in Southern Mosi the four colonial *cercles* of Koudougou, Ouagadougou, Kaya, and Tenkodogo, thus excluding the Yatênga region, known in colonial jargon as the Ouahigouya cercle. These four units were located in central Upper Volta, where the majority of the Mosi entity had developed (see Map 2). The population of these cercles was predominantly Mosi (see Table 7.1).

For Hesling and most of his successors, these relatively populated areas (by AOF standards) were central to a new economic policy.[1] In every field—urban infrastructure, road construction, railway building, production of cash crops, production of food crops, and labor conscription for the Ivory Coast—numbers were of crucial importance. Upper Volta had to prove its viability as a colony; more specifically, intensive use had to be made of its main resource, the *labor force*, the product of a dynamic population. Let us briefly examine the forms taken by these exactions (see Table 7.2).[2]

TABLE 7.2

Number of Persons Recruited by the Colonial Administration:
Southern Mosi, 1924 and 1937

Cercles/Years	Military Recruits	Railway Workers	Administrative Recruits	Prestations
Kaya				
1924	175	320	1,388	27,500
1937	270	0	2,249	60,000[a]
Koudougou				
1924	275	1,109	3,102	42,155
1937	353	175	467	80,000
Ouagadougou				
1924	475	400	7,451	64,727
1937	505	175	2,040	72,290
Tenkodogo				
1924	225	0	849	33,259
1937	187	175	30	45,724

SOURCES: Military: ANS 4D series. Others: Annual Political Reports, Upper Volta and Ivory Coast, 1924 and 1937. Annual Political Reports, Kaya, Koudougou, Ouagadougou, Tenkodogo.
a. This figure is actually from 1938.

Confronted with a decreasing metropolitan population, the French government called upon its colonies to provide manpower for its defense system (Echenberg, 1975; 1980; Chapter 6 in this book). In 1912 and 1913, colonial conscription began. From then until independence in 1960, young men were incorporated into the colonial army. Quotas were established using two parameters: (1) The *commandant de cercle* would evaluate the number of young men in the appropriate age groups, and (2) military authorities would establish needs and allocate a given number to each colony (*contingent*) and the Lieutenant-gouverneur would divide the contingent among the colony's cercles.

Mosi were also recruited for building both the Thiès-Kayes (1919-1928) and the Ivory Coast railway (1919-1931). Recruitment was left largely in the hands of the chiefs who may have encountered problems when returning workers brought back stories about death, the fatigue of the long journey (it was only in the second half of the 1930s that trucks were used to transport laborers), low wages, and poor living conditions. The *commandants* gave voice to these complaints; they were also sometimes heard at the *Conseil des Notables* (a consultative council of chiefs in each cercle). The effects were felt at the lowest and least powerful level of the administration, but orders had to be obeyed and needs had to be met.

By far the most important internal user of labor was the administration itself. Laborers were requisitioned through commandants and chiefs to work on administrative sites—such as the construction of Ouagadougou between 1919 and 1922, or the installation of trading companies between 1924 and 1927. Numbers were often large: 3000 or more men and women working for one month at very low wages. Usually the start of the rainy season marked a decline in activity, but many commandants discovered that dwindling supply did little to restrict demand. None was more informed than Commandant Michel, who supervised laborers coming in from other cercles to Ouagadougou. In 1925 (ADGRST, A III and IV), he made a list of the major labor petitioners: (1) the administration of the Ouagadougou cercle, (2) the military construction authorities, (3) merchants (Boussac) and the Catholic mission, (4) the Ivory Coast railway, and (5) porters for different services. In March 1926 he wrote a letter to the lieutenant-gouverneur imploring him to reduce these requests:

> A general fatigue has developed after the effort of the last few months. ... I am afraid the fatigue will increase and cause grave reactions from the natives. We must remember that the natives, overworked, will soon be underfed [ADGRST A IV].

These words were prophetic: 1926 *was* a year of acute famine in many areas. "To want the native to be at the same time a farmer and a *prestataire* is to desire the incompatible," he concluded. His perspective was correct; no agricultural society working at such a simple level of technology could satisfy such large demands for labor while still providing what was required for the reproduction of its producers.

To the sum of labor already described must be added *prestation,* the number of days that every able-bodied male had to give to the administration of the cercle. The general framework of regulations concerning prestation was set in 1918 before the creation of Upper Volta. Legally, use of prestataires was limited to modest projects in the vicinity of the village of residence, undertaken only by male workers between ages 16 and 60 during the off-season, for a maximum number of days fixed by the lieutenant-gouverneur and published in the *Journal Officiel* (seven or eight days in the 1920s and 1930s). Furthermore, these projects and the corresponding number of days were supposed to take account of the density of the region's population. However, the gulf between law and reality was wide and deep. Children and women were known to be enrolled, the limit on distance was rarely observed, the number of days per worker was pure fiction, work was sometimes done during the rainy season, and, most important for our concerns, there was no control on the work sites, except by chiefs and guards. So, to say the least, the numbers of workers in Table 7.2 (column 5) are a minimum. These statistics were calculated for each cercle by dividing the total number of days used by the number of days owed by the male population.

In evaluating the weight of these labor requirements one must consider both quantitative and qualitative aspects. The percentage of the total evaluated population involved in the recruitments is moderate: Kaya, 11.8 percent in 1924, 23.6 percent in 1937; Koudougou, 13.4 and 23.0 percent; Ouagadougou, 13.7 and 14.0 percent; Tenkodogo, 14.9 and 22.5 percent. For three out of four cercles there was a population increase between 1924 and 1937. Theoretically, at a maximum, only a quarter of the total population was touched. Reality was much bleaker. If we consider only the male population—legally the target population—then the percentages jump to a quarter (in 1924) and a half (in 1937). We also lack information on the structure; consideration of that variable would push our percentages higher as a fraction of adult male able-bodied workers.

Finally, during the 1930s more and more members of the colonial service came to recognize the qualitative constraints on labor exactions. The absence of able-bodied workers had clearly impeded the reproduction of the conditions of agricultural production. The long, hungry seasons of 1926 and 1930 and undernourishment in general had endangered the quality—and quite logically the quantity—of the labor force. Sorel, general inspector of AOF sanitary and medical services, noted that the efforts required from the "natives" had reached their limits; if surpassed, the future of the "race" was at risk.[3] The *commandants de cercle* were not blind to these risks. In 1931, for example, the commandant of Koudougou expressed fear concerning the effects of excess labor extortions, following in the footsteps of a predecessor who in 1924 had estimated that 18 percent of the total population were adult males fit for use by the administration.[4]

EFFECTS ON THE AGRICULTURAL WORK PROCESS

Because of the ecological and technical constraints on agricultural production in Southern Mosi, any call on the domestic labor force, whatever its level, without a prior increase in rural productivity could and would undermine nutrition. Basically, the domestic production units could not assure conditions necessary for agricultural production.

What were these conditions? The geography was harsh (Pallier, 1978), the level and distribution of rainfall were undependable. The most recent description of Yatênga characterizes the whole region (Marchal, 1983: 46): a relatively short rainy season; irregular, often brief but violent rains producing significant erosion; rapid evaporation of soil moisture. Rainfall statistics (see Table 7.3) suggest the insecure state of agriculture. In all cercles, close to a half or more months of the rainy season from 1920 to 1940 were under the average.

The technological level of agricultural production was similar to other parts of West Africa: *rudimentary* in order to respect fragile ecological conditions, and therefore *dependent* on massive inputs of labor (Dupriez, 1980; Kohler, 1971; Marchal, 1983). As elsewhere, the off-season work calendar was flexible, but when the rains arrived, time became rare, work intensified, and the calendar of operations expanded.

TABLE 7.3
Months of Rain in the Mosi Region, 1920-1940:
Number of Months Under, On, Over the Average Rainfall

Region	May	June	July	August	September	October
Kaya						
under	10	10	9	9	12	12
average	2	2	3	2	2	2
over	9	9	9	10	7	7
Koudougou						
under	11	10	10	10	10	10
average	1	2	2	1	1	3
over	9	9	9	10	10	8
Ouagadougou						
under	8	5	10	8	8	10
average	5	3	1	1	2	2
over	4	8	6	9	7	5
Tenkodogo						
under	9	9	9	11	10	11
average	3	2	0	0	1	2
over	7	8	10	10	10	6

SOURCE: Afrique occidentale française, Gouverneur-Général 1954.
NOTE: Totals do not always equal 21 because there are gaps in the data. The dividing line between the average and the others is 5 mm.

A few words must be said of the social context of agricultural production, storage, and land tenure (Ancey, 1983; Dubourg, 1957;
Gnampa, 1980; Izard-Héritier and Izard, 1959; Kohler, 1971; Lallemand, 1977; Marchal, 1983; Mesnil, 1970; Rémy, 1972; Sawadogo,
1970). Often identified as an important cause of migration, the
gerontocratic power of the male elders dominated—and still
dominates—the agricultural production process. The *yirsoba,* head
of the households, negotiated access to land. He approaches the
tengsoba, chief of the land (often *not* a Moaga [singular of Mosi] but
a member of the indigenous group called *Nioniosé*), and assures that
all household members have the land they require. The most notable
social dichotomy is found between (1) the common fields, organized
and allocated by the yirsoba—the fields' production was stocked in his
granaries, of which he is the sole manager and (2) the individual fields
(*beolgha*) given to women and other members of the *yiri,* the yield of
which is kept by these individuals. A similar division is found in land
allocation between (1) fallow bush lands and (2) cultivated fields, including those exploited annually near the huts where manure is used
and those at a distance cultivated in rotation. These social and
agricultural divisions created a complex network that was not completely under human control. The equilibrium characteristic of Moaga
history and society was a product of the astute manipulation of these
variables; it was disrupted by the imposition of new crops and new
demands made on the agricultural production units.

Cotton production gives us one example of the effects of demands
for one new crop.[5] Hesling on his arrival in Ouagadougou in 1919
launched an important cotton campaign by (1) pressing producers to
expand cultivation of the crop, (2) encouraging (between 1925 and
1927) commercial interests to build in Ouagadougou, (3) massively improving the communications networks (minimizing costs by using prestataires), and (4) creating an infrastructure to experiment, diffuse
new seeds and techniques, and control quality. In 1924 an experimental farm was established 25 kilometers from Koudougou, becoming in
1926 the *ferme-école cotonnière de Saria,* symbol of the transition
from experiment to economic policy.

Table 7.4 shows the evolution of cotton exports from 1923-1924 to
1936-1937. The lack of rainfall made 1925-1926 a year of famine; food
crop production was also disrupted by the imposition of competing
export crops. In the case of cotton, it may be easily explained. Tradi-
tionally sowed on the manured fields near the huts, cotton was usually
a personal crop, planted in small fields with other crops (beans, con-
diments). An increase in exports was generated through the interven-

TABLE 7.4
Upper Volta, Cotton Exports, 1924-1937
(in metric tons)

Years	Total Upper Volta	Mosi Cercles
1923-1924	300	100
1924-1925	3,538	1,815
1925-1926	6,238	3,259
1926-1927	2,005	842
1927-1928	3,200	1,425
1928-1929	2,758	1,535
1929-1930	4,247	2,312
1930-1931	1,664	892
1931-1932	141	51
1932-1933	313	n.d.
1933-1934	557	48
1934-1935	468	210
1935-1936	334	141
1936-1937	414	n.d.

SOURCES: ANCI R series, files 800, 826; ANS 1R 48 and 10G 9.

tion of agricultural agents (trained in Saria), pressure on commandants de cercle, collective fields imposed on village chiefs, and
distribution of (not-always-successful) new seeds (Allen, Karangani-
Garroh Hills, Budi).

At the local level we can but hypothesize as to the effects of these
policies. Given the traditional allocation of fields, a few scenarios may
be imagined.

(1) If the collective cotton fields measured, controlled, and imposed by the
    agents were on manured land near the huts, there was a decrease both
    of hungry season crops such as maize, and condiments.
(2) If they were allocated to fields farther away, they competed directly
    with the basic food crops of millet and sorghum.
(3) If cotton was relegated to bush and fallow fields (the least likely possi-
    bility given that the administration excluded this category), it often ter-
    minated the fallow period of an old field. Furthermore, cultivation of
    these outfields was time-consuming in terms of both travel and agricul-
    tural labor.
(4) When cotton quotas were not met, yirsoba had to go elsewhere to buy
    the needed supplements, spending already scarce cash resources that
    would be needed in periods of famine.
(5) The last possibility was the absence of space and time.

We know from oral and written testimonies that the proceeds from the
sale of the cotton from the collective fields were rarely returned to the

producers.[6] The system deprived cultivators of what was later to be called "exchange entitlements" (Sen, 1976). So when natural factors did contribute to famine conditions, peasant purchasing power was too low to permit access to the food crop market.

THE INSTRUMENTS OF INTERVENTION

Two points were made in the preceding sections: (1) that colonial use and abuse of Mosi labor may have been so overwhelming as to endanger reproduction strategies, and (2) that because of ecological and technical constraints, manipulation of time (by diverting domestic labor) or space (by reallocating fields) may well have drastically reduced domestic capital (food and monetary reserves). Yet the administration did attempt to compensate for the negative effects of these colonial policies. Two aspects of efforts to modernize agricultural production can be cited: (1) the geographical distribution of colonial exactions and (2) the work of the *Service de l'agriculture*.

The population census constituted the cornerstone for the French colonial administration—the number of taxpayers, prestataires, military recruits, available workers, and, indirectly, the quotas for export crops—were all established using the results of such enumerations. The Gouverneur-Général of AOF considered census taking a major priority; Bourgeois-Gavardin, head of a 1941 inspection team in AOF, summed up this goal succinctly: "The census, as recent and exact as possible, is the essential element of our knowledge of indigenous populations" (Mission d'inspection, 1941: report 15, 2). Local administrators themselves were aware of its importance when they blamed bad censuses for significant migration, noting, quite rightly, that people were fleeing an unjust tax structure; those who remained behind frequently were obliged to pay for the dead and the migrants. In the face of these problems, were the censuses reliable?

This is a difficult question and cannot be truly answered here. Only two observations will be made. First, the quality of the censuses was much too variable to permit any generalization. The debate, spanning the twenty years under study, about the necessity of nominal versus numeric censuses, as well as the harshness of criticism and orders, points to the difficulties involved and the slowness of bureaucratic response.[7] Censuses in AOF were archaic and archaeological: Archaic in methods because the lack of qualified personnel (European and African) made it impossible to organize anything approaching a modern census. The first population data were the results of either an updating of earlier estimates or a visit to chiefs who were required to provide the total population of their villages. These were numeric approximations with a low degree of reliability. In their manipulation by the administration they were archaeological: Every subdivision was considered a strata, quasi-independent of others. By "archaeological," I also mean that there was and could not be any synthesis of total numbers; population data were viewed as layers of different dates (according to the year of the last census) that had to be adjusted when time and personnel allowed.

Second, during the late 1930s, the increasing frequency of nominal censuses made results more reliable. The methodology was similar to the one used in the 1976-1978 censuses in most Sahelian countries. This method was not really operational on a large scale until the end of the period under study and never for a whole cercle. The colonial administration was, therefore, on the basis of a very approximate evaluation, organizing massive labor mobilization *with little prior knowledge of what local production units could sustain.*

Agricultural services in AOF have a checkered history and have been subject to two fundamental contradictions: (1) the often overt conflict between technicians and administrators[8] and (2) the debate over the role of each level of government services; what was the role of the AOF inspectorate, for example, and what was to be left to local services? Solutions to both problems were developed simultaneously. Administrators were given preeminence over technicians. The federation inspectorate (*Inspection générale de l'agriculture*) was incorporated into economic affairs *(Affaires économiques)* and given a coordinating role, with the exception of the management of a few experimental stations (Bingerville, Pobé, M'Bambey). Local agricultural services in the colonies were limited to experimental farms such as Saria, while administrators, without prior knowledge of the elementary problems of tropical agriculture, were charged with mobilization of production, diffusion of technological innovations, evaluation of food crop production, and export crops.

The agriculture service of Upper Volta was created in August 1923 (see Hesling, 1923: 113-114). Its role was technical, advisory, and coordinating. Hesling's (1923: 5-6) memorandum set the tone:

> Finally, the creation of this technical service corresponds at present to the urgent necessity of methodically organizing on scientific bases industrial crops whose existence and development are indispensable for the economic take off of the colony.

The service was placed under the authority of the lieutenant-gouverneur, and for technical matters it depended on the federation inspec-

TABLE 7.5

Upper Volta, Budget Allocations to Agriculture, Health,
and Administration as a Percentage of Total Expenses
1920-1932

	Agriculture	Health	Administration
1920	0.4	5.2	39.8
1921	0.8	6.4	38.0
1922	0.9	6.5	35.1
1923	1.9	7.8	34.2
1924	3.6	7.1	31.3
1925	3.1	6.3	28.5
1926	3.8	5.5	26.9
1927	3.1	6.7	22.5
1928	3.9	7.1	24.1
1929	2.8	6.8	23.9
1930	3.2	7.3	24.3
1931	3.9	8.7	24.5
1932	4.1	10.1	23.3

SOURCE: Budget de la Haute-Volta, 1920-1932.

torate. Table 7.5 quantifies the place of agriculture in resource allocations. Though the percentage was doubled when the service was created, and it continued to grow, one is struck by the fact that a maximum of only 4 percent of the budget was allocated to a sphere of activity encompassing 95 percent of the population. Budgetary reallocation went mainly to health and education. During the administrative absorption of Southern Mosi into the Ivory Coast (from 1933 to 1947), visible budgetary items point to a further marginalization. The budget of the experimental farm and school of Saria, for example, stagnated; Poundou and Banankélédaga, the other two experimental farms in colonial Upper Volta, were simply abolished.

FEEDING HUNGER:
THE DIALECTICS OF COLONIAL
DEMOGRAPHIC AND AGRICULTURAL POLICIES

I have tried to establish a relationship between the quantitative and qualitative levels of the Mosi work force under the strains imposed by colonial administration and the social and ecological constraints involved in agricultural production. Many facets of the problem can be identified. If one considers the overall logic of the colonial system, it is obvious that few options were available. The obligation of fiscal self-sufficiency brought with it the necessity to find exports. In Upper Volta from 1919 to 1933-1934 these were cotton *and* labor. I have tried to show the limits of this double dynamic. Without prior investment in the modernization of production, and without an increase in productivity, there was no room in the Mosi calendar for cotton on a large scale. Absence of reliable population estimates made it impossible even for local administrators to grasp the importance of their (and their superiors') labor requirements.

What of the numerous estimates found in the archives? They were the means used by authorities to justify the annual increases in labor exports and tax totals until a breaking point was reached: In 1926, food crops were insufficient; in 1931-1932 fiscal pressures reached a peak. The first element of the dialectical situation was the expansion of demand for one or more goods—the construction of a unilateral system of requirements without a simultaneous investment to assure the reproduction of the conditions of production.

The response of the domestic production units could only be inadequate. Over hundreds of years it had developed means of adjusting to climatic conditions. It had created the surplus required by the agricultural work process; this had been secured by adaptive techniques and massive inputs of labor. In a short period of time it was propelled into a system that deprived it of space and time; it was deprived of the management of its labor and land. Once the process was engaged, it fed itself. The cotton policy was a fiasco because techniques remained the same while demands increased dramatically. Cotton prices were very low; this pushed young men into migration to the Gold Coast in order to find tax money. In the Mosi region, hunger was created through the largely imaginary estimates of population numbers, the basis for no less imaginary quotas of export and food crops and labor recruitments. Neither could be produced because of low productivity levels and the flight of able-bodied men. As Sol so aptly put it, the system was a bargain because everything cost so little *until* the reproduction mechanisms (demographic and economic) collapsed under the accumulation of contradictions. Imagination was insufficient to overcome the crisis.

NOTES

1. Hesling's letter to the *Gouverneur-Général*, ANS 10G7 (107), January 1923; report to the President of the Republic, *Journal Officiel de la Haute-Volta* (hereafter JOHV), 1919, 5-6.

2. A complete examination of data sources and methodological problems is offered in the thesis. In this analysis, I use the term "domestic labor" to refer to the total labor

force that would have been available for agriculture had there *not* been colonial recruitment. By "reproduction of the conditions of agricultural production" I mean the reproduction of all elements of production: land (and land allocation strategies), human capital, technical capital (tools, seeds), and, finally, the means of sustaining life.

3. There are, for example, instances when the health problems of laborers were analyzed: Mission Sol, Economic report, ANS 10G19 (107); Sorel report, 1931, annex of the previously quoted report; *Inspection mobile d'hygiène,* Dr. Viala, 1932, ANS 10G9 (107); Annual medical report, Upper Volta, 1931, ANS 2G 31:26; and Report on military recruitment 1929, ANS 4D 8(81), 1931, 4D 9(81), 1933, 4D 10(81), 1934, 4D 11(81).

4. Koudougou, Annual political report, 1924, ANCI E 1763 (X-21-426), 45; Annual political report, 1931, ANCI E 1763 (X-21-426), 27.

5. See the B. Sol inspection, economic report, and the *Rapport sur la politique suivie à l'égard des produits naturels susceptibles d'une utilisation industrielle;* the agricultural reports for Upper Volta and Ivory Coast in the ANS 2G series; ANS 1Q 48. In ANCI the R series contains vital files, especially R 808, 898, 873, 882, 887, and 879.

6. See Mission Sol, Report 36, annex 39; ANS 1R 125 (158); ANS 10G9 (107); ANCI R873, reports and correspondences.

7. See the *inspections*: Demaret, 1918-1919, report 1; Picanon, 1924-1925, reports 122 and 128; Sol, 1931 1932, reports 2 and 79; Bagot, 1934-1935, report 29bis; Bourgeois-Gavardin, 1941, report 15. See *memoranda*: Hesling, 1923 in ANCI D1840; Fournier (Lt.-Governor of Upper Volta), 1932, in annex report 18 of the Sol mission; Reste (Lt.-Governor of Ivory Coast), 1934, in the annual political report of 1934, ANS 2G 34:7, 57-67. See *statements*: Reste's 1932 annual political report for Ivory Coast, ANF-SOM (Paris) *Affaires politiques,* 567, 56; Reste's exchange of letters with the commandant de cercle of Ouagadougou in ANCI E 1396 (XVII-25-12).

8. This subject was mentioned often: Mission Meray, 1921-1922, reports 109-110; ANS 1R 115(158) on the teaching of agriculture 1907, 1922, and 1934; ANS 1R 71(158) the *arrêtés* of 1920 and 1923 concerning the service; the 1921 Report of the inspectorate, just before its virtual abolition (ANS 1R 56 [158]).

8

MAKING MIGRANTS
Zarma Peasants in Niger, 1900-1920

THOMAS M. PAINTER

        The demographic regime of African peripheral capitalism is frequently characterized by high fertility and a high incidence of migrations (Gregory and Piché, 1981). The Dosso region of southwestern Niger, which will be considered here, typifies this type of demographic regime. Annual population growth was estimated to be 2.5 percent in 1978 (Niger, 1978: 22), and the current incidence of seasonal migration is high, involving two-thirds or more of the migrant-age (around 17 to 55 years of age) male population in some areas (Beauvilain, 1977; Niger, n.d.; Painter, 1985; Poncet, 1974).

        The destinations of Dosso migrants have varied over time (see Map 3). From shortly after 1900 through the 1960s, they traveled princi-

Author's Note: This chapter is based on doctoral dissertation research conducted in Niger, Senegal, France, and England in 1981-1983. My work was financed by an International Doctoral Research Fellowship from the Social Science Research Council and the American Council of Learned Societies, by Grant SES-8016409 from the National Science Foundation, and by contributions and loans from my family and several generous friends. Their support and good faith are most gratefully acknowledged. I would also like to thank the directors and staff of the Archives Nationales de France, Service des Microfilms (Paris), the Public Records Office (Kew Gardens, United Kingdom), the Archives du Sénégal (Dakar), the Archives Nationales du Niger (Niamey), and the Préfet of the Dosso departement, Niger, for permitting me to consult their collections. Thanks are due also to Jean-Loup Amselle, Michael Horowitz, and Bill Martin, who read and commented on earlier versions of this essay. Responsibility for any shortcomings in the present version is mine alone.

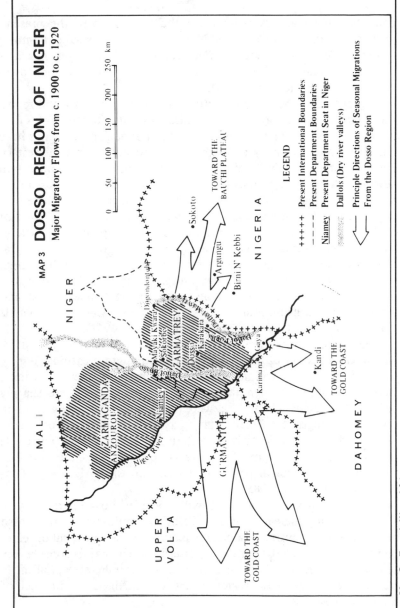

MAP 3 **DOSSO REGION OF NIGER**
Major Migratory Flows from c. 1900 to c. 1920

0   50   100   150   200   250 km

MALI

NIGER

UPPER
VOLTA

ZARMAGANDA
NZOUROU

Niger River

Dallol Bosso

Namey

GURMANTCH

TOWARD THE
GOLD COAST

TOWARD THE
GOLD COAST

Dagomdoutchi

Maduki Kauna

Sokorbe

ZARMATAREY

Dosso

Katakam

Dallol Fogha

Karimama

Gaya

Kandi

TOWARD THE
GOLD COAST

DAHOMEY

Sokoto

Argungu

Birni N' Kebbi

TOWARD THE
BAUCHI PLATEAU

NIGERIA

LEGEND

+++++   Present International Boundaries

－－－   Present Department Boundaries

<u>Niamey</u>   Present Department Seat in Niger

Dallols (Dry river valleys)

Principle Directions of Seasonal Migrations
From the Dosso Region

Map 3   French West Africa

pally to Ghana and Nigeria; from the late 1960s to the present, primarily to the Ivory Coast and Nigeria, but also in smaller numbers to Benin, Togo, and Cameroon (Niger, n.d.). Within Niger, migrants from rural areas travel to the capital, Niamey, and to smaller towns (Gregory, 1975; Sidikou, 1980a).

Migrants leave Niger from October through December and return the following April and May to prepare and cultivate their fields during the rainy season, which begins in May or June. These months have long been referred to by administrators and inhabitants of western Niger as marking the beginning and the end of the "migration season." Annual migrations of peasant cultivators from Dosso over distances as great as 1500 kilometers to the Guinea Coast, where they engage in petty trade and unskilled labor, have become a "fact of life"—a normal feature of a peripheral demographic regime (Berg, 1965; compare Gregory and Piché, 1978). So important have migrations become for western Niger's rural economy that they have been incorporated into Zarma ideology and serve as something akin to a masculine rite of passage. Having been to the Guinea Coast and returned with cash and commodities is, for many, evidence that a male is indeed an adult (Painter, 1984; Rouch, 1956, 1961).

Seasonal migrations are also very important to the Nigerien state, which had a history of heavy dependence on migrant earnings during the colonial and postcolonial periods. From 1900 when head taxes were introduced, through the late 1970s when taxes were sharply reduced (made possible by what were then rapidly increasing uranium revenues), migrations made tax payments possible for many household heads, particularly in western Niger. Head taxes (and cattle taxes) accounted in turn for a large portion of state revenues throughout the colonial period and well into the early years of independence (Painter, 1985).

In the remarks to follow, I will consider how migrants were "made" during the early years of colonial domination in the Dosso region. I hope to promote a clearer picture of the historical development of the seasonal migration pattern, which has become a key feature of demographic regimes shaped by peripheral capitalism, a pattern seen in the Dosso region, elsewhere in Niger, and in much of Sahelian West Africa.

THE BEGINNINGS OF COLONIAL DOMINATION IN THE DOSSO REGION

The French colonial presence dates from November 1898 when a military post was created in the village of Dosso. Immediately after their arrival from Karimana in Dahomey, the French military forcibly requisitioned local labor and local production (Périé and Sellier, 1950: 1060; Salifou, 1977: 451-453; ANN, "Monographie, Ancien Cercle de Djerma," Archives de Cercle de Niamey, 1901). A new era had begun in *zamratarey* (see Gado, 1980), or Zarma country (see Map 3) and with it came new burdens for the Dosso peasantry.

Within a year, the region's populations experienced a particularly violent encounter with European military forces when the Mission Voulet-Chanoine (a part of the larger Mission Afrique Centrale), passed through the region from Say on its way to Lake Chad via Zinder. The column was enormous. By one account, there were 6 French officers, 600 African soldiers, 200 women, 800 porters, and about 500 head of cattle (Périé and Sellier, 1950: 1061).

Irritated by the fears and hostility of local populations, and sorely taxed by heat and thirst, the column's leaders, captains Voulet and Chanoine, and their soldiers turned their wrath on the region's inhabitants. Staples and animals were seized or destroyed, hundreds of persons were killed, and an estimated 50 villages were burned to the ground (Périé and Sellier, 1950: 1061-1063). So ruthless were the column's *spahis* with their machetes during attacks on villages that the mission became known (and is still remembered) by the Hausa name *sara-sara* or "chop-chop" (Abadie, 1927: 315; Rolland, 1976).

The differences between the cruel methods of the Voulet-Chanoine mission and what became standard procedures of the French administration were those of both degree and kind, but violence was a frequent tool of colonial domination throughout Niger (Kimba, 1981; Salifou, 1977; compare Rash, 1972).

LAYING THE GROUNDWORK FOR SEASONAL MIGRATIONS IN THE DOSSO REGION: CONTINUITY OR DISCONTINUITY?

Appropriation by the French military of peasant production and labor was soon stepped up through imposition of a head tax. Yearly tax collections, scheduled to occur immediately after the October millet harvest, began in 1900. All persons over six years of age were subject to the tax of two francs, payable in money, millet, or livestock (Kimba, 1981: 107; Rash, 1972: 142). By 1903, however, the tax rate proved to be too much for local populations and was reduced to fifty centimes (ANF-MI, 2G-11 [200 MI 1628], Résidence de Zinder, "Rapport Politique, juin 1903"). Taxes were raised again in 1908 and reached three francs by 1920, after which rates in Niger were report-

edly much higher than anywhere else in French West Africa (Fuglestad, 1974: 22; 1983: 83). During this time Dosso peasants were under
continuous pressure from administrative requisitions and forced labor
recruitment.

The appropriation of agricultural surpluses by statelike structures
did not begin with the French occupation of Dosso. From at least the
early nineteenth century, Dosso peasants had been paying tribute
through a system that included village headmen (*kwara koyan*),
regional land chiefs (*labu koyan*), and the Dosso Zarma Chief, the
Zarmakoy, assisted by his police agents or bodyguards, the *dogari*. In
like manner, the *boogu,* a form of collective labor organization (which
persists in much of Zarmaphone Niger) provided a source of labor for
the fields of the Zarmakoy and other nobles. Finally, a great deal of
precolonial agricultural labor was supplied by captives (Olivier de Sardan, 1984: 27-60; Rash, 1972; Rothiot, 1984; Streicker, 1980: 74-75,
passim).

The imposition of taxes and *corvée* by the French thus followed
upon precolonial forms of appropriation, but these new forms were
additions to rather than replacements for the older forms (Rash, 1972;
Rothiot, 1984). Precolonial forms of appropriation also changed
qualitatively during these years. The Dosso Zarmakoy (and the
Mawrikoy in Sokorbé, to the north of Dosso) were now able to collect
their one-tenth forcibly with French military backing. The principle of
land use-fee payments (*labu albarka*) to the Dosso Zarmakoy, by virtue of his descent from the original Dosso settlers, also became a coercively sanctioned obligation.

Seizure of peasant labor by the colonial administration was
codified in 1912, when all males over 12 years of age were required to
furnish five days of labor annually. In principle, corvée labor was
remunerated, but in practice this was rare. This, too, was added to
preexisting forms of labor appropriation. In addition, for those land
chiefs who cooperated with the French and their ally, Zarmakoy
Aouta, and who were thus appointed *chefs de canton,* the precolonial
boogu became a means of coercively appropriating the labor of com-
moners, thus compensating their losses of captive labor, selectively
freed by the French.

In sum, the new forms of appropriation constituted a heavy burden
on Dosso peasants, for unlike precolonial forms, they were collected
with little regard for the peasantry's capacity to pay, and they were
collected with the backing of force as never before.

COLONIAL APPROPRIATION AND EARLY MIGRATIONS

The Context of Colonial Appropriation:
A Crisis in Peasant Production

Under optimal conditions, predominantly rain-fed agricultural production was (and remains) a marginal enterprise in much of the Dosso region (Fuglestad, 1974; Rash, 1972; Sidikou, 1974; Streicker, 1980). Rainfall is often meager and poorly distributed during many rainy seasons. The crusty, lateritic soils of the central plateau areas and the heavily leached alluvial soils of the dry river valleys *(dallols)* to the east and west are poor.

During much of the nineteenth century, however, conditions for production were far from optimal in the region. To the harsh climate was added chronic political insecurity. Tuareg and Fulbe repeatedly raided Zarma settlements, and there was strife among Zarma subgroups themselves. Reserve grain stocks were raided and seized, standing crops occasionally were destroyed by fire, and the agricultural labor force itself—whether free or captive—was subject to capture and forced migration (Beauvilain, 1977; Streicker, 1980).

Political Economy, Famines, and Early Forms
of Resistance: Migrations as Escape

Toward the turn of the century, conditions in western Niger deteriorated even further. Famines, caused by droughts and locust attacks, plagued the Anzourou and Zarmaganda to the northwest, and from 1901 to 1903 the Dosso region was also affected (Fuglestad, 1983; Sidikou, 1974: 22). It was during this nadir in the history of Dosso that French penetration occurred, severely exacerbating an already critical situation. This was not the last time, however, that political oppression, state exactions, and a particularly unfavorable phase of ecoclimatic conditions would act in concert to undermine Niger's peasantries. Very similar coincidences during the 1930s and 1970s eventually produced analyses and an overall interpretive framework that subsumed these seemingly disparate phenomena: the political economy of famine (for example, Comité d'Information Sahel, 1975; Derriennic, 1977).

Faced with administrative coercion, the Dosso peasantry yielded the grain and livestock demanded by the Dosso post. In 1902 a political report states that "the attitude of the Dosso Zarma is improving—they are beginning to understand what a tax is" (ANN, Poste de Dosso, "Rapport Politique, janvier 1902"). As the 1901-1902 taxes were collected, censuses were conducted for the next fiscal campaign. The field trips failed to produce satisfactory census information, but they did demonstrate that the administration's tax campaign and its multiple requisitions of crops and livestock, superimposed on repeated poor harvests, had already taken a toll on the region's peasants. A subsequent report notes that some Dosso inhabitants had traveled as far as Sokoto (northern Nigeria) in search of millet seed because they had nothing more to plant (ANN, Poste de Dosso, "Rapport Politique, mai 1902").

There can be little doubt that villagers would travel considerable distances from their home regions in search of food and seed when pressed, but this was only part of the picture. Growing numbers of Dosso peasants who crossed into British territory were *fleeing* French territory. As a form of resistance and a means for coping with serious disorder caused by a combination of environmental disruptions and French demands, migration as escape was increasingly practiced by the region's peasants. This reaction was not new. It had been observed several years earlier among Gourmantché to the southwest and was to be a recurrent theme in Niger and in other French territories during the early years of occupation (ANS, 11G-1, Résidence de Say, "Rapport Politique, avril 1898"; Fuglestad, 1974; Kimba, 1981; Rothiot, 1984; compare Asiwaju, 1976; Cordell and Gregory, 1982). Thus, during the first years of French occupation, the Dosso countryside began to move, and by 1903, an estimated 10,000 people left southwestern Niger as a whole (ANF-MI, 2G3-11 [200 MI 1627], Troisième Territoire Militaire, "Rapport Politique, mai 1903").

Eventually, even colonial administrators acknowledged the destructiveness of French policies, and one described the countryside in western Niger as "ruined by years of successive requisitions," concluding that "emigration is the almost natural result of the heavy burden of French occupation" (ANF-MI, 2G2-13 [200 MI 1625], Troisième Territoire Militaire, "Rapport Politique, Troisième Trimestre 1902"). Reports during much of the first two decades of French occupation echo this theme: Oppressive tax and labor recruitment policies were major causes of massive emigration into British territory.

FURTHER CONSEQUENCES OF COLONIAL APPROPRIATION

Forced Sale of Agricultural Production:
Forced Exchange of Cowrie Currency

The character of colonial appropriation changed in 1906 when efforts began to replace tax payments in kind by payments in currency, and within three years the administration also sought to disallow tax payments even in the local cowrie (*Cypraea*) currency. By 1909 cowries were "mercilessly refused" as tax payment in the Dosso *cercle,* and this became a territory-wide policy in 1910 (ANN, Cahier des Rapports, Cercle de Dosso, "Rapport Politique, mars 1909"; Baier, 1980: 107).

Concurrent with measures to force tax payments in specie was a chronic shortage of French currency (ANN, Cahier des Rapports, Cercle de Dosso, "Rapport Commercial, 1er Trimestre 1909"). This hindered timely tax payments and led to greater harassment of local populations by the administration. These recurring shortages, particularly of small-denomination coins, also slowed the insertion of the peasantry into circuits of cash exchange, so vehemently desired by the French, for once taxes were paid, little money remained among the region's populations (Rothiot, 1984: 274-278; compare ANN, Cahier des Rapports, Cercle de Dosso, "Rapport Commercial, 1er Trimestre 1909").

The pressing need for French currency helped to push peasant production for use-value further into the sphere of exchange and into new geographic areas (compare Cordell and Gregory, 1982: 212; Rothiot, 1984: 274-279). Comments of the following kind become frequent in administrative reports written during the first months of tax collection campaigns:

All over the natives have begun to look for tax money, and have gone to different markets in the region [in order to sell their livestock and millet] [ANN, Cahier des Rapports, Cercle de Desso, "Rapport Politique, février 1908"].

They were traveling to Niamey to the west, to Kandi in Dahomey, and to Sokoto and Birni N'Kebbi in Nigeria. Through administrative coercion, the commoditization of production increased in tempo but in a manner decidedly disadvantageous to local populations. Peasants were forced to accept extremely poor terms of exchange for their cowries, grain, and livestock from the traders who were the major sources of coin (Rothiot, 1984: 277-280; ANN, Cahier des Rapports, Cercle de Dosso, "Rapport Politique, mars 1909"; ANF-MI, 2G5-19 [200 MI 1637], Cercle de Dosso, "Rapport Politique, 1er Trimestre 1905").

These devaluations and what amounted to forced sales of production *did* bring in tax revenue, but they also further undermined the peasantry's narrow margin for maneuver under precarious conditions of subsistence.

Forced Labor in the Service of
Colonial Domination

A second source of French currency was the administration itself, although its supplies were often low. Effective colonial penetration of the Niger territory required a minimum of infrastructural development. Administrative offices, quarters, warehouses, granaries, and other out-buildings were required, as were stables, wells, and even gardens. Roads were necessary as were encampments for traveling administrators. Telegraph lines were needed for more efficient communication. Once constructed, these all required maintenance and repair.

These works programs created a sporadic demand for labor in areas adjacent to administrative posts. During the second half of 1908, for example, construction began on a telegraph line between Niamey and Zinder to the east. Laborers were needed to carry and install the posts, crowns, insulators, and wire, and many of the workers were supplied by the Dosso and Dogondoutchi cantons (ANN, Cahier des Rapports, Cercle de Dosso, "Rapports Politiques, septembre 1908; mai 1909").

The laborers were paid one franc per ton-kilometer, which permitted most taxes to be paid in coin during the two years of the line's construction in the Dosso region. In fact, most of the money paid to the workers quickly returned to the administration's coffers in the form of head tax payments during 1908 and 1909 (ANN, Cahier des Rapports, Cercle de Dosso, "Rapports Politiques, mars 1909 and mai 1909"; Rothiot, 1984: 273).

The Search for Money:
Toward a Consolidation
of the Seasonal Migration Pattern

While fiscal liability was widespread among rural populations, access to the means of relieving it was not. Persons who were beyond the perimeter of the telegraph line's short-term effects, for example, were forced to search elsewhere for tax money.

Peasant mobility increased as people sought to sell their production to secure tax money, but more was moving than physical objects, destined for transformation from use value into exchange value. The peasantry's labor itself was becoming mobile, also moving under duress toward commoditization as migrant labor power. This was possible only in distant areas where the possibilities for accumulation existed and the subsequent development of capitalist production relations was such that what was domestic (household) labor in one sphere could be freely bought and sold as a commodity in another.

The Zarma were forced to migrate over greater distances in their quest for cash. By 1910 they were traveling as far as the Gold Coast gold mining areas where African labor in European mines increased from 2400 in 1894 to about 19,000 in 1910 (Greenhalgh, 1974: 239-240; Kay, 1972: 336-337; Rouch, 1956: 51). There is evidence that these early Zarma migrants, along with Mossi from Upper Volta, provided a disproportionately large share of labor for the dangerous underground work in the gold mines (Ampene, 1967; Keita, 1978: 184; Rouch, 1956: 80). The round trip from the Dosso region to the southern Gold Coast covered a distance of more than 3000 kilometers, was made on foot, and lasted two months or more. For Dosso peasants in need of tax money, there were few options. They were forced to travel.

The results of these long trips were mixed. The early migrants, and many who followed them, did return with tax money. This was the time described in administrative reports as the *rentrée des migrants*—the migrants' return. Significant but unknown numbers of these men also returned with silicosis and tuberculosis, chief among the occupational hazards they encountered, the other being death, for accidental death rates were very high for underground workers in the Gold Coast mines (PRO-CO 97/770, File 31034, Gold Coast, 1941-1943).

Dosso peasants also traveled to Northern Nigeria where tin was being mined from about 1904 and railroads were being constructed beginning in 1908. From 5832 in 1911, African tin mining labor on the Bauchi plateau almost quadrupled by 1920 and was composed largely of migrants (Freund, 1981: 76-78, 214; PRO-CO 657/4, Nigeria, "Annual Report on the Mines Department, Northern Province, for the Year 1916"). By 1912 Zarma peasants were among those who migrated to the mines, and the importance of labor from French territories (Niger and Chad) and from the German colony of Cameroon grew apace (Freund, 1981: 84-85).

Construction of the Baro-Kano and the Bauchi Light Railways to link the tin mines with the coast also required large numbers of laborers in Northern Nigeria from 1908 until about 1915 (Freund, 1981: 85-86; Mason, 1978: 71; PRO-CO 446/10 Northern Nigeria, "Report on the working of the Baro-Kano and Bauchi Light Railways for the half-year ending 30 June 1912": 6, 12). Once again, peasant cultivators from the Dosso region were among the railroad workers (ANN, "Monographie de la Subdivision de Dosso, 21 février 1913"). From 1910 Dosso peasants were also being recruited for work in Dahomey on the 480-kilometer road link between the Savé railhead of the Cotonou line and the Niger River to the north (ANN,

"Monographie de la Subdivision de Dosso, 21 février 1913"; ANF-MI, 2G14-38 [200 MI 1677], Colonie du Dahomey, "Rapport d'Ensemble sur le Service de la Route du Niger, no. 105, 23 mars 1915").

Migrations between 1911 and 1921 were given added impetus by several serious droughts (1911-1914; 1915-1917; 1920-1921), the effects of which further compounded the difficult situation of the Dosso peasantry, aggravated by more than ten years of taxes and requisitions.

From the 1920s savanna peasants were migrating to the Gold Coast diamond mines, and Zarma migrants from the Dosso region were among them (Greenhalgh, 1974: 238-240, 486; Keita, 1978: 184, 202-209; Rothiot, personal communication). Dosso peasants were also traveling to cocoa-growing areas of southern Gold Coast where they provided piecework and share-crop labor in the production of cocoa, and staple crops, particularly corn (Painter, 1985; Rouch, 1956). Finally, large numbers engaged in a wide range of unskilled nonagricultural wage labor, including porterage, and petty trade (Rouch, 1956).

SUMMARY AND CONCLUSION

Shortly after each year's harvest, many Dosso men packed a few belongings and began the long trek on foot to *kurmi* (south in Zarma) or *yamma* (west in Hausa), to the Gold Coast or Nigeria. These were the *kurmizay* and the *yammizey,* as the migrating peasants were called: literally, children of the south, children of the west. They, and the households of which they were members, became increasingly dependent on earnings from the distant Guinea Coast. The beginnings of this continuing transformation, from peasant cultivators to semi-proletarians (or, as some would argue, to proletarians), was not the collective result of multiple rational choices. These children of the south and the west, and the seasonal migration patterns that they collectively created—and recreated—were born of violence.

The coercive policies of the colonial administration superimposed upon a social formation situated in a habitat where the physical conditions of production were extremely harsh had several effects on the peasant societies of the Dosso region during the first two decades of French domination.

First, Dosso peasants were forced to convert increasing portions of use-value production into exchange value and to exchange it and local cowrie currency at disadvantageous terms as they sought tax money.

Second, they were forced to provide labor power for administrative works programs in Niger and Dahomey. Third, they were forced to move—often to flee—into neighboring or more distant British territories as they sought the money demanded by French administrators. The result during the period from about 1900 to 1920 was a pattern of cyclical migrations that helped to transform many thousands of peasant cultivators each year into migrant laborers in areas of capitalist development in the southern Gold Coast and northern Nigeria.

What primitive accumulation provoked during the early years, a growing dependence on cash income—to satisfy an increasing number of life's needs—perpetuated and deepened during subsequent years. What began as an anomaly—seasonal migrations among the region's largely sedentary peasant cultivators—was consolidated into what would be for many a life pattern over several generations.

PART III

CENTRAL AFRICA: FORCED MIGRATION AND THE DEMOGRAPHIC REGIME

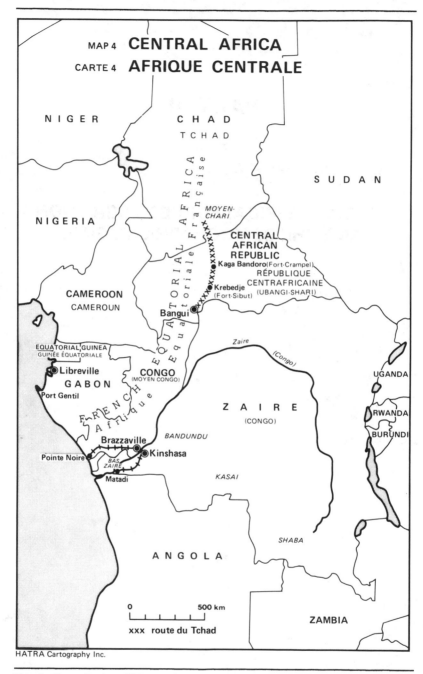

MAP 4 **CENTRAL AFRICA**
CARTE 4 **AFRIQUE CENTRALE**

NIGER

CHAD
TCHAD

SUDAN

NIGERIA

MOYEN-
CHARI

EQUATORIAL AFRICA
Equatoriale Française

CENTRAL
AFRICAN
REPUBLIC
RÉPUBLIQUE
CENTRAFRICAINE
(UBANGI-SHARI)

Kaga Bandoro (Fort-Crampel)

Krebedje
(Fort-Sibut)

CAMEROON
CAMEROUN

Bangui

EQUATORIAL GUINEA
GUINÉE ÉQUATORIALE

Zaire

(Congo)

UGANDA

Libreville
GABON

CONGO
(MOYEN CONGO)

Port Gentil

FRENCH
Afrique

ZAIRE
(CONGO)

RWANDA

BURUNDI

BANDUNDU

Brazzaville

Pointe Noire

BAS
ZAIRE

Kinshasa

Matadi

KASAI

ANGOLA

SHABA

0   500 km

ZAMBIA

xxx route du Tchad

HATRA Cartography Inc.

Map 4   Dosso Region of Niger

9

EXTRACTING PEOPLE FROM PRECAPITALIST PRODUCTION
French Equatorial Africa from the 1890s to the 1930s

DENNIS D. CORDELL

Equatorial Africa lacks labor for its development. This deficit is the result of three factors ... : the low population density; the difficulty of deploying labor; and the misfortunes which have stricken the population and have diminished ... its capacity, already so restricted, for production [M. Rondet-Saint, *L'Afrique équatoriale française, 1911*].

EXPLOITATION AND MIGRATION
IN FRENCH EQUATORIAL AFRICA

The French arrived in Equatorial Africa (today's Gabon, Congo, Central African Republic, and Chad; see Map 4). toward the end of the nineteenth century in search of wealth. Shortly, however, they faced a dilemma that bedeviled them for fifty years: how to compel Africans to provide labor for the development of the colonies without at the same time undermining future demographic growth. They faced the same problem elsewhere—in Indochina (Scott, 1976) and in French West Africa (see Chapter 6 by Echenberg, Chapter 7 by Ger-

Author's Note: I would like to express appreciation to the American Council of Learned Societies, whose Study Fellowship Program allowed me to take courses in the département de démographie at the Université de Montréal in 1982 when I wrote a preliminary version of this chapter; to the National Endowment for the Humanities (United States), whose Travel to Collections program provided funds for archival research in Aix-en-Provence and Marseille in 1984; and to Dedman College, Southern Methodist University, which generously allowed me a semester's leave for work on this and other projects.

vais, and Chapter 8 by Painter, this volume). What made French Equatorial Africa (FEA) different was its small population (see Table 9.1).

The most dramatic feature of these data is the great drop between the totals of 1912 and 1921, the result of genuine decline and a more realistic estimate of early population. However, it is also important to note the seemingly slow growth of the population in the interwar period, *after* the downward revisions. The data for 1921 and 1946, for example, suggest that in Gabon the population remained the same, and in two others, Ubangi-Shari and Moyen-Congo, it grew quite slowly. Only Chad and Cameroon registered significant increases; in the case of Chad this was mainly the result of an upward revision of estimates.

Beyond this, FEA suffered in comparison with other French colonies. French West Africa, for example, was endowed with a population twice as large and growing, as well as an economy already supplying exports to the world market (especially peanuts, palm oil, and cocoa). In the face of such contrasts, the French in Equatorial Africa opted for immediate gain. Pressured by both the metropolitan government and private interests, the state attempted to maximize revenue and minimize expenditures. It also opened the doors to a violent and disruptive penetration of capital: In 1899, 70 percent of FEA (excluding Chad) was distributed among forty concessionary companies. In exchange for promises to invest in infrastructure, they acquired monopoly trading privileges, as well as ownership of all natural products within their concessions (Coquery-Vidrovitch, 1972: 51-70).

In the early years the companies forced people to collect these products (ivory, rubber, wax, and even honey) by imposing head taxes in kind. Forced collection obliged Africans to divert substantial labor from the domestic economy; it also implied substantial mobility because the required items were not always near villages. The policy produced little in terms of "development," for the companies invested little capital. Forced collection, however, did constitute a first effort to "liberate" African labor for capitalist production.

But forced collection was far from the only form of labor coercion. During the first two decades of colonial rule, the state initiated forced labor, public and private porterage, head taxes, *regroupement,* military recruitment, forced cash crop cultivation, and the recruitment of workers for private enterprise.

Migration played a central role in many of these policies. On the one hand, it was the mechanism whereby the population was spatially re-

TABLE 9.1
The Evolution of the Population, French Equatorial Africa
and Cameroon (in millions)

Colony	1903	1905	1906	1912	Year 1921	1931	1946	1951	1960
Gabon					0.4	0.4	0.4	0.4	0.5
Moyen-Congo	15	8	10	15	0.4	0.7	0.6	0.7	0.8
Ubangi-Shari					0.8	1.1	1.1	1.1	1.4
Chad					1.2	1.1	2.0	2.2	3.1
Cameron		After 1918			2.2	2.2	2.8	3.1	3.5
Total	15	8	10	15	5.0	5.5	6.9	7.5	9.3

SOURCES: For the years 1903-1912, Sautter (1966: vol. 1, 19). Other data come from Amin and Coquery-Vidrovitch (1969: 156).

arranged to fit the needs of capitalism. This mobility was usually intended to be temporary or circulatory; often, however, it resulted in permanent change of residence. On the other hand, African resistance to colonial demands often took the form of flight—another form of migration. Again, such mobility often began as temporary relocation, later becoming permanent.

Views of Migration in Former French Equatorial Africa. A survey of the demographic literature on former FEA inevitably begins with French geographer Gilles Sautter. In a major study (1966) of the human geography of Gabon and Congo, he offered three explanations for the "underpopulation" of Equatorial Africa. First, a "call of the void" attracted people toward the Atlantic coast during the precolonial era. Population equilibrium is the moving force here—all things being equal, a population will migrate to a less populated region (vol. 2: 990). Second, he refined his analysis by identifying factors of repulsion and attraction, which, he believed, governed recent migration. He wrote of the social needs of migrants and the attraction of the cities ("the bright lights" theory of population mobility). Third, he added cultural determinants, theorizing that "behavior differs, notably according to ethnicity and distance" (vol. 1: 47-48, 61-62). Sautter placed little weight on interregional and rural-urban economic differences. Where he raised such issues, his analysis suggests that regional economies were closed; he did not raise the issue of connections among regional economies and the way different forms of production relate to each other (vol. 2: 1013, 1023). But despite limitations, it is important to acknowledge two major contributions of Sautter's work. First, his research brought to light a significant body of demographic data. And second, he noted the need for a historical perspective:

> Gabon and Congo are unintelligible if one ignores their colonial and precolonial antecedents. . . . Many of the most significant characteristics are the result of negative events (the destruction of populations, mass emigration, failed agricultural experiments, economic failures) whose only traces are void and absence, and whose existence is only recorded in accounts written at that time [vol. 1: 9].

Migration itself was not new. With several notable exceptions, populations in this part of Africa were apparently quite mobile—although for different reasons. People living along rivers in the south traveled to trade and to fish; societies in the forests of Gabon and Congo often combined hunting, gathering, and itinerant agriculture that required frequent moving about (Dupré, 1982). In the savannas farther north, low population density and ample land encouraged mobility (see Burnham, 1980; Cordell, 1983b). Upheavals associated with slave raiding and the slave trade were less routine, but, nonetheless, important causes of migration, particularly in the second half of the nineteenth century. While much of this traffic was directed to the fringes of the area—north and northeast towards the Muslim Sahel or southwest toward the commercial system of the Congo River—there was probably a substantial internal slave trade that redistributed part of the population (Cordell, 1985a; Harms, 1981; Vansina, 1983). In addition, the violence of raiding provoked flight and depopulation in some regions.

Familiarity with migration does not seem to have made it easier for people and societies to adjust to mobility demanded by the colonial state, although it may have made flight a more conceivable alternative. These two forms of migration are the subject of the two central hypotheses of this chapter. The *first* is that migration between the conquest and the depression in French Equatorial Africa was engendered mainly by capitalist penetration. As Rey (1976: 51) noted,

> The problem is relatively simple during the colonial phase: it is forced recruitment that furnished the mass of workers and which explains the "free" sale of labor by the minority that escaped forced recruitment (Congolese signing up to work in the forestry industry to escape forced labor on the Congo-Ocean railroad, Voltaics migrating to the Gold Coast to avoid being recruited for the Ivory Coast, etc.)

But migration was also a form of resistance. Hence the *second* hypothesis is that forms of mobility changed as a result of African resistance and when capitalism became dominant.

THE EXTRACTION OF LABOR AND MIGRATION

During the period of conquest in French Equatorial Africa—from the occupation of coastal areas in the 1870s to the fall of Wadai in Chad in 1911—the colonial regime had two major aims: (1) the installation of an effective French presence, which required regular communication, and (2) the extraction of sufficient revenue to defray costs (see Amin and Coquery-Vidrovitch, 1969: 24). Ironically, colonial ideology presumed that such objectives were good for the people as well as the colony:

> Forced labor is necessary to bring the natives out of the inferior state in which they find themselves [in order to render them] more apt for the work of colonizing the country. We can only hope to give these peoples a taste for work by first imposing it on them [Coltrat de Montrozier, 1903, cited in Coquery-Vidrovitch, 1972: 104].

Administrative Porterage

Early in the colonial era, the most important form of imposed migration was porterage, necessary for conquest and the subsequent functioning of the administration (Coquery-Vidrovitch, 1972: 190-191). Access to the interior presented a formidable challenge. From the Alantic, the major route was overland to Stanleypool on the Congo (to avoid rapids), assured by porterage; and then northeast up the Ubangi River to Bangui. The itinerary then became the "route du Tchad," turning north for 100 kilometers by land or water to Krebedje (today's Fort-Sibut), and finally overland for another 500 kilometers to Chad itself, a link also requiring porters (see Map 4).

In the 1890s private and military expeditions recruited porters through local authorities. Ammunition, rifles, trading goods, and other items arrived on African heads (Goutalier, 1979). By 1900 the colonial state had established a regular transportation network based in large part on porterage. But if porterage nourished European administrative posts, it deprived African villages along the way of a large part of their labor. Two examples illustrate the weight of this burden. In the south, the Marchand expedition of 1896-1897 required the transport of 9 tons of provisions, or 3000 headloads of 30 kilograms each, within several weeks; Loango and Bakongo villages along the itinerary were drained of population (Coquery-Vidrovitch, 1972: 187; for a similar effect in the Congo Independent State, see Lututala, Chapter 10, this volume). A second example comes from the opposite end of the network, in Manza country along the "route du Tchad":

> The [administrative] subdivisions crossed by the route were responsible for furnishing porters. The working conditions were difficult: loads of 30 kilos; daily journeys of 25 kilometers; a salary of 1 franc. Given constantly expanding transportation needs, porterage eventually repelled the best volunteers. No food was provided, and most porters . . . had to cover 80 or 100 kilometers racked by hunger. And later, one went so far as to deduct [money] from their meager salary to pay village taxes [Daigre, 1947: 111].

During this period, it was necessary to transport 3000 headloads per month to supply the troops in Chad (Amin and Coquery-Vidrovitch, 1969: 123). Suret-Canale estimated the total population subject to porterage at the two ends of the system at 120,000, but noted at the same time that there were only about 12,000 real candidates, "given that women, children, the elderly, chiefs, and notables were exempted from the *corvée*" (Suret-Canale, 1964: 44). Overall recruitment in these zones probably took about half of the male work force.

As for the period of engagement, in 1902 and 1903 the state required 112,000 and 101,066 days of porterage, between nine and ten days per male recruit (Suret-Canale, 1964: 44). To this must be added the time necessary for travel between villages and assembly points. Although perhaps exaggerated, one estimate suggests that recruits were absent for eighty days each year (Fourneau, 1904: 121-124, cited in Suret-Canale, 1964: 44).

Although migration was the direct result, porterage also had an impact on other demographic variables. Death was common. In 1889 de-Brazza estimated the mortality rate among porters at 150 per thousand. Azevedo's research among the Sara of Moyen-Chari (in today's southern Chad) revealed that during a five-day trip, the mortality rate was 50 per thousand (Azevedo, 1976: 21, 248). Applied to porters along the "route du Tchad," working ten days a year, the death rate would double to 100 per thousand. With a pool of 12,000 potential porters, such a rate translates into the death of 1200 porters annually—10 percent of the adult male population!

Another way of evaluating the impact of porterage is to assess its effect on a single population—in this case the Manza, many of whom

TABLE 9.2
Manza Population, 1903-1960

Year	Place of Residence	Population
1903	around Fort-Crampel (today's Kaga Bandoro), regional seat	16,000 - 18,000[a]
1920	population of the region of Kémo-Gribingui (largely Manza)	23,404 men 24,928 women 5,867 children 74,199 total
1959-1960	Manza	84,940

SOURCES: For 1903, Fourneau (1904: 121-124). For 1920, AN-SOM (Aix), 4 (3) D27, **Rapport politique, 1920.** For 1959-1960, INSEE (1964: 32).
a. Manza porters, January-July 1902: January, February, and March, 5,629; April, 2,205; May, 2,137; June, 1,645; July, 1,034; total porters, 12,650 (Coquery-Vidrovitch, 1972: 189).

lived along the "route du Tchad." The population was relatively small (see Table 9.2). Although these figures do not refer to the same unit, they are generally comparable, giving an idea of the impact of porterage before 1914.

The estimates of the total number of days furnished by these 12,650 porters fluctuate widely. Coquery-Vidrovitch (1972: 189) suggests an average absence of six to eight days per person, whereas Fourneau suggested a maximum of 80 days; hence a minimum of 88,550 days' absence ($7 \times 12,650$), and a maximum of 1,012,000 days. The former figure is probably too low, and the latter too high. Compared with the total Manza population, the burden represented by recruitment of these dimensions may or may not appear overwhelming. However, given that porterage affected small units (that is, villages) in a limited region (that is, areas near the routes), the impact was probably devastating in some areas. The reaction of the Manza gives some idea of the effects:

For a year now the dispersal of the tribes has continued. Villages fall apart, families split up, each abandoning tribe, village, family, fields to live in the bush like a hunted animal to avoid recruitment. The result is famine, and it is by the hundreds that the Manza have died these past few months.... Everything has been tried.... Everything fails today in the face of the collapse of the Manza, only a few years ago rich, numerous, and distributed in large villages [ANF-SOM (Paris), G-C, XIX, dossier 4b, deRolle, *Rapport,* 1902].

The *Regroupement* of Villages

Among the myriad forms of forced migration was regroupement, initiated in the 1910s (ANF-SOM [Aix], 4[3]D24, 1917; Sautter, 1966: vol. 2; 1018-1020; Burnham, 1975). Regroupement had four major aims: (1) making people available for the maintenance of the transportation system, (2) allowing greater control over the population, (3) permitting easier collection of taxes, and (4) promoting recruitment of laborers for the public and private sector (Coquery-Vidrovitch, 1972: 192-194). Villages were moved to sites along streams, paths, and, later, roads. Relocation was determined by the perceived needs of the state (ANF-SOM [Aix], 4[3]D23, *Rapport politique,* 1916: 8), and Africans often found themselves living far from the best agricultural land (ASSC, *Rapport médical,* 1934: 65).

Although initiated by the state, private companies encouraged the policy. In Gabon, for example, forestry enterprises encouraged the government to create settlements near their worksites (Sautter, 1966: vol. 2; 1018-1020). Regroupement also created a longer-range threat. Precolonial agricultural was itinerant in the savanna regions of FEA, an adaptation to abundant land with soils of limited fertility (Guillemin, 1956: 61; Prioul, 1981: 165-166). Settlement in one place for more than a few years exhausted the soil, produced smaller yields, and led to subsequent nutritional decline.

Military Recruitment

Military recruitment was important throughout the colonial era, but especially during World War I and World War II. During World War I, Africans from FEA were recruited for Cameroon and Europe. In Cameroon, they were used mainly as porters for military columns and 50,000 died. Along the Cameroon-Gabon border, recruits from Ubangi-Shari and Moyen-Congo suffered mortality rates of 330 per thousand. As for Europe, 3000 men were recruited in Ubangi-Shari in 1918-1919; 1065 died before combat (355 per thousand; Azevedo, 1976: 73).

Interwar figures are incomplete. Unlike the case in French West Africa, where recruitment was more generalized (see Echenberg, Chapter 6, this volume), particular populations were targeted for military service in FEA. As a result, the impact of recruitment differed dramatically from one society to another. Azevedo's research gives a general impression of the impact of military recruitment on an individual population, the Sara of southern Chad (see Table 9.3).

Comparison of the numbers of recruits (mostly Sara, regardless of the sometimes vague indication of origin), with the population of

TABLE 9.3
The Population of Moyen-Chari Compared with Data on Military Recruitment in Chad

Year	Men	Women	Children	Total	Recruits	Region of Origin
1910	60,101	57,474	71,674	400,000		
1920				189,244		
1922	60,199	57,799	74,099	192,097	1,350	Chad
1923				197,900	1,000	Chad
1924	61,400	62,574	57,656	181,630	1,000	Moyen-Chari (Sara from southern Chad)
1925				180,000		
1926				180,000	600	Moyen-Chari
1927					800	Moyen-Chari
1928				162,562	7,000	Moyen-Chari
1930				175,000	300	Moyen-Chari
1931					300	Moyen-Chari
1934				155,000		
1938				162,274	1,500	Chad
1941				174,992		
Total recruitment					13,850	

SOURCES: Population data: Archives nationales du Tchad, Série W, cited in Azevedo (1976: 78). Recruitment data: Azevedo (1976: 68; 1981: 1).

Moyen-Chari (also predominantly Sara), suggests the impact of this policy. Data on both population and military recruitment are available for seven years (1922, 1923, 1924, 1926, 1928, 1930, and 1938). Dividing the average recruitment of 1979 by the average population for these years (178,780), results in an overall rate of 11 per thousand. Among adult males the annual rate would be 33 per thousand, if it is assumed that they made up about one-third of the population. Labor lost was, in fact, substantially greater. Recruits usually were absent not one, but two or three years; some, of course, did not return.

The Recruitment of Workers for Forestry Companies

Exploitation of the tropical forest in FEA began in the 1920s and also stimulated migration. Again, private capital solicited the aid of the colonial state to recruit labor (Sautter, 1966: vol. 2, 1003-1005). Although less violent than the policies of the concessionary companies that preceded them, forestry companies often appealed to agents of the state, who in turn pressured village chiefs to recruit workers.

Overall, the companies in Gabon estimated their needs at 20,000 to 30,000 workers between the ages of 20 and 30 annually, which is to say nearly all males in these age groups for a population of 150,000 to 180,000. But between 1925 and 1947, they never attained these goals. Their demands were cut by an administration that needed workers for other sectors. Nor did Africans sign up in desired numbers. A partial accounting is found in Table 9.4.

The demographic impact was important—because of both the numbers of people involved and the working conditions. First, recruitment took place not only in the immediate forest regions delegated to the companies but in a much larger surrounding area. Recruits signed two-year contracts, which were often extended. Such employment thus often required long-distance migration, along with the absence of a considerable number of men for several agricultural seasons. Often recruits did not return, especially if they were not married:

> Thousands of unmarried workers were transferred to the coast, of which 75 percent were never reintegrated into their home regions; thus was born, around the zones of exportation, an uprooted proletariat having severed all links with ancestral customs [Balandier, 1971: 167-168].

Failure to return home was not the only direct demographic effect of long range migration and lengthy contracts. Mortality among forestry workers was also probably high. One example for which we have

TABLE 9.4
Recruitment for Forestry Companies

Year	Workers Requested	Workers Accorded	Workers Recruited
1925	16,300	12,500	6,500
1926	18,940	9,350	4,120
1927	18,736	7,996	4,500
1928	17,300	6,750	6,000
1933	5,299	5,095	?
1947	14,030	3,120	?

SOURCE: Balandier (1971: 166).

data is the worksite at Oyem. During the single month of January 1922, 30 workers died out of a group of 175 new recruits, a monthly rate of 171 per thousand (Balandier, 1971: 167).

In addition, the absence of men had an important impact on the sex structure of the rural population. In the subdivision of Makakaou in the 1920s, for example, the sexual imbalance was very large. There were 7018 women for 4603 men, a sex ratio of 65.6 men for every 100 women (Balandier, 1971: 166-167). Later on, in the period subsequent to that depicted in Table 9.4, the data on sex structure became more detailed (see Table 9.5).

Without reconstructing the social organization of rural Gabonese societies during the period, it seems probable that this imbalance had a major effect on the division of labor by sex and age. Balandier described the effects of such disequilibrium in a more recent era when the recruitment of miners accompanied that for forestry:

> The impoverishment of villages and demographic disintegration ... left villages with too little labor, brought atomization and increased mobility [Balandier, 1971: 60].

The Congo-Océan Railroad and Forced Migration

Of all the topics on historical demography in FEA, the impact of the Congo-Océan railroad is the most studied (see Sautter, 1967: 219-299; Azevedo, 1981). Built between 1921 and 1934 by the Société de Construction de Batignolles between Pointe-Noire on the coast and Brazzaville in the interior, a distance of 510 kilometers, the project employed a total of 127,500 Africans for 138,125 person-years (Table 9.6).

Apart from capital, which came largely from French public revenues (Azevedo, 1981: 4-5), the colonial administration promised

TABLE 9.5
Sex Ratios, Age 15 and Over
(Number of Men per 100 Women)
Gabon, 1951

| | Zone | |
Former Districts	Zone of Exploitation	Reserve Areas
Libreville and Commune	119.8	
Port Gentil	103.6	
Lambrene	118.3	
Oyem		74.8
Bitam		69.3
Booue		70.8
Makokou		70.9

SOURCE: Calculated from Balandier (1971: 170).

to furnish 8000 construction workers annually along with supervisors and cooks—some of whom were women. In 1926, after a reduction in the length of the work day from ten to nine hours, the administration raised this number to 8800 (Sautter, 1967: 240).

The state had hoped to recruit workers in the neighborhood of the itinerary. But with a population of only 70,295 adult males, the zone of recruitment soon had to be enlarged. By 1925 the administration imposed levees of 1000 workers annually for Moyen-Logone and Moyen-Chari, *circonscriptions* in Chad, and another 1000 for Ubangi-Shari (Sautter, 1967: 242-244; Azevedo, 1981: 6). Overall Ubangi-Shari and Chad furnished 37 percent of the labor.

In the face of low salaries—there were those who earned only 1 French franc per day—and long contracts, recruitment became increasingly difficult. While early contracts were for six months, a reflection of the proximity of the labor supply, they soon stretched to a one to four year period with expanded use of migrant labor.

But it was working conditions rather than wages that made recruitment difficult. First, a contract implied migration—absence from a familiar milieu, and for many a migration of several weeks just to reach the construction zone. Near Brazzaville, where the population was relatively dense, most workers were recruited locally and came with their families (Sautter, 1967: 247, 279). At the other end, the local population was very sparse; the Société imported migrant laborers, most of whom arrived alone. In addition, the work was arduous. In the Mayombe region, for example, the laying of each kilometer of track required 107,000 person-days; it thus took 10,000 workers three

TABLE 9.6

Workers Recruited for the Congo-Ocean Railroad, 1921-1932

Origin	1921	1922	1923	1924	1925	1926	1927	1928	1929	1930	1931	1932	Total
Moyen-Congo													
Number	4,750	5,425	9,600	8,825	9,050	7,300	6,600	8,400	8,050	5,500	4,825	1,525	79,850
Years absent	1,575	1,800	5,075	4,775	6,400	5,450	4,625	7,025	6,125	4,425	4,125	1,100	52,500
Ubangi-Shari													
Number	—	—	—	—	1,425	6,800	6,700	6,075	5,800	6,025	5,600	3,550	41,975
Years absent	—	—	—	—	2,100	10,200	10,025	12,150	11,600	12,050	11,200	5,325	74,650
Chad													
Number	—	—	—	—	925	—	—	600	725	1,150	1,525	500	5,425
Years absent	—	—	—	—	1,525	—	—	1,325	1,575	2,475	3,250	825	10,975
Total													
Number	4,750	5,425	9,600	8,825	11,400	14,100	13,300	15,075	14,575	12,675	11,950	5,575	127,250
Years absent	1,575	1,800	5,075	4,775	10,025	15,650	14,650	20,500	19,300	18,950	18,575	7,250	138,125

SOURCE: Sautter (1967: 258-259).

and a half years to cross the ninety kilometers of forested hills in the area (Sautter, 1967: 236).

These conditions produced high mortality, although there is debate over its dimensions. Sautter suggests a total of 14,100 deaths among the 127,250 recruits, or 111 per thousand (Sautter, 1967: 271). To this total must be added deaths during travel. Among a sample of 6832 people recruited north of Brazzaville, 1338 (370 per thousand) never reached the worksites. Those who died between the worksites and their villages after completing their contracts must also be included (Sautter, 1967: 253, 269; see Cordell, Gregory, and Piché, in press). Serious illness was also common. Laborers often lacked adequate clothing and food, both while traveling and on the worksites, and shelter was frequently minimal. As a result many died of respiratory diseases such as tuberculosis and pneumonia, contracted on the worksites but aggravated by poor housing (ANF-SOM [Aix], 4[3]D37, 1927).

Azevedo suggests much higher losses. While restricted to southern Chad, his conclusions are striking. Half of the 20,000 Chadian men who worked on the railroad never returned home (Azevedo, 1976: 189; 1981: 12). A close examination of Moyen-Chari gives a clear indication of the impact of recruitment. Between 1924 and 1932, the years for which data are available, 13,300 (1478 per year) workers were recruited in Moyen-Chari. Comparing this figure with the total population (Table 9.3), a recruitment rate of 8 per thousand may be calculated for the population as a whole, or 25 per thousand for adult males.

FLIGHT AS MIGRATION AND RESISTANCE

Apart from being a mechanism for the reorganization of economies for the needs of capitalism, migration was also a major form of African resistance. Local flight was common. In the early decades of colonial rule, particularly in Ubangi-Shari and Chad, the state did not effectively control all of its territory. People fled in large numbers to remote locations and managed to avoid authorities for months or even years (see, for example, ANF-SOM [Aix], 4[3]D19, *Resumé, mois de mai,* 1912; 4[3]D22, *Rapport, 1er trimestre,* 1915; 4[3]D23, *Rapport politique, 2e trimestre,* 1916).

Other people sought alternative employment in places such as Gabon where the population was not subject to railroad recruitment, the result of pressure from the forestry industry, which wished to retain its own labor force. In addition, many people from Chad and eastern Ubangi-Shari fled to the Anglo-Egyptian Sudan where tax and labor burdens were less onerous (Santandrea, 1964). People also sought refuge in the Cameroon and Nigeria.

Workers also fled on the way to their worksites. In 1927 among the 6832 railroad recruits who were to arrive by way of Brazzaville, 585 "escaped." There were also desertions; in 1926, 431 of the 7031 workers at Mayombe fled (Sautter, 1967: 247-248). While refugees often did not intend to stay away permanently, this, in fact, very often happened.

CONCLUSION

The Depression in French Equatorial Africa

In his massive study on Gabon and Congo, Sautter concludes that "severe colonization" came to an end after 1930. It is true that several changes eased the demands made on Africans. First, working conditions on the railroad improved after 1931, and the project ended in 1934. Second, in the wake of excesses, the state limited the powers of the concessionary companies, most of which by this time had either gone bankrupt or become trading houses. Third, in the absence of war, the volume of military recruitment diminished. Fourth, the depression closed several forestry enterprises. Finally, Gouverneur-Général Antonnetti, known for his draconian labor policies, left office (Sautter, 1966: vol. 2, 985-986).

However, the effects of this relaxation of colonial authority should not be exaggerated. The first three decades of colonial occupation had provoked major changes in both population distribution and relations of production. From the state's point of view, the problem was no longer one of forcibly extracting work and workers. Colonial policies had by this time seriously undermined the ability of local societies to produce what they needed; hence the necessity for cash produced migrant workers without direct coercion. In addition, the forced production of cash crops such as cotton had begun to transform agricultural production from within (Guibbert, 1949; Stürzinger, 1983). And, finally, earning money to pay higher head taxes imposed by the administration during the depression forced people to sell either their labor or market crops (Coquery-Vidrovitch, 1976: 408, 410-411). In FEA the depression was indeed a watershed, marking the end of the era of primitive accumulation. Colonial violence and African resistance had transformed local societies. Henceforth violence became structural:

The impoverishment of the countryside and the flight of rural people to the city, state capital, and finally the internal cycle in the public domain of aid and indebtedness, and in the private domain of the flight of profits . . . made the period 1931-1936 . . . the key phase of the genesis . . . of a specific phenomenon, the underdevelopment of the Third World [Coquery-Vidrovitch, 1976: 422].

The Demographic Regime

Apart from considering how colonial policies created labor migration in FEA, it is important to remember that migration also influenced mortality and fertility as well as the overall capacity of populations to renew themselves; migration is only part of the larger demographic regime. In several places this chapter emphasizes the deadly implications of migration for mortality. In addition, although many of the policies analyzed above aimed at extracting male labor, they nonetheless directly affected female labor. Many societies experienced multiple demands for labor. In southern Chad, for example, it may be hypothesized that the extraction of adult males for military service and railroad construction (as well as recruitment for local needs) would have profoundly affected the organization of work. The limited research already completed suggests that the sexual division of labor changed, with women assuming new agricultural tasks (Azevedo, 1976: 1981).

Fertility and/or fecundity levels may also have been modified. The absence of large numbers of men may have decreased the chances of women becoming pregnant. In fact, the high incidence of migration probably brought increased sexual mobility, which, in turn, facilitated the spread of sexually transmitted diseases. Such maladies reduced fecundity and raised sterility in many societies (Retel-Laurentin, 1974; Frank, 1983; Cordell, 1985c).

The increased physical burdens on labor may also have lowered resistance to disease, with negative consequences for female health in general, and maternal health in particular. Such changes would also have affected children. Poor maternal health might have increased the chances of spontaneous abortions, stillbirths, and the birth of unhealthy infants. Once born, children may have been subjected to higher morbidity and mortality levels, given the fact that their mothers had less time for child care, food preparation, and general sanitation. Fragmentary evidence suggests that more extensive research may verify these hypotheses for FEA (see Cordell, Gregory, Piché, in press).

10

LES ORIGINES DES MIGRATIONS MODERNES DANS L'OUEST DU ZAIRE

LUTUTALA MUMPASI

Les populations du Zaïre (voir Map 4) accusent une dynamique qui affole et le phénomène migratoire est unanimement—ou presque—considéré comme celui qui y a le plus contribué.[1] Avec l'infécondité, la littérature coloniale y a consacré l'essentiel de ses investigations démographiques. Ryckmans (1953: 5), parlant des premières enquêtes démographiques,[2] nous dit qu'elles furent instituées en vue d'établir les disponibilités de la main-d'oeuvre et d'étudier les contrecoups des recrutements.

L'importance du phénomène n'a donc pas manqué de susciter l'intérêt des chercheurs; ceux-ci l'ont expliqué par la "push-pull theory" (Lamal, 1954; Denis, 1956). Ces auteurs considéraient que des facteurs tels que la pauvreté et l'épuisement des sols, la forte densité, les exigences excessives des chefs ou des anciens, le taux éleve de la dot et l'appât de l'argent poussaient les populations à partir de leurs milieux de naissance. Seul Lamal mentionnait les cultures obligatoires et des "causes anciennes" notamment l'abus des corvées et le taux de

Author's Note: Ce texte est une version, remaniée et enrichie, d'une communication que nous avions présentée au 25e Congrès des Africanistes Américains, Washington, novembre 1982 et au 13e Congrès des Africanistes Canadiens, Québec, mai 1983. C'est une introduction à une recherche doctorale plus vaste où nous examinons la "dynamique des migrations au Zaïre." Nous voudrions remercier le Centre des Recherches pour le Développement International qui a financé notre participation à ces congrès, ainsi qu'à la "Chaire Quételet 1983," Université de Louvain, que nous avons mis à profit pour compléter notre recherche documentaire.

l'impôt. La recherche d'emploi, l'attrait de la vie urbaine et la pour-suite des études étaient considérés comme des facteurs attractifs.

Nous proposons ici une antithèse à ces stéréotypes que certains des travaux contemporains continuent de reproduire.[3] Evacuant la dimen-sion historique, ces recherches se concentrent sur l'individu-migrant et ne montrent pas que les facteurs dits répulsifs n'ont été généres qu'à la suite des processus de coercition, et que dans les lieux de destination, les facteurs dits attractifs n'ont été dans un premier temps que des pro-cessus de stabilisation des migrants. En effet, la reproduction de la force de travail, primordiale pour l'accumulation, avait conduit à l'une des contradictions fondamentales du système colonial belge,[4] à savoir faire des villages à la fois le réservoir de la main-d'oeuvre et les camps des travaux forcés (Jewsiewicki, 1981a: 73). Cette double pres-sion n'avait pù porter fruits qu'au prix de multiples stratégies, à cause notamment de la triple rareté de la main-d'oeuvre (Lux, 1961: 44-46): (1) une "rareté absolue naturelle" à cause de la réticence des autochtones de fournir une réponse spontanée favorable à une oeuvre aussi étrangère, (2) une "rareté absolue délibérée" qui traduisait un réflexe de défense contre ces assauts capitalistes, et (3) une "rareté relative" qui traduisait un sous-peuplement et une dichotomie entre la localisation des ressources exploitables et celle des ressources hu-maines, un décalage entre l'augmentation annuelle des besoins en main-d'oeuvre (de l'ordre de 5.4 pourcent de 1925 à 1930, par exem-ple) et l'accroissement de la population (qui ne devait pas excéder les 2.3 pourcent l'an pour la même période).

Pour vaincre la rareté dite absolue de main-d'oeuvre, les autorités coloniales mirent sur pied des mécanismes de coercition. Contraire-ment aux allégations des tenants de la "push-pull theory", c'est à la Trilogie coloniale belge (Administration-Missions-Grandes sociétes) que revenait, en cette phase primaire de l'accumulation,[5] le rôle de dominer les structures en place, de les intégrer au nouveau mode de production capitaliste et d'amorcer ainsi le processus de dépendance dont les facteurs dits répulsifs ne furent que, et sont encore, des tares. Comme le reconnùt plus tard, Lux (1966: 303), nous pensons que tant qu'une offre de travail n'est pas spontanée ou que les autochtones se présentaient "non pas comme ouvriers offrant leur service contre rémunération, mais en colonisés qui ressentent leur situation globale de dépendance", on doit parler de recrutement forcé et non de marché d'emploi. Ces contraintes (voir la prochaine partie) eûrent un impact direct et indirect sur les migrations.

La typologie migratoire de l'Ouest du Zaïre, et probablement de tout le pays, durant l'époque coloniale peut être schématisée en six

points (voir Figure 10.1). Aux premiers moments de l'oeuvre coloniale
se développent des besoins en main-d'oeuvre qui donnent lieu à des
mécanismes de coercition (temps-évènement 1 sur la figure) et occa-
sionnent des migrations temporaires forcées (2). Celles-ci impliquent,
bien entendu, des migrations de retour. L'oeuvre coloniale va se poursuivre avec l'exploitation des richesses grâce entre autres aux travaux
forcés, qui constituent en même temps des mécanismes de répulsion
(3) et favorisent des migrations temporaires semi-forcées (4). L'intensification de l'exploitation fait accroître les besoins en main-d'oeuvre,
renforce les mécanismes de répulsion et développe des mécanismes
d'attraction (5). Ce qui va se solder par le soi-disant jeu attraction-
répulsion (6) qui favorise des migrations à la fois spontanées, ''volontaires'' et ''définitives''. Même affranchies de ces mécanismes qui leur
avaient donné naissance, les migrations demeuraient et demeurent encore une stratégie collective de survie qui s'impose à ces inégalités que
par ailleurs elles renforcent.

Pour sa part, la rareté dite relative donna lieu à des mesures de
régulation démographique diverses:

(1) des mesures pro-natalistes pour élever (Bezy, Peemans, et Wautelet,
1981: 26) la main-d'oeuvre nécessaire: réglementation de la durée du
''contrat'' du travail migrant, surimposition des polygames, allocations
familiales, travaux d'assainissement publics pour parer aux épidémies,
location-vente des maisons aux chefs de ménages stabilisés en villes,
érosion des tabous et interdits sexuels, ''reconstitution'' des ménages
urbains;

(2) une politique migratoire assujettie à la conjoncture économique, se
traduisant tantôt par des engagements massifs des travailleurs ou la

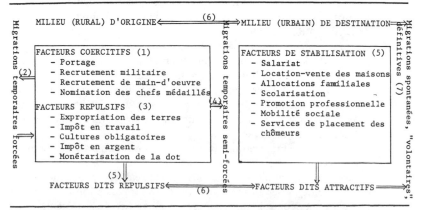

Figure 10.1 Fecondation des migrations modernes dans l'ouest du Zaïre

libéralisation de la circulation des personnes, tantôt par leur déportation, tantôt encore par des mesures restreignant la circulation, même à l'intérieur d'un milieu donné.

Cette batterie de mesures visait le maintien de la vitalite des milieux ruraux, postulat de base, selon le Gouverneur Général Ryckmans, des politiques démographique et de main-d'oeuvre (Dhanis, 1953: 490). Lorsqu'on analyse les diverses sources (Lututala, 1982) on s'aperçoit que les caractéristiques de la dynamique démographique du Zaïre durant l'époque coloniale correspondent avec les buts visés mais souvent dissimulés par ces mesures:

(1) Une fécondité qui est demeurée à la hausse depuis les années 1920, comme le montre l'évolution des taux de fécondité selon les générations (calculés à partir des données de l'EDOZA, Enquête démographique dans l'ouest du Zaïre, 1975-1977).

(2) Une surfécondité urbaine par rapport à la fécondité rurale: cette caractéristique, ainsi que la première, vient démentir la théorie de la transition démographique selon laquelle la modernisation ferait passer la fécondité des niveaux traditionnels élevés vers des niveaux modernes relativement bas.

(3) Une baisse importante de l'infécondité: celle-ci est généralement considérée comme l'élément explicatif de l'évolution de la fécondité décrite ci-dessus (Sala-Diakanda, 1980), alors que la dynamique de la lutte contre cette infécondité, que nous privilégions, est laissée pour compte.

(4) Une surmasculinité régressive des populations urbaines qui dénote le caractère sélectif des recrutements des travailleurs et le souci de maintenir la vitalité rurale. Cette sélectivité conditionnerait, nous semble-t-il, d'autres caractéristiques notamment la prostitution en villes, le maintien de la polygamie en milieux ruraux, les maladies vénériennes et la division sexuelle du travail, à cause soit des déséquilibres sexuels, soit de la séparation des époux.

(5) Un rajeunissement progressif des populations urbaines qui reflète le passage de la formule du travail migrant plutôt d'hommes adultes valides (H.A.V.) à la libéralisation des migrations.

(6) Des creux et des palliers dans l'evolution des populations urbaines aux moments même des crises économiques, soit dans les années 1929 et 1955, qui dénotent la forte corrélation entre conjoncture économique et politique démographique.

(7) Des échanges migratoires plutôt unidirectionnels, où les villes l'emportent largement sur les milieux ruraux.

(8) Enfin une migration internationale négligeable, ce qui dénote la préférence de puiser et maintenir la force de travail à l'intérieur même de la colonie, contrairement au cas du Ghana et de la Côte-d'Ivoire,

par exemple, où la main d'oeuvre devait, dans une bonne proportion, se reproduire et être puisée au Burkina Faso, et aux autres pays voisins (voir chapitre 7 par Gervais et chapitre 8 par Painter).

Il apparaît donc qu'outre les eléménts de réponse aux multiples interrogations sur les causes profondes de la dynamique démographique et notamment le rôle de la migration qu'elle apporte, l'étude du processus de libération de la force de travail des économies traditionnelles et de reproduction d'une main-d'oeuvre salariée permet de comprendre comment concrètement le phénomène migratoire a été peu à peu imposé, accepté, intériorisé et adopté comme stratégie de survie.

EXTORSION AU TRAVAIL ET TRAVAIL MIGRANT

Lorsque Stanley finit par rencontrer les appétits capitalistes du roi des Belges Léopold II, il se fit confier la responsabilité de l'expédition surnommée plus tard par les autochtones *Bula Matari* (Casseur de pierres, en langue kikongo de l'Ouest du Zaïre). Sa mission etait d'ouvrir un chemin caravanier, d'établir un poste à Vivi et à Stanley-Pool (actuel Kinshasa) et de remonter le fleuve avec des bateaux démontables (Eynikel, 1984: 34). Notons quelques points sur le système colonial belge qui aideront à comprendre les mécanismes d'extorsion de la force de travail.

(1) Le pacte colonial belge se distingue du modèle classique dans ce sens que la colonie n'avait pas comme vocation exclusive de fournir des matières premières à la métropole et de consommer le surplus de sa production manufacturée; elle devait en outre assumer le financement de ses exploitations, la Belgique ayant refusé de supporter les charges financières (Mulambu, 1974: 10). En conséquence, il y eût non seulement un afflux très important et diversifié des capitaux, mais aussi un "autofinancement", à partir des ressources locales. Pour faire face à la concurrence mondiale (Lux, 1966), il fallut maximiser les profits et ... l'exploitation de la population.

(2) La "politique des zones economiques" (Tshund'olcla, 1984), que les économistes post-coloniaux vont consacrer par leurs fameux trois pôles de développement économique du Zaïre (Kinshasa, Kisangani, et Lubumbashi), fit des milieux ruraux les périphéries où devait se reproduire l'armée de réserve se faisant engager presque gratuitement et au besoin.

Il nous paraît important d'ajouter que la population de l'Ouest du Zaïre, en particulier avait déjà été victime, depuis le 16e siècle, de l'esclavage et ses conséquences (dépopulation, dépravation des moeurs, appât des produits et de la civilisation occidentaux, etc.) lui imposés par les Portugais (voir aussi le chapitre 15, de Heywood et Thornton). Certaines de ces conséquences furent récuperées par Stanley et ses successeurs pour y bâtir leur ruse en vue de gagner la collaboration autochtone.

Les Mécanismes de Coercition

C'est le portage qui a été la première forme d'utilisation massive de la main-d'oeuvre autochtone. En effet, alors que, de Vivi dans le Bas-Fleuve, Stanley devait faire transporter par tête 1,830 charges (64 tonnes), il n'avait à son service que 190 hommes (Zanzibarites et autres Africains recrutés a grands coûts sur les côtes). Les autochtones, eux, "donnaient juste un coup de main: ils refusaient de s'éloigner à plus de cinq, six kilomètres" (Wauters, 1892: 19). Mais la mise sur pied d'un personnel blanc chargé du recrutement avec la collaboration des autorités coutumières, la nomination des "capitas" (chefs de caravane) et l'introduction du salaire changèrent les choses.

En 1892, on signalait mille porteurs par jour sur la route des caravanes de Vivi à Kinshasa (Wauters, 1895: 20). Et le service leur aurait rapporté, jusqu'à date, dix millions de francs (1892: 19). Les besoins en porteurs augméntèrent rapidement. Nous avons estimé[6] à 57,200 le nombre annuel des porteurs qui devaient avoir été mobilisés pour 1885, à 251,666 pour 1892 et à 503,333 pour 1893.

Ces effectifs devaient avoir considérablement diminué à partir de 1898, année de la mise en service du chemin de fer Matadi-Kinshasa qui venait d'être construit (1889-1898) pour faciliter l'écoulement des produits et remplacer le portage. Mais il faut noter le conflit entre besoins en porteurs et en travailleurs pour le chemin de fer. Le problème fut résolu en allant recruter au Liberia, en Guinée, au Ghana, au Sierra-Leone, en Chine, en Haïti, au Sénégal, etc. Cette main-d'oeuvre étrangère sera nettement plus nombreuse jusqu'à la fin des travaux. Ainsi, sur les 7,921 travailleurs qui étaient sur le chantier en 1897, 1,607 étaient des Sénégalais, 4,559 venaient des colonies anglaises, et seulement 1,688 étaient des autochtones (Cornet, 1948).

Ces mêmes faits seront observés en ce qui est du recrutement des militaires: les premiers soldats étaient recrutés ailleurs que dans la colonie. Seulement, ici les méthodes changèrent radicalement par la suite; un décret fut promulgué en 1891 selon lequel les soldats devaient être recrutés par des engagements "volontaires" et par des levées annuelles (tirage au sort ou simple désignation). Ainsi, de 100 Zanzibarites qu'était l'effectif de l'armée de Stanley en 1879, on dénombrait 6,000 autochtones dans la Force Publique en 1895. Ceux-ci étaient recrutés pour sept ans et demeuraient réservistes pour cinq ans (Cattier 1906).

En même temps commençaient l'implantation des industries, l'exploitation minière et d'autres investissements publics et privés. Le chemin de fer Matadi-Kinshasa était un préalable à l'implantation de ces autres activities: aménagements portuaires (1914), firmes commerciales et industrielles belges, anglaises, portugaises, italiennes, services administratifs, écoles et missions à *Kinshasa*; construction du chemin de fer du Mayumbe (1898-1919) et exploitation forestière dans le *Bas-Fleuve*; industries du ciment (1926), de la canne à sucre (1925), d'huile de palme dans les *Cataractes*; aménagement portuaire à *Matadi*; exploitation des palmeraies et industries d'huile de palme (1911) dans le *Bandundu;* exploitation minière (1912), du caoutchouc et construction du chemin de fer Bukama-Dilolo (années 1920) dans le *Kasaï*. On peut comprendre, dès lors, que les besoins en main-d'oeuvre se soient considérablement et progressivement accrus.

Comme les lieux où se développaient ces exploitations étaient déterminés par la qualité du sol, les conditions climatiques et les ruptures de charge de transport plutôt que le potentiel démographique, et comme ces endroits étaient souvent moins peuplés, on mit sur pied un système de recrutement. Ce fut d'abord les chefs coutumiers qui, moyennant divers cadeaux, devaient fournir le quota exigé par les agents de "l'Etat Indépendant du Congo." Ceux-ci devaient avoir compris que la gérontocratie pesant de tout son poids dans ces sociétés, il suffisait de corrompre les chefs pour dompter les masses. Mais la contrainte était encore plus forte à l'endroit de ces chefs qui osaient ne pas s'exécuter: ils etaient fouettés dans les moindres des cas, démis et remplacés par des chefs couronnés dans les pires des cas. Ces derniers étaient des anciens soldats, des anciens travailleurs ou des anciens "boys" ayant "fait la preuve de leur soumission à l'autorité européenne" (Demunter, 1975: 65).

La demande de main-d'oeuvre atteignit des proportions telles qu'on créa des institutions chargées de recruter les travailleurs et de les répartir entre employeurs: la Bourse du Travail du Kasaï (1922) et l'Office du Travail de Léopoldville (1922). De plus, il y eût la création des zones de recrutement dans lesquelles des conflits d'intérêt, tranchés par l'Administration, ne manquaient pas de surgir en cas de violation (Tshund'olela, 1984). La formule était celle du travail migrant: navette plus ou moins régulière des travailleurs entre le village et le centre d'emploi.[7] Deux raisons justifiaient cette formule (Lux, 1961: 28-31). Elle permit une plus-value plus grande; les entreprises étaient dispensées des frais d'installation des travailleurs, et ceux-ci ignoraient les règles du jeu quant à la rémunération de leur travail. Elle permit aussi le maintien des milieux coutumiers car ce retour du migrant permettait d'entretenir la fécondité et la survie de la société. En plus du devoir de reproduire d'autres travailleurs, les milieux coutumiers devaient fournir aux entreprises des vivres pour la reconstitution physique des travailleurs migrants. En 1917, par exemple, on instaura les cultures obligatoires en vue, entre autres, de ravitailler les centres d'emploi (nous y reviendrons).

Le degré de coercition des opérations de recrutement peut se jauger à travers le prix de leur succès: des ravages. De crainte qu'ils n'hypothèquent la vitalité des milieux ruraux, ces ravages donnèrent lieu à la création d'une "Commission chargée d'étudier le problème de la main-d'oeuvre".[8] Celle-ci fixa à 25 pourcent d'H.A.V. la proportion pouvant être mobilisée, 15 pourcent devant être utilisés dans le territoire et 10 pourcent au loin. En réalité cependant, ces proportions furent largement dépassées; ce qui ne fit que renforcer cette dévitalité que l'on voulait éviter. Des enquêtes démographiques furent alors menées en vue de connaître le nombre de contribuables pour faciliter la fixation du taux de l'impôt et ... de la main-d'oeuvre[9] (voir aussi le chapitre 7 de Gervais).

La crise de 1929, dont les effets se prolongèrent jusqu'à 1934, conduisit à une diminution des besoins en main-d'oeuvre. De nombreux travailleurs furent alors renvoyés dans leurs villages. De Kinshasa, par exemple, on renvoya 6,000 en 1930 et 7,000 en 1932 (Denis, 1956: 575). Ceux qui restaient virent se détériorer leurs revenus. Ils connurent une exploitation si insupportable que des révoltes, dont celle des Bapende en 1931 (Mulambu, 1971) et des marins à Matadi en 1930 (Sabakinu, 1981: 495) furent déclenchées. Les travailleurs licenciés, migrants de retour, constituèrent par la suite une "réserve de main-d'oeuvre qui viendra librement, lors de la reprise économique, se faire embaucher" (Makwala 1966-1967: 10).

La Genèse des Facteurs de Répulsion

Les Conséquences des Mécanismes de Coercition. Soulignons d'abord cette assimilation des autochtones au travail salarié, qui offrit une alternative plus alléchante aux conditions de production et de vie, déjà dominées. Au moment où l'on voulait remplacer le portage, on ne s'en doutait d'ailleurs pas:

On peut, dès maintenant (1892), affirmer que ces populations de la région des Cataractes, qui depuis l'origine du service (du portage) jusqu'à ce jour ont gagné plus de dix millions de francs à transporter des charges ... sont aujourd'hui convertis.... Ils fourniront des bras à l'agriculture quand les transports viendraient à leur manquer.... Les indigènes transporteurs, qui auront appris à ne plus se passer des produits de notre industrie, qui se sont créés des besoins, devront aussi se créer des ressources. Ils offriront alors leurs bras aux industries locales qui viendraient à se former [Wauters, 1892: 10].

Cette assimilation bouleversa les structures, par la réquisition d'H.A.V. et l'abandon, par ces derniers, fût-il temporaire, des activitiés economiques domestiques. Il s'ensuivit des disettes et une perte de vitalité des sociétés autochtones. Les départs d'hommes adultes séparèrent les conjoints, renforcèrent le déséquilibre démographique et la division sexuelle du travail et, commc lc signale Makwala, marquèrent le retard les femmes dans l'accès au nouveau mode de production (1966-1967: 7).

Qui plus est, la population perdit ses droits fonciers, à cause d'une loi de 1885 qui fit considérer toutes les terres "vacantes" (non occupées par les autochtones) comme domaniales. Demunter (1975) signale qu'en réalité cette spoliation concernait les meilleures terres et les plus fertiles. Pourtant, l'utilisation des techniques rudimentaires nécessitait beaucoup de terres car la jachère devait être longue. Il s'en était suivi une réduction de celle-ci, une marginalisation des terres à cause des érosions et du manque de souplesse dans la rotation des cultures (Lukoki, 1984).

Soulignons en plus que les porteurs et d'autres salariés de retour furent les propagateurs des éléments de la civilisation européene et des maladies (Makwala, 1966-1967). Les récits des anciens migrants, comme le dira si bien Chrétien (1978) dans le cas de l'Ouganda, firent peu à peu entrer la migration dans les habitudes sociales; elle fit l'objet de conseils pratiques et de jugements de valeur.

L'Impôt en Travail. Il fut institué en 1891 en vue d'obliger légalement la population aux premières activitiés lucratives. Il consistait en une remise d'une quantité de produits dc cucillette (caoutchouc, noix palmistes, ivoire) ou agricoles (maïs, sorgho, etc.) représentant 40 heures de travail par mois. Le succès de ces opérations, qui auraient fourni à l'Etat jusqu'à 55.3 pourcent de ses revenus annuels (Cattier, 1906) était dû aux moyens de coercition. Des expéditions militaires et même punitives (d'où otages des femmes et enfants, arrestation et châtiment des chefs autochtones, viols, confiscation des vivres) étaient utilisés. Plusieurs auteurs (Cattier, 1906; Boute et de Saint-Moulin,

1981, etc.) pensent que cet impôt avait causé une importante dépopulation et une rareté (relative et absolue) de main-d'oeuvre qui faillirent hypothéquer la réussite de l'oeuvre coloniale. La population du Zaïre aurait en effet été d'environ 15 millions d'habitants au début de l'ère coloniale (1885).[10] Mais les premiers recensements de 1914 ne donneront que 4 millions d'effectifs. Quoique ces statistiques souffrent de surestimation ou de sousestimation, il reste qu'il y a une dépopulation certaine. Van de Pute (1946: 16) parlera même d'indice de survivance de la population plutôt que d'indice d'accroissement. Il fallait donc vite changer le fusil d'épaule!

L'Impôt en Argent. Il fut institué en vue: (1) de généraliser le travail salarié en se procurant le numéraire "dans les factoreries, contre les produits commerciales créés par son travail, ou en mettant ses bras à la disposition du fisc et des particuliers" (Cattier, 1906: 124), (2) "de promouvoir le développement quantitatif et qualitatif des cultures et d'améliorer l'alimentation des populations" (Mulambu, 1974: 13), bref (3) de pallier aux ravages et insuffisances de l'impôt en travail. Son impact fut considérable: jusqu'à 50 pourcent des migrants partaient pour gagner de quoi payer l'impôt et la dot (Lux, 1958: 693). Demunter (1975) fait observer que l'acquittement de cette fiscalité, qui se serait élevée à 2.5 francs belges en 1925, à 10 francs en 1928 et à 18 francs en 1931, nécessitait 3 à 6 mois de travail salarié. Pour ceux qui se résignaient à rester dans les villages, il y avait nécessité de développer davantage des cultures de rente, avec comme conséquence un surtravail et la négligence des cultures vivrières. Notons d'ailleurs que, durant les années de la crise (1929-1934), la chute des prix payés pour les produits agricoles et la hausse continue du taux de l'impôt renforcèrent ces conséquences. Notons aussi que les hommes polygames payaient plus d'impôt que les monogames; l'emprisonnement servait de sanction aux récidivistes.

Les Cultures Obligatoires. Celles-ci ont revêtu, comme le signale Mulambu (1974) une plus grande importance qu'on ne le dit. Elles offraient: (1) des possibilités fiscales immédiates et illimitées, (2) un soutien aux effets de la crise: "il suffisait de comprimer les prix d'achat aux producteurs pour sauver les entreprises" (Mulambu, 1974: 25), (3) une plus-value plus grande aux entreprises, qui payaient à des prix très bas les produits agricoles versés comme part en nature des salaires aux travailleurs migrants, (4) un soutien à l'expansion démographique, (5) une occupation intégrale du territoire, et (6) une source de revenus monétaires.

Introduites en 1917, elles consistaient en une obligation d'exécuter des travaux de cultures vivrières (2 jours par semaine) et d'exportation (5 jours par mois), en complément des "travaux d'utilité publique" imposés en 1910 "pour combattre spécialiement la maladie du sommeil qui avait ravagé des villages entiers et diminué la main-d'oeuvre" (Mulambu, 1974). Vers 1929, elles devinrent en plus un élément de rachat pour ceux qui ne pouvaient payer l'impôt faute du numéraire. Ces cultures furent intensifiées durant les années de la crise en vue d'occuper les migrants de retour et surtout de compenser la perte des entreprises minières par l'augmentation des exportations agricoles (Merlier, 1962: 144; Jewsiewicki, 1983: 49). Elles contribuèrent ainsi à la survie de l'économie industrielle. D'abord parce que ces entreprises s'étaient assurées le monopole d'achats des produits. Ensuite parce qu'elles rémunéraient le paysan à un prix parfois plus bas que celui du portage (Jewsiewicki, 1983: 41).

Les cultures obligatoires aggravèrent la dévitalisation des milieux ruraux, qui furent alors de véritables camps de travaux forcés. En effet, les insoumis (11,383 sanctions prononcées à la Cour d'Appel de Léopoldville en 1932, contre 49,998 en 1938) étaient punis à sept jours de servitude pénale et/ou 200 francs d'amende (Mulambu, 1974). De plus, pour y maintenir la population, qui n'avait plus d'autre choix que d'accepter la faible rémunération de son travail agricole ou de quitter le village et vendre sa force de travail (Jewsiewicki, 1983: 50), on promulgua le décret du 5 décembre 1933 qui imposait l'obligation d'un passeport de mutation à quiconque quittait son lieu d'origine pour plus de 30 jours. Le poids des travaux contribua à la prolifération de la polygamie et à la hausse de la fécondité, les ménages devant, à leur tour, s'assurer une main-d'oeuvre familiale plus importante pour y faire face. Il occasionna des érosions et un épuisement du sol.

DES MIGRATIONS FORCEES AUX MIGRATIONS SPONTANEES

Le Renforcement des Mécanismes de Répulsion

Les années 1940-1945 furent marquées par ce qu'on a appelé "l'effort de guerre". Il se traduisit dans les faits par une augmentation des travaux forcés pour les paysans, des exportations et des revenus pour les entreprises. C'est en effet au cours de ces années que ces exportations connurent leur apogée. Le nombre de jours à consacrer aux cultures obligatoires par an fut doublé. L'effort exigé des paysans fut tel que le Gouverneur Ryckmans reconnut en 1946 que "les populations sont fatiguées, on ne peut leur demander de soutenir pareil effort" (Demunter, 1975: 243).

La Genèse des Mécanismes d'Attraction et la Stabilisation des Travailleurs

La décennie des années 1930 fut charnière entr^ les recrutements forcés et les migrations spontanées. Elle s'était terminée, nous l'avons vu, par un regain de prospérité économique qui fit reprendre de plus bel les recrutements. Mais il s'agissait cette fois-ci des offres spontanées: les règles du jeu étaient si bien établies que la contrainte administrative pût être relâchée.

C'est cependant durant la deuxième guerre mondiale que le regain d'emploi va s'amplifier. La demande de main d'oeuvre devint encore plus intense. Le nombre de migrants, durant ces cinq années, aurait augmenté de 50 pourcent (Infor-Congo, 1959: 20). Comme le montre la Figure 10.2, la population urbaine connut une forte croissance, que le mouvement naturel ne peut, à lui seul, occasionner.

La croissance urbaine dépendait de la conjoncture économique, l'allure des deux courbes étant la même pour tous les milieux urbains. Cette croissance fut soutenue jusqu'aux années 1955. Cela s'explique par un regain encore plus grand de l'activité economique. Réinvestissements des profits réalisés pendant la guerre, demande de maitières premières pour restaurer l'Europe, afflux de nouveaux capitaux dû en partie aux garanties de rentabilité qu'offrait le Zaïre contribuaient à ce regain. Les engagements spontanés se multiplièrent. Certains villages Yaka dans le Kwango accusèrent des taux d'engagements volontaires allant jusqu'à 84 pourcent de la population mâle adulte en 1952 (Dhanis, 1953: 494). Chez les Basuku, ils étaient de l'ordre de 61 pourcent d'hommes adultes célibataires (Lamal, 1954: 375). A ces proportions, nous dit Dhanis, il faut ajouter les migrants clandestins qui ne se souciaient plus de demander un "passeport de mutation". Capelle nous dit qu'on aurait accordé à Kinshasa 1,300 nouveaux permis de séjour par mois en 1946.

On accusa une certaine pénurie de main d'oeuvre vers 1950 (Makwala, 1966-1967). La migration continuait d'être temporaire et circulaire dans beaucoup de cas. Chez les Bayaka, "elle durait le temps nécessaire pour la constitution de quelques économies" (Ngondo, 1979: 25). Lamal note la même chose chez les Basuku qui ne voulaient "pas se lier par un contrat à long terme" (1954: 371).

Tout cela donna lieu à la politique de stabilisation qui devait permettre un volume certain et régulier de main-d'oeuvre et pallier aux

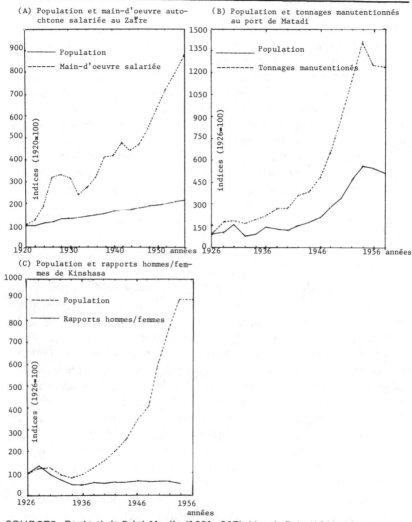

(A) Population et main-d'oeuvre autochtone salariée au Zaïre

(B) Population et tonnages manutentionnés
au port de Matadi

(C) Population et rapports hommes/fem-
mes de Kinshasa

SOURCES: Boute et de Saint-Moulin (1981: 307); Van de Pute (1946: 19); Sabakinu
(1981: 630); Romaniuk (1959: 575); and Capelle (1948).

Figure 10.2   Population et industrialisation au Zaïre (1920-1960)

désavantages du travail migrant: manque de spécialisation et perte du
bénéfice d'entrainement des travailleurs; dénatalité, divorce et
polygamie dans les milieux ruraux; polyandrie, libertinage et prostitution dans les milieux urbains. On procéda à l'augmentation des
salaires et au renforcement des infrastructures sociales: écoles,

hôpitaux, services d'hygiène. Les droits des "évolués" s'élargirent. Une politique de logements demarra en 1944. En 1951, on instaura un système d'allocations familiales en vue d'inciter les travailleurs au mariage et/ou à une forte fécondité. On procéda également à une reconstitution des ménages en ville, en permettant aux travailleurs seuls de se faire rejoindre par leurs femmes et enfants. On exigeait même à l'Etat d'accorder au mari stabilisé en ville un "moyen légal de contraindre sa femme à le rejoindre" afin de parer à l'opposition des parents de celle-ci (Lamal, 1954: 367).

Cette politique de stabilisation permit ce que nous appelions la normalisation progressive de la pyramide d'âges et du sex-ratio (voir introduction et la Figure 10.2c). La surmasculinité qui predominait pendant toute la période du travail migrant devint un "mal démographique" qu'il fallait plus que jamais endiguer dans les villes (Charles, 1948: 901).

L'Héritage Colonial

Les cinq dernieres années avant l'indépendance (1955-1960) furent marquées par une récession qui se traduisit par un tarissement progressif des investissements. Le marché du travail fut saturé et le chômage prit de plus en plus d'ampleur dans les villes, alors que s'affirmait une bourgeoisie nationale qui servait désormais de trait d'union entre les colons et les prolétaires. Les mesures de contrôle des chômeurs et des déplacements dans les villes furent de nouveau renforcées. A Kinshasa, la création en 1956 d'un "Bureau public de placement" visait entre autres choses de faire disparaître le parasitisme. De nombreux chômeurs vont alors être rapatriés dans leurs villages. Des mesures furent prises pour réglementer de nouveau l'exode rural. Mais la colonie faisait déjà face à la crise de la décolonisation et l'afflux en ville n'était plus uniquement lié à une conjoncture économique favorable. La migration devint un mode de vie et le migrant quelqu'un qui s'en allait tenter sa chance là où il pouvait survivre, même s'il n'y était vu que comme un "trouble-fête." Trois ans avant l'indépendance, Bezy (1957: 109) résumait cet héritage:

> S'il a fallu en de nombreuses régions exercer une certaine pression jusqu'à la dernière guerre pour obtenir des populations qu'elles se déplacent pour s'intégrer dans le circuit de l'économie européenne, il n'en va plus de même aujourd'hui. Les hommes adultes des milieux coutumiers ... affluent dans les centres au point que l'on voudrait plutôt en refouler une partie, devant les difficultés que provoquent les déplacements massifs.

CONCLUSION

Comme ce fut le cas avec la capture des esclaves africains dont le travail a permis l'essor du capitalisme américain, ou celui du Burkina Faso qui a servi de réservoir de main-d'oeuvre pour une accumulation réalisée au Ghana et en Côte-d'Ivoire, l'histoire des migrations dans l'Ouest du Zaïre montre aussi comment et combien les besoins capitalistes avaient contraint la population à vendre sa force de travail, contribuant ainsi, malgré elle, à implanter et perpétuer le phénomène migratoire. Cette implantation progressive est étroitement associée à la pénétration du capitalisme Léopoldien d'abord puis international ensuite. Parce que, d'une part, le capital ne s'investissait que là où les conditions de rentabilité étaient réunies ou accumulées, et que des mécanismes de paupérisation des milieux ruraux furent mis en branle d'autre part, la population a été et s'est vue contrainte de migrer vers les nouvelles sites capitalistes.

L'importance quantitative de ces mouvements ainsi que leur caractère sélectif expliquent en plus la périphérisation des milieux ruraux, car les migrations n'ont constitué ni plus ni moins qu'un transfert des capacités de production qui a renforcé les inégalités. Même affranchies des mécanismes de coercition qui leur ont donné naissance, les migrations demeurent une stratégie de survie devant ces inégalités qu'elles renforcent. Une recherche psychosociologique dans l'Ouest du Zaïre n'a-t-elle pas montré que cette partie du pays (et vraissemblablement tout le pays) n'est plus qu'un espace de paysans résignés et découragés, et des citadins qui monopolisent les profits du ''développement'' socio-éconmique, quoiqu'étant eux-même des ''dominateurs dominés'' (Schwarz, 1980: 125-129)?

La particularité de ce processus pour le Zaïre consiste en cette double fonction imposée aux mêmes sociétés: fournir la main-d'oeuvre (l'offrir et la reproduire) et les ressources naturelles pour l'accumulation. Ainsi, vecteur de l'accumulation des richesses, les migrations ont aussi été le vecteur de la dynamique démographique durant l'époque coloniale. La vitalité des milieux ruraux, postulat de base de la politique démographique et de la doctrine en matière de main-d'oeuvre avait effectivement permis de soutenir des niveaux élevés de fécondité, d'améliorer la morbidité et de diminuer la mortalité, par des mesures d'assainissement sanitaire, et du lutte contre l'infécondité et la polygamie. Il n'est donc pas surprenant que la fécondité accuse une augmentation régulière durant l'époque coloniale. Ce postulat avait aussi conduit à l'assujettissement des migrations au rythme de la conjoncture économique et des besoins en main-d'oeuvre. Et lorsque, dans les années cinquante, ce postulat fut relâché au profit de la stabilisation des travailleurs, c'est-à-dire de ce que Peemans (Bezy, Peemans, Wautelet, 1981) appelle la cogestion par l'Administration et les Grandes sociétés des espaces d'élevage de la main-d'oeuvre, la fécondité urbaine ne tarda pas à prendre le dessus sur la fécondité rurale. A leur tour, les migrations connurent alors une sorte de "boom" qui s'accentuera dans les premières années d'indépendance et se poursuit encore.

Ces relations entre développement capitaliste, implantation des migrations et dynamique démographique constituent une allerte: aucune recherche ne peut les négliger se l'on veut comprendre tant soit peu la dynamique démographique en général, et migratoire en particulier, du Zaïre néo-colonial d'aujourd'hui.

NOTES

1. Faisant le bilan des vingt premières années de l'indépendance, Huybrechts et al. (1980: 59) reconnaissent que "la principale transformation profonde qu'ait connu la société zaïroise depuis l'indepéndance du pays est sans conteste celle résultant du phénomène migratoire. ... Déjà, sous la colonisation, le phénomène était présent et seules des mesures restreignant la liberté individuelle parvenaient à le limiter quelque peu."

2. On a connu trois grandes sources des données demographiques pendant l'époque coloniale: les enquêtes démographiques appelées "coups de sonde" depuis 1925, les recensements sur fiches ou l'enregistrement continu et l'Etat civil depuis 1933. Elles sont de qualité inégale et s'améliorent dans l'ensemble avec le temps. Leur exploitation invite toujours à la prudence. Voir Ngondo (1974), Boute et de Saint-Moulin (1981), Ryckmans (1953).

3. Voir notamment Mbumba (198?). Cette approche est encore dominante pour expliquer les migrations africaines. Pour une critique théorique, voir Amin (1974b) et Gregory et Piché (1982).

4. Nous faisons remonter la colonisation depuis 1885 même si, en réalité, la colonisation belge ne commence qu'en 1908 lorsque Léopold II lègue à la Belgique sa "propriété," jusque là Etat Indépendant du Congo.

5. Jewsiewicki (1983: 168) la définit comme étant un "processus social de production du travail salarié obtenu par la destruction de l'autonomie socio-économique et culturelle des communautés de producteurs ruraux."

6. La méthode a consisté à convertir les tonnes à transporter en charges (1 charge = 35kgs) puis en nombre de voyages nécessaires (1 charge = 1 voyage), et à diviser le résultat par 6 (nombre moyen de voyages par an). Voir Wauters (1895: 20).

7. Les départs successifs des travailleurs après leur retour au village étaient néanmois assurés. Sabakinu (1981: 483) nous parle du mécanisme utilisé pour attacher les ouvriers de l'Offitra-Matadi à leur emploi: jusqu'à expiration du contrat, ils ne percevaient que les 2/3 du salaire, le réliquat constituait le pécule de licenciement.

8. D'autres commissions furent créées par la suite: Commission consultative de la main-d'oeuvre indigène (en 1928) et Commission de la main-d'oeuvre indigène (1930-1931).

9. Cette triple fonction de l'agent recenseur compromettait largement le succès des opérations, à cause d'un trop grand intérêt porté sur les hommes adultes valides, la fuite de ceux-ci et, phénomène encore observé aujourd'hui, leur tendance à rajeunir pour ne pas être étiquetté H.A.V. (Homme adulte valide).

10. Stanley parle même de 30 millions dans ses récits (Duc de Castries, 1960).

PART IV

EAST AND NORTHEAST AFRICA: CONQUEST AND THE READJUSTMENT OF FERTILITY AND MORTALITY

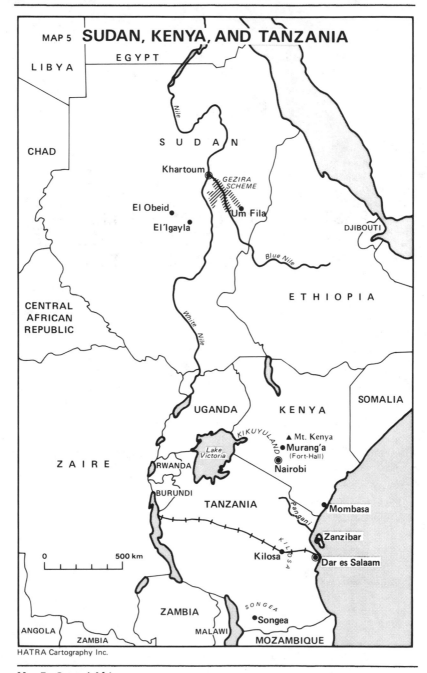

MAP 5 **SUDAN, KENYA, AND TANZANIA**

LIBYA

EGYPT

CHAD

S U D A N

Khartoum

GEZIRA SCHEME

El Obeid

Um Fila

El 'Igayla

Nile

Blue Nile

DJIBOUTI

CENTRAL
AFRICAN
REPUBLIC

E T H I O P I A

White Nile

UGANDA

K E N Y A

SOMALIA

KIKUYULAND

▲ Mt. Kenya

Z A I R E

Lake Victoria

RWANDA

Murang'a
(Fort-Hall)

Nairobi

BURUNDI

TANZANIA

Pangani

Mombasa

Zanzibar

KILOSA

0   500 km

Kilosa

Dar es Salaam

ZAMBIA

SONGEA

●Songea

ANGOLA

ZAMBIA

MALAWI

MOZAMBIQUE

Map 5   Central Africa

11

DIFFERENTIAL HIGH FERTILITY
AND DEMOGRAPHIC TRANSITIONS
Peripheral Capitalism in Sudan

JAY O'BRIEN

Conventional wisdom is always refractory, and nowhere is this truer than in African population history. Etched in stone is the notion that African populations were characterized by high fertility rates and high mortality rates until colonial European medicine reduced the latter, leaving the former high. Although there is no shortage of evidence that contemporary African fertility and population growth rates are very high, evidence concerning precolonial population dynamics is skimpy indeed. This circumstance makes the unanimity among observers that earlier African fertility rates were extremely high curious, but at the same time makes it exceedingly difficult to win support for alternative analyses. This chapter will nevertheless attempt to argue that this conventional wisdom is wrong and that the more common impact of colonialism in Africa was to *increase* pressures for high fertility. The argument will be indirect, drawing principally on the analysis of differential reproductive strategies of two contemporary Sudanese villages to suggest that high fertility rates in these cases represent aspects of farmers' responses to the specific

Author's Note: Fieldwork in Sudan was carried out between 1975 and 1979 under grants from the Ford Foundation-sponsored Manpower Research Project of the University of Khartoum. I was assisted in the field by Salah Eddin el Shazali, Haj Musa Kuku, Mohamed Yousif Ahmed el Mustafa, Mohamed el Dukheiri, and Mohamed Azim Abu Sabah. See O'Brien (1980) and Ali and O'Brien (1984).

pressures of capitalist penetration (see Map 5). The villages are Um Fila in Blue Nile Province and el'Igayla in Northern Kordofan Province.

THE CONVENTIONAL WISDOM

Before examining colonial effects on African population dynamics, it is necessary to ask why, in the absence of relevant evidence, the conventional wisdom has come to dominate discourse on the subject. The ruling general concepts in this field are those of demographic transition theory as formulated by Notestein (1945), systematized for the Third World by Davis and Blake (1956), Coale and Hoover (1958), and others, and modified by Caldwell (1976, 1981, 1982). The central proposition of transition theory is that human fertility rates were universally high—except in special circumstances of scarcity (e.g., the San of the Kalahari desert) or life on a small island (e.g., Tikopia; see Caldwell, 1976)—due principally to the prevalence of high mortality rates. With the invention and spread of modern medicine, mortality rates dropped, pulling down fertility rates once these effects were felt (see the first section of the Introduction to this book). The specificity of the contemporary Third World is that mortality decline is said to occur through the exogenous introduction of modern medicine from Europe rather than as part of an organic process of technological, economic, social, and cultural "modernization." Thus, current high population growth rates in Africa are regarded as resulting from a lag between mortality decline and a drop in fertility rates that stems from the perseverance of archaic cultural "props" for high fertility.

In its more sophisticated variants (e.g., Caldwell, 1976, 1982), transition theory admits that there was more to high fertility than compensation for high mortality and associated cultural props, and that persistence of high fertility after mortality rates have declined may be a "rational" adaptation to economic conditions in which net intergenerational wealth flows favor parents of many children (see Cain, 1977). Nevertheless, the "naturalness" of high fertility and its universality prior to the development of modern medicine are taken as given.

Some of the flaws in demographic transition theory and its apologetic stance toward capitalist development have been noted (e.g., by Seccombe, 1983). In Europe, the high fertility rates of the early phases of the Industrial Revolution appear to have risen above those of the late feudal period, and the onset of the decisive downward trend in fertility considerably antedates the general diffusion of modern medicine—apparently having more to do in urban areas with the adoption of relatively simple public health measures at the instigation of the trade union movement. Such evidence suggests the possibility that the persistence of transition theory owes most to its ideological function of providing an alternative to Marx's analysis of capitalist population dynamics, as embodied in the theory of the industrial reserve army, in order to explain poverty and unemployment under capitalism as precapitalist remnants that capitalist development gradually overcomes (Marx, 1976; see also Meek, 1971).

While this bit of conventional wisdom achieved formalization in the framework of the demographic transition, the basic ideas are much older. This fact forces us into a more fundamental confrontation with central aspects of bourgeois social thought. Historical understanding in general is embedded in a variety of oppositional models taken to represent past and present. Whether articulated in terms of natural versus market economy, community versus contract, tradition versus modernity, or other polar pairs, such models represent pseudohistorical constructs intended to present history as transition from one to the other. Historical analysis then proceeds on the basis of sorting the mixed elements of any concrete reality into those left over from the past and those belonging to the emergent future. Rather than reconstructing history, such an exercise reproduces a pseudohistorical process with implicit evolutionist assumptions. Thus, characteristics such as community, self-sufficiency, other-directedness, religious attitudes, simplicity, functional diffuseness, and high fertility are assigned to the past while another set of characteristics such as individualism, market integration, self-motivation, scientific attitudes, complexity, functional specificity, and low fertility are seen as emergent modern traits. History is thereby removed from time and placed firmly in an abstract realm of sociocultural evolution. Real societies sharing temporal space are radically separated from their interrelationships on the basis of their possession of lesser or greater numbers of modern traits and assigned to different abstract evolutionary stages. The traits themselves are represented as changing independently; population dynamics thus become a bounded set that changes in response to technology and education. Their imbrication in historically specific social relations is abolished.

Unfortunately, similar oppositional models have also dominated critical discourse, albeit in different forms. Thus, Marxists identify precapitalist "modes of production" articulated to and dominated by a capitalist mode in Africa. Which is which is decided by the presence or absence of the relevant diagnostic traits. Where we find wage labor, commodity markets, and class differentiation we have capitalism.

Where we encounter household production, subsistence orientation, and kinship relations we are to speak of some kind of "precapitalist" mode of production. The classification and definition of these precapitalist modes of production have been characterized by fractious debate largely because the conceptual field is defined negatively in terms of the absence of supposedly capitalist characteristics that render organic commodity production and state formation conceptually impossible. One need only refer to the debates over African feudalism, domestic modes of production, the Asiatic mode of production, and tributary modes of production to grasp the gravity of the conceptual problems (see Meillassoux, 1972; Amin, 1976; Goody, 1969; Coquery-Vidrovitch, 1978; Dupré and Rey, 1978). Without entering into these debates here, it is important to register the contention that they stem from the assimilation into the Marxist problematic of the evolutionist schema of bourgeois historical thought.

DISSENTING VOICES

It behooves one undertaking an oppositional exercise to search out and identify respectable intellectual parentage. Of course, the risk of discovering oneself to be an intellectual orphan or bastard always lurks behind such a project, as appears likely in this case. All the elements of my argument are present in one stream or another of Marxist discourse, but to my knowledge they have so far not cross-fertilized into a comprehensive and coherent refutation of demographic transition theory as applied to Africa. Marx himself was clear about the historical specificity and contingency of capitalist population dynamics, although many of his followers have been less careful about accepting the antiquity of high fertility rates. Faris (1975) has noted the relatively low fertility rates under primitive conditions of producer control and has distinguished the structural logic of population dynamics of precolonial African states from capitalist population dynamics but does not treat the respective fertility conditions in detail. Many have noted the operation of specifically capitalist pressures for high fertility in the Third World, such as Gregory and Piché (1981) and Cordell and Gregory (1980) for Africa, Mamdani (1971) for India, and de Janvry (1981) for Latin America. De Janvry argues that fertility rates in Latin America have recently been on the rise, but the antecedents remain unclear. For Africa, Meillassoux (1983a) has argued that capitalism has actually brought about increasing fertility rates in the labor reserves, but the argument remains little more than an assertion unsupported by evidence.

The more common position is that of Caldwell (1976, 1982), who posits a two-state model of fertility—high or low—with anything in between being transitory or structurally insignificant. This position recognizes that the high fertility state may exist in the context of either precapitalist or capitalist relations, but sees high fertility under capitalism as basically a continuation of precapitalist rates. A more sophisticated view, articulated by Romaniuk (1980), has the unusual merit of acknowledging for the case of Zaire that fertility rates actually rose under the impact of colonialism. Romaniuk, however, attributes this rise to effects of modernization, which he argues removed "checks" on fertility through undermining such "traditional" practices as postpartum sexual restrictions and polygyny and making bottled milk available as a substitute for long-term breast-feeding. No consideration is given to the possibility that positive factors may have been introduced by "modernization" itself that increased pressures on fertility and altered reproductive strategies.

In contrast, I argue that fertility is a continuous variable dependent on class relations, that it may be high without being maximal (as I argue was the case in much of precolonial Africa), and that similar fertility rates may result from vastly and significantly different pressures and reproductive strategies. The two cases I analyze below both exhibit high fertility rates, but the reproductive strategies and the consequences for children differ greatly between them. In Um Fila the dominant strategy aims to maximize the number of healthy and productive adult men in an extended family production unit, while the dominant strategy in el'lgayla strives to maximize the number of children between the ages of about 6 and 13 in a household. Each strategy has arisen out of a different pattern of incorporation into peripheral capitalism.

THE DEVELOPMENT OF CAPITALISM IN SUDAN

The vast irrigated Gezira Scheme dominated the colonial economy of Sudan. Farmed by thousands of tenant families assisted by annual infusions of seasonal labor from peasant villages and pastoralist groups, it produced cotton for the mills of Lancashire. Through the imposition of taxes payable in cash, the undermining of indigenous craft production, aggressive marketing of new consumer goods, and other devices, the colonial regime sought to tap the labor supply of rural Sudan on a seasonal basis while allowing peasant and pastoral production to continue to supply their basic subsistence needs (see O'Brien, 1980, 1983, 1984). Local communities responded to these pressures in varying ways, which included production of cash crops desired by the British as well as different patterns of involvement in wage labor. Following independence in 1956, capitalist agriculture expanded rapidly, spreading irrigation and moving into the rainlands as well. This expansion relied on the same general formula of strategic use of machinery and massive reliance on migrant seasonal labor.

Every wave of expansion brought new areas of peasant and pastoral production into the orbit of capitalist markets for labor and products as market forces penetrated rural productive systems through the stimulation and expansion of cash needs. Although altered by this penetration, many peasant and pastoral systems remained basically self-sufficient in the limited sense that local production of subsistence and cash goods, irregularly supplemented by seasonal wage labor, generally sufficed to reproduce the community from one year to the next. Wholesale disarticulation of domestic economies was not widespread in the first several decades, and was generally restricted to the core labor supply areas. Instead, there was a variety of responses to the pressures of partial incorporation into the capitalist political economy based on differing local conditions, including divisions of labor and attitudes toward work.

Within the range of variation two broad patterns of response were particularly important (O'Brien, 1983): (1) Members of some groups, especially nomads and recently settled former nomads, among whom women took prominent roles in agricultural production, became regularly involved in cotton picking in family groups; and (2) members of strongly patriarchal groups and others in which women did little or no agricultural work most frequently sought to intensify local agricultural production and produce cash crops rather than seek wage labor. Among the latter groups, seasonal migration tended to be irregular, with only men migrating while women and children remained at home.

What is of central importance is the fact that the development of the peripheral capitalist political economy, and the agricultural labor force in particular, proceeded in such a way that the manner and extent of incorporation of individual communities depended largely on their location and internal characteristics. Initial stages of incorporation were achieved not through profound transformation of existing production but through tapping the potential within precolonial structures for expanding production. Thus, the early stages of penetration were based on absolute rather than relative surplus value (see O'Brien, 1983).

A crucial consequence for the colonial labor force was a diversity of forms of incorporation that allowed participation in wage labor and commodity production in ways that were compatible with the continued reproduction of the social relations in specific communities. These different social forms in turn gave rise to pressures to increase fertility in order to raise the absolute amount of labor within production units and to variable reproduction strategies corresponding to different patterns of demand for labor.

UM FILA: OPTIMIZING HIGH FERTILITY

Um Fila is a Zabarma village in northeastern Blue Nile Province that in 1974 numbered 426 people whose ancestors had come to Sudan from West Africa over a century before (see Painter, Chapter 8, this volume). Most of the village is organized in large extended family production/consumption units composed of a father, his wife or wives, and his married sons and their wives and children living together in fenced compounds. These family groups work common fields together and consume from common stores and a unified treasury managed by the patriarch. The ability of men to build and maintain large extended family production units has depended on their reproductive success—particularly their luck in fathering an appropriately spaced group of sons. Such reproductive success is consolidated through strategically timed polygynous marriages (see Gruenbaum, 1979; O'Brien, 1980).

The village productive system centers on the cultivation of rainfed fields of sorghum (for household consumption) and sesame (for sale). Land is relatively abundant and accessible to all men by virtue of their membership in the community. These fields are cultivated by the men and boys of an extended household unit. Married women do not participate in the work in these fields, but remain in strict seclusion within the family compound (where they may, however, cultivate small garden plots).

In addition to cultivating the main rain-fed fields, some units also cultivate vegetable gardens along the seasonal Rahad River and a nearby tributary, and herd animals (mainly goats and sheep, with some cattle). However, successfully combining all three activities requires a large group of cooperating men able to spare an adult (preferably aided by a boy) for each garden and herd. Large units, consisting of at least three grown men and three boys over 6 years old, are thus able to afford a more balanced year-round diet and greater security for their members than are smaller units.

Pressures on the reproductive powers of women and the management abilities of patriarchs have recently been increasing as markets and wage-earning opportunities in the area expand. Such pressures already began to be felt from at least the 1920s when taxation and the suppression of indigenous textile production increased the need for cash. To defend their patriarchal authority, the elders expanded cash crop (sesame) production as an alternative to labor migration. The increased labor required made it more difficult for smaller units to maintain vegetable cultivation and herds at the same time, thereby placing a greater premium on the ability to father many sons.[1] The minimum size of the cooperating group of men and boys necessary to maintain a balanced production of vegetables and animal products in addition to grain and cash crops was thus increased.

The accelerating penetration of the village productive system by capital since the 1960s has begun to intensify these pressures. Capital has penetrated village production in a number of ways in addition to the long-standing marketing of cash crops and the purchase by villagers of an increasing array of consumer goods. From the early 1960s, many households started, primarily at the instigation of junior men, to hire tractors to plow their fields. The use of tractors has resulted in a more extensive pattern of cultivation and an improved ability to balance food and cash crop production through removing the labor demand bottleneck previously imposed by the arduous task of hand-turning the heavy clay soil. Units able to hire tractors are thus able to accomplish their work in seven- to eight-hour workdays in contrast to the eleven- or twelve-hour workdays of the past. But raising the required cash requires having working sons.

Several agricultural tasks—especially the sesame harvest, which must be completed within about seven to ten days after the crop ripens—require more labor than most households can field independently. In the past such labor was mobilized through reciprocal cooperative work parties, in which families worked in each other's fields in return for meals and tea provided by the host. As pressures to earn cash have increased, many men have come to demand monetary compensation for this labor, and even then may refuse to work for farmers who are not close kin. Small families suffer most from this change, as their need for supplementary labor is greatest and their resources for mobilizing it (mainly grain surpluses) poorest.

By the mid-1970s, escalating inflation was increasing the costs of all goods purchased and new cash needs were proliferating rapidly. Urban merchants had begun sending crews to the forest just outside Um Fila to make charcoal, with the result that this source of firewood and building materials began to disappear. Villagers either had to neglect other work to collect these necessities from farther afield or else had to spend cash to obtain them.

All these circumstances conspire to make an increasingly large group of men indispensable to maintaining a satisfactory diet and standard of living while at the same time increasing the difficulties of keeping such a group together. Inflation, the threat of sons breaking away from their fathers, and the instability of the higher consumption standards of even the largest extended family units lead some patriarchs to attempt to convert group assets to cash for trade, additional polygynous marriages, and so on. Their sons in turn feel pressures to field a larger work team through having large numbers of sons of their own. Women share this interest in bearing many sons, especially in polygynous households, where having grown sons is their only guarantee of support in old age. Since pressures for high fertility focus on male heads of extended family units, the high frequency and intensity of polygyny in Um Fila represents an aspect of men's strategies for maximizing their fertility.

The consequences of these pressures on fertility are a characteristic reproductive strategy. The core of the productive work force is a group of men; thus, sons are favored over daughters. Villagers say that a boy will be breast-fed for two years after birth, with pregnancy being avoided in the interval, in order to maximize his health and potential for growing into a productive adult. The birth of a girl is the occasion for disappointment, unless she has been preceded by sons, and it is said that she is generally weaned within a year of birth, at which time her mother hopes to become pregnant again.

That these priorities have some impact on actual reproductive patterns is indicated by the results of reproductive histories I collected for 54 women who had ever given birth.[2] These women had produced 239 children in 237 births. The mean interval between the birth of a son and the next birth was 3.0 years, while the mean interval following birth of a daughter was 2.7 years. The interval following a male birth before the next birth was more than 2 years in half of the cases, while following a female birth the interval was over 2 years in approximately one-third of the cases.

I do not have adequate direct data to assess the possibility of differential effects of birth intervals on the life chances of males and females. Recollection and reporting of infant and child deaths were vague, and there seemed to be a tendency to remember deaths of sons, especially those who lived more than a year, better than those of daughters.[3] Given the small size of the total village population and the fact that the overall sex ratio—100.8 males per 100 females—was remarkably balanced, there seems to be little basis for concluding that differential birth intervals result in significantly higher mortality rates for girls than for boys. Nevertheless, boys are favored over girls and the predominant reproductive strategy and fertility regime in Um Fila clearly support a pattern of response to capitalist penetration that seeks to maximize the number of healthy and productive males in an extended family.

EL 'IGAYLA: MAXIMIZING FERTILITY

El 'Igayla is a Joama' Arab village founded in 1898 near the route later followed by the western rail line in central Kordofan (see O'Brien, 1980; Ali and O'Brien, 1984). Initially cultivating millet and small amounts of cotton for local consumption, these people, who in 1977 numbered about 750, now cultivate sorghum as a staple food and sesame and groundnuts as cash crops. Drastic changes in village production patterns occurred in the 1920s. When the Gezira Scheme opened in 1925, large numbers of migrant workers—many of whom came from Chad and West Africa to settle permanently—began to move through the area by rail and on foot. At the same time, the British began to push taxation and other policies more aggressively in order to stimulate cash needs and a flow of labor to Gezira.

The local people responded in a number of ways, which included abandoning cotton cultivation in favor of the purchase of imported cloth. Spurred by new cash needs and drought in 1925-1926 and 1926-1927, most villagers went to pick cotton in Gezira in its first two seasons. This source of cash gave the villagers another idea. Many of them set about clearing the surrounding forest and using cash earned picking cotton to hire some of the labor circulating in the region to cultivate new fields. At the same time, they began to shift from millet to sorghum and sesame, which enjoy higher returns to labor. Cash-cropping assumed increasing importance, to the extent that by the 1970s most families directly produced only a portion of their food, paying for the remainder with cash.

El 'Igayla exhibits much more extensive and complex social differentiation than Um Fila. Immigrant families were encouraged to settle as a source of labor through grants or loans of small plots. Others settled as sharecroppers without access to plots of their own. As the result of individualization of landownership and the settlement of immigrants, el 'Igayla developed a significant permanent (but seasonally migrant) population of landless families and other families with only tiny holdings. By 1977, 13 percent of the married men held half of the land owned by men, while at least 9 percent of married men were landless (see O'Brien, 1980; Ali and O'Brien, 1984). At the same time, 95 percent of the married women cultivated land separately from their husbands.

With the emergence of a local wage labor market in the context of an increasingly skewed distribution of land, many found it difficult to mobilize large family work groups. By 1977, teenage children could command the going wage for their labor, even from their own parents. As command over teenage labor became tenuous, parents often encouraged offspring to seek wage work and to assume responsibility for part of the family budget (often clothing for their younger siblings). In this way they hoped to sustain a contribution to household income from these increasingly autonomous children.

These developments have also affected patterns of seasonal outmigration for wage labor. From 1925 until recently, most families in el 'Igayla annually migrated as family groups to pick cotton, with each member earning a cash income. The dominance of the cotton-picking labor market by such family groups resulted in a prevailing wage rate that was substantially lower than rates available in other activities (see O'Brien, 1983). As higher-wage jobs became more widely available and pressures on cash resources increased in the 1970s, family members who could earn the higher wages began to leave cotton picking. Adult men began to work in the more remunerative sorghum harvest in the rain-fed schemes while boys from about the age of 13 began to seek work in the towns. Family cotton-picking groups were thus reduced to women and their children under 13, plus a few old folks.

These developments within village agriculture and seasonal labor migration have progressively reduced the unpaid labor force within the family to the parents (working largely independently of one another) and their children under 13. Children contribute labor at below market rates of compensation only between the ages of about 6 and 13. Such a condition has dramatic implications for reproductive strategies; whatever the consequences of doing so, reducing the interval between births is the only way in which a family can field a large work team and avoid paying relatively high wages to hire labor. This problem is not simply a matter of direct cost/benefit calculations. Cultivation entails cash outlays right from the start of the season, such as for seed and land rent, in addition to labor hire. In particular, the high cost of seed is often an obstacle to cultivation of groundnuts, the crop with the highest return on cash and labor invested. Thus, having children available to work without a wage may make the difference between a family being able to plant groundnuts and not being able to do so.

The effects of the resulting fertility strategy can be seen quite clearly. Women in el 'Igayla state that they wean babies of both sexes after about six weeks and attempt to become pregnant again as soon as possible. The mean interval between births for 117 women who had ever given birth was 2.2 years, with little difference discernible between the sexes.[4] This contrasts sharply with Um Fila, where the overall mean birth interval was 2.9 years. The contrast is even more dramatic than these figures indicate. In el 'Igayla, 17.1 percent of recorded birth intervals were a year or less, compared with 3.1 percent for Um Fila. In el 'Igayla, only 21.9 percent of the birth intervals were longer than two years, in comparison with 44.6 percent in Um Fila.[5] Women in el 'Igayla who had ever given birth averaged 5.6 children each, while women in the same category in Um Fila averaged 4.4 children each. In el 'Igayla, 74 of 117 women surveyed (63.2 percent) had had at least one child die before reaching the age of 16, while in Um Fila 13 of 54 women (24.1 percent) had suffered such a loss. Very rough calculation of the rates of death before the age of 16 yield a figure of 207 per 1000 in el 'Igayla and 154 per 1000 in Um Fila.[6] Such evidence suggests that the pressures on families to field work teams of children aged 6 to 13 have led to a regime of maximum fertility, with consequences including a relatively high child death rate.

CONCLUSION

In the above comparison of the reproductive strategies of families in Um Fila and el 'Igayla, I have tried to show how fertility patterns—and, secondarily, child mortality as well—are related to differential patterns of incorporation of the two villages into peripheral capitalism. Despite the lack of positive evidence concerning their precolonial population dynamics, I would argue that an analysis of their differential incorporation by capitalism is sufficient to explain their contemporary reproductive strategies and behaviors. For Um Fila, the relative isolation of the village—actively sought by the elders in response to capitalist encroachment—and the form of the patriarchal extended family led to pressures for the increase in the number of men and boys within each extended family unit. Reproductive strategies favoring boys were adopted, although apparently not to the extent of introducing serious threats to girls' life chances. Men also sought plural marriages as another means of increasing their available labor force. In lieu of evidence from precolonial times I cannot say whether fertility rates or the frequency and intensity of polygyny significantly increased. However, to maintain that they did not increase would require demonstration of precolonial forces that could have resulted in similar pressures to those observed under capitalist penetration.

It would seem to me that the need for such demonstration would be even more obvious in the case of el 'Igayla, where the consequences of the pattern adopted under the pressure of capitalist penetration have been much more painful—the heavy burden imposed on women and the high incidence of child death. Moreover, the greater pressures on fertility in el 'Igayla can be traced directly to factors such as the railway and earlier penetration of markets, both attendant upon more precocious and complete incorporation into the colonial capitalist economy. Recent developments in Um Fila, associated with the acceleration of capitalist penetration in that corner of Blue Nile Province—the opening of the Rahad Scheme across the river, dramatic price inflation, and the escalation of cash needs as sources of firewood and building materials have begun to disappear—suggest that conditions very like those shaping el 'Igayla's reproductive patterns are beginning to emerge there as well. I expect that all but the wealthiest families in Um Fila will lose the ability to sustain the large extended family form of production and that the resulting nucleated units will feel increasing pressures to maximize fertility, perhaps even at the sacrifice of their children's health.

This comparison is admittedly insufficient as historical reconstruction. Um Fila was less deeply penetrated partly because community leaders deliberately resisted capitalist encroachment on their patriarchal authority through relocation and institutional adjustments. The internal economy of the village and its reproductive patterns were nevertheless affected by this resistance and the articulation of the village to the wider political economy. By the late 1970s, this resistance was rapidly being undermined, with results similar to those experienced in el 'Igayla decades earlier. In this sense, then, the comparison lends plausibility to the contention that, in broad outline, the fertility regimes of Um Fila and el 'Igayla approximate stages in the response to capitalist expansion. The significance of the sort of analysis attempted here does not, however, lie in demonstrating changes in fertility patterns, or even necessarily in demonstrating measurable differences in fertility. The central aim is rather to show the necessity of understanding reproductive strategies—whether they are successful or not—as aspects of people's responses to the socioeconomic conditions in which they live, and particularly to the conditions of capitalist penetration.

NOTES

1. The same pressures probably led to the present virtually exclusive cultivation of sorghum and the abandonment of millet as a food crop due to its greater field labor requirements. This change in turn may have increased pressures for the exclusion of women from field labor and increased seclusion because more labor is required to process sorghum than to process millet.

2. These results are reported only for their suggestiveness. Due to the seclusion of women, the information was obtained from male heads of households and supplemented by limited information obtained from women by Ellen Gruenbaum (see Gruenbaum, 1979). While various checks and observations led me to regard the information as generally accurate, there are gaps that lead me to regard anything beyond indicative numbers as unwarranted in analysis of the reproductive data.

3. A census of the village in 1974 found sex ratios in the younger age classes that are suggestive—perhaps misleadingly—in this regard. There were 103.7 males for 100 females in the 0 to 5 age class—about the proportion expected at birth—but 121.2 per 100 in the 6 to 11 age class (Galal-el-din, 1975; see O'Brien, 1980).

4. These women among them had produced 671 children in 655 pregnancies. If twins are counted as two births occurring at an interval of zero years, then the mean is only 2.1 years.

5. At this stage in my analysis of the data for el 'Igayla I have not been able to verify differential reproductive performance by class; I expect this would reveal even closer birth spacing among poorer families in this highly differentiated village.

6. The overwhelming majority of these deaths occurred before the age of 5, but informants were often vague about the ages of children who had died, especially when those deaths had occurred several years earlier. In fact, I suspect that deaths of children, particularly those who failed to survive more than a few weeks, were in some cases forgotten or otherwise not reported. The sample is thus skewed. For this reason, plus the fact that age at death figures are too imprecise to allow calculation of years lived for children who have died, the rates given should be taken as proxies for rather than estimates of child mortality rates. Actual child death rates in both cases are probably higher, though perhaps in roughly the same proportions. It is interesting to note also that if one woman in Um Fila who was a member of the poorest family in the village and lost 8 children is not counted, the child death rate for that sample would be reduced to 129 per 1000.

12

POPULATION GROWTH AND THE DETERIORATION OF HEALTH
Mainland Tanzania, 1920-1960

MEREDETH TURSHEN

This chapter explores new explanations for twentieth-century demographic change in Africa to see how they can help to reconcile population growth with deteriorating health in British-ruled Tanzania. The chapter is divided into two parts: in the first, theoretical work is discussed and new hypotheses are proposed; in the second, empirical examples from Tanzania (see Map 5) are studied to test theory.

THEORY, APPROACH, AND HYPOTHESES

In the Absence of Benchmarks

In Africa there are no national demographic data for the precolonial period, and we do not know the size of the population of Tanzania before 1900. Even major demographic events are difficult to quantify. For the slave trade, there are no firm estimates of the population captured or exported, the numbers killed in raids or dead of diseases contracted as a result. We do not know the long-term social impact of slavery on societies decimated by the loss of their able-bodied young. Historians such as Fage (1969) minimized the effects of slaving, but new scholarship in historical demography speculates on its reproductive impact (Manning, 1981; Thornton, 1983).

Classic Demographic Views of the Colonial Period

Conventional wisdom holds that current high population growth rates are consistent with traditional high rates of fertility among African women (see Cantrelle, 1974, for example). The theory of demographic transition is based on the assumption that high death rates were the only check on high fertility, and that Western scientific medicine introduced by colonists and missionaries brought mortality decline, which accounts for increasing population growth rates since the beginning of colonial rule. This theory is both factually and theoretically wrong.

First we must establish the relation between ways of life and ways of renewing life—between reproduction and what Marxists call "modes of production." Some observers believe that hunter-gatherers and fisherfolk had population patterns that differed from those of pastoralists and settled agriculturalists: Hunter-gatherers had fewer children, spaced further apart, than agriculturalists; they also had lower infant mortality rates and longer life expectancy (see Howell, 1979).

These differences can be related not only to labor demands (as Cordell, Gregory, and Piché have done in the introduction to this volume), but also to disease patterns and ecological niches. Agriculture on well-watered plains and plateaus supported larger populations than did herding in dry areas; but herders were often nomads who left their wastes behind them (to be "burned" in hot desert sands); their environment was more sanitary. When hunters or herders lived in relatively self-contained groups and had little contact with others, they developed immunity to many communicable diseases.[2] And, except in extreme circumstances probably not frequently experienced before European conquest, their food supply was adequate and rich in protein. Agriculturalists were more dependent on their immediate environment, but at the same time they enriched it. The supposition is that agriculturalists, living in constant contact with their own refuse, experienced more disease, which in turn made them more vulnerable during food shortages. However, the availability of land in East Africa suggests that famines were localized and of short duration; most groups probably recovered their vitality with the next harvest (see Gervais, 1982, for similar findings in Niger). In short, there were few long-range obstacles to population growth, but during famines, reproductive powers failed, and fewer children were born. Crisis mortality was highest among the very young and the very old, sparing young adults of childbearing age.

There is a further element—in addition to disease and ecology—often ignored by demographers: the power of African women, which derived from their productive activities as much as from their reproductive capacities. Throughout East Africa, according to early ethnographers, women were the principal agriculturalists and enjoyed a great deal of autonomy. Because a measure of economic independence has been found elsewhere to be a key to women's control of their fertility, the autonomy of African women farmers, particularly among matrilineal groups of Tanzania, is presumed to be consistent with reproductive control. Although labor was divided along gender lines, there is little evidence that women were treated as inferiors or that they were controlled closely by older men as Meillassoux (1975b) believes or as occurred after European conquest.

The Impact of Capitalism on the African Family

There is little work relating the dynamics of African family formation to the introduction of capitalism. Elsewhere family reconstitution has proven fruitful in analyzing the relationship between demographic behavior and socioeconomic change at the individual level. This method allows the reconstruction of families of origin (demographic units of production) through reference to parish registers of baptisms, burials, and marriages. Levine (1977) used the technique to raise questions about links between early industrialization and increased population growth in eighteenth-century England; Kitching (1983) has explored the implications of Levine's hypotheses for Africa.

Because Christianity was not widely accepted and parish registers were not common, changes in family formation in Tanzania cannot be deduced from African parish registers alone, and evidence must be pieced together from many scattered sources. The studies by Levine and Kitching allow speculation that population growth in Tanzania after 1920 resulted from real increases in fertility that added to the base of the population pyramid, following a breakdown of cultural controls that had kept marriage age high and fertility lower. Growth after World War II was thus a consequence of the enlarged base. (Declining age at marriage also shortens the interval between generations, so that more children are born per unit of time with an increase in age specific fertility at younger ages.) Kitching (1983: 229) considers key the transition to monogamy from polygyny, which predates the slave trade and is thought to be correlated with lower fertility among individual wives.

According to Thornton (1983), nineteenth-century slaving reinforced polygyny because a surplus of women was created when men were captured and women left behind, or when women were captured, retained by raiders, and incorporated into their societies. In the colonial era, capitalism produced the opposite effect: By raising demands for labor and creating economic opportunities, capitalism weakened polygyny, which previously had been the prerogative of older men. Young men working as migrant laborers could earn dowries; they no longer had to wait for an inheritance on the death of a parent or depend on years of accumulation. While access to bridewealth cattle enabled men to marry earlier, it did not affect women's age at marriage; however, it reduced the number of unmarried young women and thus brought a decline in polygyny. The decline was accelerated by Christian missionaries, often the advance agents of capitalism, who imposed monogamy wherever they were influential. The effect of this new family formation on fertility was to increase the age-specific fertility of individual women (Kitching, 1983).

The new mode of production also increased demands for child labor, providing monogamous couples with incentives for larger families. The question arises whether higher fertility was associated with increased maternal and infant mortality; in other words, whether monogamy affected health adversely. Higher female than male mortality in adulthood has been noted in areas where men migrate to work in another environment and women remain in the original environment to bear and raise children (Turshen, in press). In general infant mortality rates are predictive of life expectancy, but discontinuities are possible, especially among children born in one environment who live as adults in another. This may account for increases in adult life expectancy where infant mortality rates remain high.

Men are thought to have higher adult mortality than women because they are exposed to more health hazards in their work (Waldron, 1983). This may have been the pattern in the period of the worst colonial oppression, lasting through World War I, when men and not women made up the work force (this sexual division of labor did not obtain everywhere). But from the 1920s, the deteriorating environment of labor reserves may have been as lethal as that of mines, plantations, and the (peacetime) army. Women's work burdens increased as male/female sex ratios fell and dependency ratios rose. Probably both sexes faced greater occupational health hazards for different reasons with the oppressive restructuring of the sexual division of labor. One might hypothesize that increased workloads, poorer nutrition, more pregnancies, and declining social and political power contributed to rising mortality among women in the reserves.

I have been thinking for some time about the African custom of married women bearing economic responsibility for themselves and their children, wondering whether this custom predates European contact. The work by Thornton and Manning on women and slavery suggests that this familial arrangement was a consequence, not so much desired as necessary, of the absence of men. The question then becomes, Why did it persist after colonial rule was established and slavery curtailed? One answer is that European use of male labor in colonial Africa differed little from slavery as far as women were concerned; the absence of migrant men had a similar impact on family formation, age and sex structure of families, availability of labor, dependency ratios, and sex ratios. Also, women's economic, social and political power declined after colonial rule was established, while men's power (in newly constructed or restructured tribal[3] hierarchies and in the new colonial economy) was reinforced by capitalist opportunities and Victorian beliefs in male superiority. It was advantageous to Europeans to pay men a single man's wage and believe that African families were self-supporting subsistence farmers. It was also advantageous to African men to believe that their women were self-supporting in the transition to a new mode of production under colonialism. African men, therefore, would have attempted to preserve this new-found power over women.

THE IMPACT OF COLONIALISM ON THE TANZANIAN POPULATION

Some demographers have used colonial statistics to extrapolate precolonial birthrates, life expectancy, and death rates. But these figures are crude and misleading, as a close study of the methods shows (Turshen, 1984: 45-49). There are two hypotheses about the precolonial period: According to Coupland (1938) and other historians, between 1850 and 1890 the population of East Africa was stable and grew slowly; after 1890 population growth was greater, thanks to the peaceful conditions accompanying Europeans, which put an end to intertribal warfare. Accordingly, after 1920 the population grew rapidly. The second hypothesis, put forward by Kuczynski (1948) and elaborated by Kjekshus (1977) is that, despite the slave trade, population grew between 1850 and 1890, but the ecological catastrophe accompanying European partition in the last decade of the nineteenth century resulted in decline; population did not grow again until 1925. For the period before 1890 all authors agree that the population increased. For a period after 1890 the evidence is rather clear and supports the second hypothesis.

The sole verifiable fact is that after 1925 the population of Tanzania, by then under British rule, was growing. The problem is to reconcile this growth with the theory of the "development of underdevelopment," which holds that people suffered irreversible damage under colonialism, including injury to their health and nutritional status that affected their reproductive capacity. To understand these contradictions, we must analyze not only the common components of population dynamics—mortality, fertility, and migration—but also changes in the mode of production, the impact on the ecology, changes in disease patterns (which were not medically researched but are documented by social science methods), and changes in family patterns and the power of women (usually studied only in relation to fertility).

Ecological Catastrophe

The East African slave trade, which reached its height in the 1850s and 1860s, with the export of perhaps 65,000 persons per decade, disrupted settlement patterns in the interior (Lovejoy, 1983: 151). People dispersed to avoid capture or retreated to mountain strongholds for collective security. Dispersion meant regression to less sophisticated (that is, less labor-intensive) agricultural methods, whereas retreat created high population densities, land scarcity, soil erosion, and other problems in the highlands. Raided groups experienced higher dependency ratios, the brunt of which were borne by women.

The wars of conquest between 1860 and 1900 also took their toll on settlement patterns and productivity, scattering some groups into the bush and uniting others behind stockades. Nor did colonial rule beginning in the 1880s bring peace. A major revolt occurred in Tanzania in 1905-1906, twenty years after Germany claimed hegemony. The Germans used a scorched-earth policy in their military campaigns: Although their weaponry was superior, they were heavily outnumbered and destroyed food resources in order to starve the population into submission (Iliffe, 1979). These military tactics had short-term effects on health, disease patterns, and mortality, and long-term effects on the ecology.

Slave trade and wars brought new groups into contact, moved indigenous people around at a rate not previously experienced, and introduced diseases that decimated populations with no prior immunity. War and slavery also gave rise to epidemics of diseases indigenous to Africa but latent in precolonial conditions. Invading European troops spread these diseases. Famine accompanied war, especially given German war tactics, making people more vulnerable to disease. The disruption of communal life affected nursing and healing roles, which must have slowed the recovery of survivors (Turshen, 1984). Epidemics of animal as well as of human diseases had long-lasting consequences: Rinderpest and trypanosomiasis nearly wiped out East African cattle herds.

Ecological catastrophe was a compound of loss of herds, which caused an exodus from affected areas and spelled the end of pastoral life for some, and environmental change, which resulted from the reversion of cultivated and grazing lands to bush. The bush, which Africans had been at pains to keep at bay, was the habitat of the tsetse fly, which carried the trypanosome responsible for human and animal sleeping sickness. The abandonment of land also resulted in an explosion of the game population, which overran new farms and damaged crops, and constituted a reservoir of parasites that were the source of repeated epidemics.

European rule, established throughout East Africa from 1898, disrupted intercourse between African groups, affecting traditional patterns of food exchange, markets, and commerce in salt, iron, cloth, and crafts. Also, the natural frontiers created by Africans to contain such diseases as sleeping sickness, were destroyed when colonial powers drew new boundaries (Kjekshus, 1977).

The ecological catastrophe of the last decade of the nineteenth century depopulated many East African lands. Devastating attacks of measles (not a childhood disease in Africa at that time) and syphilis followed epidemics of smallpox, chiggers, and sleeping sickness. Malaria spread from coastal swamps that had been foci of the disease to new areas and new people. Coastal peoples had developed a measure of immunity to malaria, and mountain people cultivating the plains knew the breeding habits of mosquitoes and retreated to their homes before nightfall, avoiding contact; but the armies and work gangs impressed by Europeans could not choose where and when to work. All of these diseases became endemic in the twentieth century, periodically flaring up in epidemics under the adverse conditions.

On this weakened and disrupted population, Germany imposed a harsh colonial regime. All the by now well-known forms of exploitation were used to force African men into wage labor—taxes, military conscription, *corvée,* and so on. Two types of export production were attempted: European plantations that employed wage labor, and communal farms on which Africans were forced to work. The communal farms, in particular, were a source of discontent that grew into the full-scale revolt of 1905-1906 (Iliffe, 1979). The Maji Maji War was brutally suppressed, resulting in a famine that lasted more than two years, and, in its aftermath, a peculiar pattern of uneven regional development emerged.

The ability of capitalism to transform Africa was tied to the political power of colonial rule. Capitalists might establish an export sector, but it was the colonial rulers who enforced the new commodity relations in land and labor that made plantations feasible and economically viable. Colonial legal systems institutionalized private property, individual tenure, labor contracts, and master-servant relations, and the colonial military and police enforced these laws.

The German experiment was short-lived, however. World War I erupted less than a decade after the suppression of Maji Maji, and the country was the theater of most East African war operations. Belgium and Britain both invaded, conscripting Africans wherever they passed and commandeering goods and supplies. The British were reinforced by the South African army, which lived off the land in much the same way. The Germans, blockaded on the Indian Ocean, had no choice but to feed off African food reserves. The results were devastating— by official count the population was lower in 1920 than it had been in 1911. Troops and porters died more often of diarrhea and malaria than of gunshot wounds, and famine made the civilian population more vulnerable to the 1918-1919 worldwide influenza pandemic.

Under the 1919 League of Nations mandate, the British took up where the Germans left off. They recreated the plantation economy, promoting sisal, which had proved suitable to the climate and profitable in world markets. As a mandate, the country was somewhat better protected against pillage than Kenya or Zimbabwe, where white settlers dominated internal politics. No formal system of labor reserves was ever established in Tanzania, but, through a process of uneven development, de facto reserves were created.

Population Patterns in Labor Reserves

This section of the chapter illustrates changes in Tanzanian population dynamics with case studies of two districts—Songea, a source of migrant labor from the south of Tanzania, and Kilosa, a district of sisal plantations on the central plateau.

Songea was originally settled by stateless agriculturalists who were overrun in the nineteenth century by a group of Ngoni pushed north by Europeans occupying southern Africa. The Ngoni were highly stratified and centralized pastoralists; in their march north they incorporated several subject peoples. In Songea they incorporated Ndendeuli agriculturalists and adopted a mixed system of farming and herding. Reports of early European travelers to Songea tell of a flourishing society of as many as 166,000 people (Kjekshus, 1977).

Little is known about precolonial Ngoni fertility, but some idea can be gathered from ethnographic studies, which indicate that cultural controls may have kept fertility low. The age at first marriage was 30 to 35 for men, who had to complete military service before they were eligible to marry. Women also married comparatively late—after age 25. The Ngoni appear to have enforced a strict ban on premarital intercourse and severe punishment for adultery. For growth, they may have relied upon incorporation rather than biological reproduction, a strategy Cordell (1983a) noted in Central Africa.

This demographic regime ended with the retribution following the Maji Maji War. Ngoni leaders were executed and their military and social organization was crushed. The Ngoni disbanded male age sets after the war and eventually discarded other customs that had served to control fertility. Because the Germans destroyed land and food reserves and prohibited planting, famine raged for two years after the war. Kjekshus (1977) quotes missionary reports noting that starvation and migration reduced the population to 20,000. Some Ngoni captured during the war were sent north to work on sisal plantations, inaugurating the pattern of labor migration that persisted through the 1950s. Men and women began to marry at younger ages, raising fertility rates. Adultery and premarital sexual relations became more common, as more and more men were absent for longer and longer periods of time. Germany had turned the district into a labor reserve.

After World War I the British reconstructed a tribal hierarchy to conduct Ngoni affairs under indirect rule; certain customs became institutionalized even though they were no longer functional. Land allocation remained in the hands of a defunct aristocracy that discriminated against women; the resultant land scarcity accounts for some of the agricultural involution observed in the 1950s. Women tended to remain on old farms, rather than shift to new ones, despite diminishing returns. With as many as one-third of the adult males away at any one time (Gulliver, 1955), women reverted to less labor-intensive farming techniques and crops like cassava (Turshen, 1984: 124-125). Protein sources were scarce: Cattle were practically nonexistent after the epidemics of rinderpest and trypanosomiasis, and tsetse belts had expanded to cover more than one-fourth of the area. By the 1950s, chronic malnutrition was widespread (Robson, 1962).

An underdeveloped district, Songea had few governmental medical or educational services; missions supplied both. Missionary medicine was clinical curative work, in keeping with Christian healing traditions and the desire to acquire new converts. One public health exception was maternal and child health care; its function seems to have been to ensure the physical reproduction of the labor force. Post-World War II census data from 1948, 1957, and 1967 indicate slow population growth in Songea, with higher-than-average (for Tanzania as a whole) mortality and slightly lower-than-average fertility (Henin and Egero, 1972).

Population Patterns in Plantation Economies

The health and population effects of the plantation economy are contradictory. Kilosa District, in central Tanzania, was the site of large sisal estates and an area to which many Ngoni migrated. It was relatively well endowed with roads, railways, medical facilities, and schools—infrastructure lacking in Songea. African workers employed on the estates had access to medical care but were exposed to accidents and injuries and the diseases of a new environment. The trade union movement created an increasingly nationalist community, but migrants living under new stresses and without family support were at high risk of mental illness.

Young migrants usually returned home once they had saved enough to marry. Some older migrants deserted the wives and families they were not allowed to bring from the labor reserves and started new families in Kilosa, eventually leaving estate employment and taking up farming. Others returned periodically or permanently to Songea because they were laid off during recessions, or because they were disabled or too old to meet the daily work quotas on which rates of pay were calculated. A study by Gulliver (1955) showed that this group returned with little more than new diseases. Migrant remittances were small; most men brought back only a few pieces of cloth and no useful skills, and were often broken in body or spirit—adding to the burdens of reserve life.

The contradictions of the plantation economy extended beyond the estates, which were established on alienated land—usually the most arable, best irrigated, and well sited to transport crops to world markets. One effect was land scarcity among Africans, which the planters exacerbated by their inefficient use of land and neglect of fertilizers; their short-term solution to problems of soil exhaustion and reduced yields was the acquisition of more land. Plantations also undermined the marketing of local goods. Planters tended to encourage food imports rather than local production, depressing the indigenous economy. The British discouraged African trade, in order to inhibit the development of alternative livelihoods that would compete for the estates' labor.

Travel from the sisal estates around Kilosa town to outlying divisions in the district revals the lingering effects of plantations. An oral history (Mkundunge, 1973) of food shortages in northern Gairo Division describes famine directly attributable to colonial rule; increasing frequency of food shortages reveals the growing vulnerability of the economy. The first remembered famine occurred in 1860-1861, about the time of the initial European explorations. Large caravans crossed the area trading for local provisions; these exchanges may have caused food shortages, compounding the effects of a drought. The second, in 1893-1894, coincided with a smallpox epidemic and occurred when Germany was already fighting to establish hegemony in the territory. People attribute the third, in 1918-1919, to the requisitioning of food by the German and allied armies; it coincided with the influenza pandemic. Throughout the Great Depression there were famines and food shortages, and during World War II the story is repeated. In recent memory there were fewer deaths (presumably because government relief reached the area), but almost annual food shortages. In a history that extends over 110 years, good harvests were reported in 15 years.

After World War II, in an effort to promote cash crops and increase food production, the government introduced maize monoculture, which, in the absence of pesticides, was more prone to insect damage than was intercropping, the traditional practice. Without fertilizer, maize exhausted the soils; without irrigation, it was more vulnerable than traditional cereals to drought. The result was decreasing yields. Maize was also less nutritious than millet.

The demographic impact of the plantation economy is also contradictory. Population grew fairly rapidly because of the influx of migrants and the increase in the birthrate. The 1957 census listed more than seventy tribes in an area originally settled by four; the presumption is that migrants married local women. As Christian missions were active in the area, monogamy was probably replacing polygyny and more women were available for marriage. There appears to be positive correlations among migration, conversion to Christianity, and intertribal marriage (see the evidence for Pangani, a sisal district in northeast Tanzania, in Roberts and Tanner, 1959). Although the death rate fell, it has been shown above that levels of health deteriorated as malnutrition became chronic.

CONCLUSIONS

Deteriorating health should logically result in more deaths and reduce population growth rates. However, some explanations for population growth are compatible with deteriorating health. First of all, I would argue that although periodic famine in the precolonial period raised death rates, it did not affect the long-term health of survivors; but the opposite was true in the colonial period of chronic malnutrition, which lowered health and vitality, yet was not a primary cause of death. Famine and chronic malnutrition also affect reproduction differently. Unlike famine, chronic malnutrition does not halt reproduction; malnourished women continue to bear children even at the expense of their own health.[4] By instituting famine relief the colonial regime created the problems of chronic malnutrition and rapid population growth. Lower death rates resulted, not from medical services that reached barely 5 to 15 percent of the population, but from famine relief that reduced crisis mortality caused by starvation. Unfortunately, the food distributed was not sufficient to maintain good health.

Second, I believe the conditions that stimulated population growth were the very ones that undermined health. The evidence for Tanzania in the colonial period indicates that the population grew because birthrates rose. Commercial agriculturalists need more labor than subsistence farmers and therefore have an incentive to bear more children; but sisal, like so many other cash crops, cannot be consumed when world market prices fall and there is no money to purchase food. Therefore, larger families were now affected by malnutrition. Child labor may have been of even greater importance to groups from which men migrated; in the labor reserves, the subsistence farmer's incentive to bear children is directly disproportional to the ability to raise them in good health.

Third, I think that European contact disrupted the balance between the sexes, not only by withdrawing men from villages, but also by withdrawing power from women, with the result that new importance was attached to male infants. (This trend may have been reinforced by the spread of Islam.) Where migration was sex specific—as it was in Tanzania until the 1950s, when trade unions forced plantations to substitute permanent family labor for male mirgrants—one must ask whether male children were preferred and how families realized this ideal. In areas such as Songea, where the Catholic church was active, infanticide was presumably unacceptable and abortion not openly practiced. High birthrates may in part have been the result of needing many pregnancies to produce male offspring.

Fourth, the declining power of women also relates to deteriorating health and rising fertility. This decline is directly attributable to colonial rule. We can document the transfers of land from women to men, eroding the independence of women. We can show, too, that when land sales began to take place women rarely had the necessary cash. The failure of colonial authorities to develop local markets also reduced women's economic opportunities by curbing outlets for their surplus. The exclusion of girls from colonial education prevented new generations from adapting to the capitalist economy. In contrast, men's power was everywhere increased and encouraged. Men's authority was supported by the church as well as by the state. Not only did boys receive education, but men were trained in new agricultural techniques. Men were eligible for credit and were registered with cooperatives, even though women provided the labor on these farms. Women, who were expected to provide their own farm implements as well as to maintain themselves and their children, either were denied access to wages or were the worst paid when taken on at the estates. In 1959, at the very end of colonial rule, most women were excluded from the political arena; the election ruling that year gave the vote to all male adults but only to literate women and women who owned homes. It cannot be a surprise that women lost control of their fertility and produced more children than they could support in good health. This accounted in part for increased birthrates and falling levels of child health. If one adds the effect of government and missionary campaigns to eradicate traditional medicine, one sees that women had few credible medical skills at a time of greater demand for them to nurse and care for the sick.

A materialist approach to demography must consider women not only in relation to fertility, as in traditional demographic studies, but also in relation to mortality and migration; the way to measure changes in women's contributions is to examine productive as well as reproductive activities. Ideally this should be done in a perspective of class analysis, requiring more refined data than we possess. For precolonial stratified societies such as the Ngoni, one wants to know whether captured and incorporated women controlled their fertility in the same ways as royal women. For the colonial period, one wants to separate the effects on fertility of conversion to Christianity, monogamy, and education, which offered entry to government employment and a higher standard of living. For the postcolonial era in which class differentiation is the legacy of regional inequality, one wants to know how the position of women in rich peasant households differs from that among landless laborers, and how fertility is controlled by the wives of urban elites. Clearly the wives of rich peasants face a set of constraints different from those of their landless sisters. And women in towns have yet other opportunities and constraints.

NOTES

1. Stage 1—high birthrates and high death rates; stage 2—high birthrates and low death rates; stage 3—low birthrates and low death rates; See Chapter 1. See also O'Brien (Chapter 11), for a critique of transition theory.

2. Because infectious diseases produce long-lasting immunity, they do not become endemic in small groups living in relative isolation. For a discussion of the principles of immunization, see Burnet and White (1972).

3. The term *tribe* is an ideological creation of colonial rule that does not reflect African reality; unfortunately, in discussions of the colonial past, one cannot avoid its use.

4. Studies of formerly healthy European populations reduced to starvation diets during World War II revealed that menstruation ceased in women and sperm production ceased in men. In contrast, chronically malnourished populations in Asia and Africa continue to record crude birthrates above 45 per 1000 population and total fertility rates of 6 or more children per woman. Gopalan and Naidu (1972) and Frisch (1978) show that malnutrition impairs but does not halt reproductive ability.

13

HEALTH, NUTRITION, AND POPULATION IN CENTRAL KENYA, 1890-1945

MARC H. DAWSON

Kenya's current estimated annual population growth rate of over 4% is one of staggering proportions. This dramatic rate has attracted the attention of both demographers and historians. Unfortunately, many studies give the history of Kenya's population cursory treatment, usually based on a limited number of colonial documents and on "common sense" knowledge about demographic change. These studies attribute the rise in population to the persistence of precolonial patterns of high fertility and a reduction in mortality from the introduction of Western biomedical care, and improvements in hygiene and nutrition (Herz, 1974; van Zwanenberg, 1977; Mott and Mott, 1980).

Two problems are apparent in this common sense approach. First, there is little evidence to support the supposition of major improvements in health, hygiene, standards of living, or nutrition. Second, the analysis suggests that the demographic variables of mortality and fertility can be examined in isolation. Yet, the first part of this century saw indigenous Kenyan societies undergo significant social and economic changes because of colonialism. The implications of these changes in terms of health, nutrition, and population were numerous.

A more promising line of inquiry would suggest that the first three decades of the twentieth century were ones of rising mortality and

Author's Note: Some of this research was done with the financial support of the Fulbright-Hays International Doctoral Research Program and the Social Science Research Council. I deeply appreciate their financial support. The opinions and ideas expressed in this work are those of the author alone.

declining population. This change would be the result of the disruption caused by colonialism. The 1930s and 1940s would see modest declines in mortality resulting from the establishment of a new homeostasis between humans and their parasites and improved famine relief capabilities. This later period would also probably see increases in fertility resulting from new patterns of marriage and sexual practices and a reduction of birth spacing.

These hypotheses will be explored through a case study of Kenya's largest ethnic group, the Kikuyu, who live largely in Central Province (north of Nairobi), with an estimated population of 3.3 million in 1979 (see Map 5). The rainfall and soil make the area agriculturally productive and capable of supporting a dense population. The Kikuyu were heavily involved in the colonial economy and thus offer an excellent case study for demonstrating the interrelatedness of demographic and socioeconomic change. The Kikuyu were among the first to participate in the colonial agricultural market. As early as 1902, they traveled from as far away as Fort Hall to trade their crops in the new city of Nairobi. Those farmers who could expanded production of maize, planted wattle trees or grew vegetables for sale. The Kikuyu rural reserves also became one of the main sources of migrant labor.

Some of the consequences of the Kikuyu involvement in the colonial economy between 1890 and 1930 were serious epidemics of smallpox, cerebrospinal meningitis (hereafter CSM), and influenza. World War I saw the Kikuyu lose many young men in the Carrier Corps as the result of disease. Also during this period, plague spread slowly throughout the Kikuyu reserves with serious local mortality. Similarly, the diseases responsible for the bulk of morbidity and mortality—respiratory infections, malaria and so on—felt the effects of colonial socioeconomic change. Colonial medicine's limited attempts to deal with these problems experienced few successes and many obvious failures.

LABOR MIGRATION

The intensification of population movement during the colonial period was in terms not only of the numbers of people involved, but of distances traveled. By the 1920s, thousands of Kikuyu left rural reserves to look for work. They traveled perhaps only as far as Nairobi, but also east to coastal Mombasa, or west to the Rift Valley or Kisumu. Migrants risked their health working in foreign environments (highland workers in malarious lowlands or rural workers in urban environments), under harsh working conditions with poor housing and diet, and traveling under dangerous conditions. They also risked the lives of their families, since returning workers frequently brought back diseases.

This last problem was not insubstantial. Between 1910 and 1930, almost all the smallpox outbreaks in Kenya Province were traced to returning labor migrants (Dawson, 1979, 1983). Similarly, returning Kikuyu migrants brought back CSM in 1913 and Spanish influenza in 1918. Both colonial records and Kikuyu oral sources agree that syphilis was a disease contracted by labor migrants and carried back to the reserves. The data are scant and unclear, but colonial medical authorities also suspected that tuberculosis was imported from urban areas such as Nairobi.

The clearest example of the adverse impact of labor migration on the health of families in the reserves is the experience the Kikuyu suffered during 1916. In that year, the British sent the survivors of the Carrier Corps back to Kenya Province, regardless of their health. The result was that many died upon reaching or trying to reach home. Others required long convalescence. Their return also sparked 100 outbreaks of smallpox and 2 serious epidemics of dysentery (KNA, East Africa Protectorate [hereafter EAP], Kenya Province Annual Report, 1916-1917). Clearly, male labor migrants were the first victims of these afflictions, but they were then passed on to women and children in the rural reserves.

The mortality of labor migrants was significant, with no major precolonial counterpart. Deaths among young males were characteristic of colonial mortality. Precolonial long-distance traders, such as the Kamba, also faced some of these health risks, but their numbers were smaller and the epidemiological impact was thus diluted. Colonial labor migrants had to travel through and work in unfamiliar disease environments. The Kikuyu reserves were located in highland areas near the Nyandarua Mountains and on the slopes of Mount Kenya, areas that were malaria free. In 1911, for example, Kikuyu migrants working at the Coast suffered a mortality rate of 145 per 1000 from malaria, six times that of the rate for the coastal population (KNA, EAP, Nature Labour Commission, 1912-1913). Similarly, the migrants traveled under dangerous conditions, such as locked railway boxcars. The opportunity for the spread of disease in this situation is obvious. Many Kikuyu walked to the coast and reports were frequent of semistarved and ill men on the roads.

Similarly, once men found work the conditions were usually less than ideal. Food and housing were inadequate and of poor quality. In one instance, a labor recruiter took 500 Kikuyu to work on the railway spur to the salt works at Lake Magadi. Of that group, 80 Kikuyu died the morning after their arrival, and the remainder died shortly afterward. They had been fed a diet consisting solely of whole mealies (KNA, EAP, Kikuyu District Record Book). Such inappropriate diet, combined with polluted water and poor sanitation, frequently resulted in dysentery epidemics.

Housing both on plantations and in the cities was inadequate. For example, on one coastal plantation, a labor inspector found that 50 Kikuyu were living in seven huts, not one of which was large enough to stand up in. Additionally, plantation workers frequently were forced to share accommodations with the sick. In the cities, Kikuyu labor migrants had to crowd into scarce accommodations in the poorest sections. In Nairobi's Indian Bazaar, a shop with a back room was discovered to house 75 Kikuyu. An infectious disease introduced into either of these housing situations would spread rapidly. In fact, the Indian Bazaar featured prominently in almost all of Nairobi's epidemics (Dawson, 1983).

TRANSPORTATION, URBANIZATION, AND ECOLOGICAL CHANGE

The colonial transportation network contributed indirectly to the deterioration of health during the first three decades of this century. With the railway spanning the colony and roads connecting major administrative outposts, infections spread with unprecedented speed. For example, when the 1892 influenza pandemic struck precolonial East Africa, the infection took a full nine months to spread from the Taita Hills to Fort Smith in Kikuyuland. In 1918, influenza arrived by ship in Mombasa, reached Nairobi several days later, and Kisumu on the shores of Lake Victoria shortly thereafter. The railway also made possible the export of grain and probably carried the black plague rat, *Rattus rattus,* into the interior, both of which had serious ecological and health consequences (Dawson, 1983).

By 1914 in Kenya Province, good roads connected all trade centers, government outposts, and chiefs' camps. A road had also been built connecting Fort Hall and Nairobi. Many Kikuyu who lived near the roads found them to be an economic benefit; many also found them to be a health risk. In 1913 in both Fort Hall and Kiambu Districts, the areas of the Kikuyu reserves nearest the Fort Hall-Nairobi Road suffered the heaviest mortality from CSM. The same finding holds for the 1918 influenza epidemic and, in the case of Fort Hall District, for the 1923 plague epidemic (Dawson, 1983). The location of the road could also be significant. A Church of Scotland medical missionary testified before the 1913 Native Labour Commission:

The Nairobi-Fort Hall road alone was annually responsible for more deaths than would supply the present demand for labour in this country. The sickness on that road was chiefly malaria and dysentery [KNA, EAP, Native Labour Commission, 1912-1913].

Over this road, through the flat and malarious lowland areas, thousands of Kikuyu, Embu, and Meru labor migrants and traders passed.

The growth of colonial cities had important epidemiological consequences. The larger and denser populations meant that the cities became reservoirs of diseases, which then spread to rural Kikuyu communities. Administrative centers, such as Fort Hall, and mission stations also acted as foci of disease. For instance, the first incident of CSM in Fort Hall District broke out at the Githumu mission. Cities were also transportation and trading centers. Thus, many Kikuyu labor migrants passed through Nairobi looking for work or on their way home to buy goods. Full of strangers and their diseases, colonial cities were dirty and the water supplies polluted. Nairobi had no sewers or drains. During the rains, storm water lay in the streets, providing ideal breeding grounds for mosquitoes. The 1912-1913 Nairobi Sanitation Commission reported the following situation:

One of the irrigation trenches receives all the foul water sewage of the Indian Bazaar, River Road, and surrounding district. This trench is used for irrigating the market gardens where large quantities of vegetables are grown for the use of the town. Such of the sewage as is not absorbed by the market gardens runs directly into the river which is used for drinking and domestic purposes by Natives and Asiatics [KNA, EAP, Nairobi Sanitary Commission, 1913].

Not surprisingly, dysentery accounted for 16 percent of recorded African deaths in Nairobi for 1912 (KNA, EAP, Nairobi Sanitary Commission, 1913).

Central Kenya underwent significant ecological change, mainly as a result of the clearing of forest and bush for cultivation, which had a range of further epidemiological effects. For instance, the clearing of vegetation affected the composition of the wild-rodent population, the ecological balance swinging in favor of these hosts of plague. Combined with the introduction of *Rattus rattus* and an increased amount of stored grain, the incidence of plague increased (Dawson, 1983).

Similarly, evidence suggests that deforestation may have had an impact on malaria. Large parts of the Kikuyu highlands had been malaria free, yet by the 1920s, many parts of the highlands suffered from malaria epidemics. Kikuyu labor migrants worked at the Coast and other regions, where malaria was endemic; many would have been infected and would have carried the disease back home. The remaining necessary link for introducing the disease is malaria's vector, the *Anopheles* mosquito. The clearing of bush and forest for cultivated fields and the overgrazing of the limited amount of pasture would allow rainwaters to form into stagnant pools, which *Anopheles* mosquitoes prefer for breeding. The mosquito may well have arrived on the railway or, more likely, on the trucks and buses that traveled the colonial roads (Anderson, 1930; Matson, 1957). The introduction of malaria would have had important demographic implications. The adult population would have little or no immunity and would risk heightened mortality and morbidity. The group who would suffer the most, however, would have been infants. In many African communities, malaria kills 10 percent of those under 1 year of age. Thus, areas of the Kikuyu highlands must have suffered an increase in both adult and infant mortality.

MEDICAL SERVICES AND PUBLIC HYGIENE

There is little medical evidence to support a belief that Western biomedicine substantially reduced mortality in the 1920s, 1930s, or even part of the 1940s. The main charge of the Medical Department was not caring for the health needs of the African population, but to protect the European population and to ensure that epidemic disease did not significantly disrupt the colonial economy. For instance, in 1925 the Principal Medical Officer (hereafter PMO) described the plight of staff responsible for Africans' health:

> In the Native reserves the position was that to any one district one medical officer was usually posted and he would have under his care a very large stretch of country with a population in some cases of as many as 300,000. He was expected to manage a hospital sometimes of one hundred beds and to supervise or to carry out the treatment of the patients in the hospital, to be responsible for the inauguration and control of measures against outbreaks of epidemic diseases such as plague and small-pox, to supervise out-dispensaries and to check and exercise con-

trol over the expenditure of stores. In addition he was responsible for the sanitary inspection of townships and trading centres and the district generally, [KNA, EAP, Kenya Colony Annual Medical Report, 1925].

The PMO pointed out "the work was naturally beyond the powers of a single officer." The Medical Department was usually understaffed and poorly funded. As late as 1932, colonial authorities still could not station a medical officer in every district (17 physicians for 34 districts). Additionally, these officers were routinely transferred from post to post, losing whatever familiarity they had gained with particular peoples and areas. Given the scarcity of funds and personnel, Medical Department physicians limited their efforts to trying to contain various epidemic diseases, delivering medical care to European and non-European government employees, and conducting periodic safaris through the rural African reserves.

The undue attention devoted to antiplague efforts demonstrates the true purpose of the colonial medical service. Plague was a disease of fairly insignificant morbidity, but considerable funds and time were expended to combat outbreaks. The layout of colonial cities—a wide *cordon sanitaire* separating the European section from the rest of the city—is the result of antiplague measures. Inoculation campaigns began at the first evidence of an urban outbreak in order to protect the European population. In rural areas, plague received attention only because it was spreading rapidly in the main African cash-crop growing regions, which were also the major sources of labor migrants.

Colonial medical authorities also spent much time examining and immunizing labor migrants to ensure a flow of relatively healthy workers into the colonial economy. Medical records reveal the considerable attention devoted to the health problems of labor migrants, and relatively little to rural women and children. Even if officials had wanted to work in the reserves, until the 1930s physicians were incapable of curing most infections, other than giving quinine for malaria and chemotherapy for treponemal infections. Also the epidemiology of some of the diseases was not completely understood.

Two diseases, yaws and smallpox, are usually cited as examples of the positive impact of Western biomedicine. Since yaws had an insignificant mortality rate, it is not of major demographic importance. The 1920s anti-yaws campaign appeared to have dramatically reduced the disease, but had hidden mixed results (for more detail, see Dawson, 1981b). There is little question, however, that smallpox was infrequent in the Kikuyu reserves by the 1920s. Yet these two seeming successes do not demonstrate that colonial biomedical care had any important impact on the health of the vast majority of the African population.

The confusion over the significance of controlling smallpox arises from a misunderstanding of the disease in Africa (Dawson, 1979, 1983). The success of Jennerian vaccination had important demographic implications for Europe and North America, where *variola major* was the dominant strain. Fairly infectious, this strain exacted a steady toll of victims in eighteenth and nineteenth century European cities. The African strain of smallpox was very different. In its epidemic form, the disease spread rapidly, with frequently fatal results. These epidemics usually came in the wake of famines among populations weakened by severe malnutrition. In its endemic form, African smallpox was a disease of low mortality and required fairly close contact for transmission. Thus, in the absence of a major famine what real impact did colonial vaccination campaigns have on the disease? Additionally, these campaigns suffered from numerous problems: loss of potency of the vaccine, getting vaccinators to use proper techniques, local opposition to the procedure, and so on. Vaccination campaigns among the Kikuyu had some positive effects, but the demographic significance was marginal.

These "successful" campaigns also share another characteristic of colonial biomedical efforts. Plague, smallpox, and yaws all were treated with relatively cheap and easy-to-administer injections. The most effective way, however, to deal with the major causes of morbidity and mortality such as malaria, dysentery, helminthic infections, and schistosomiasis, was an improvement in the standard of living and sanitary conditions of rural Africans. While medical officials wrote about the importance of such reforms, these efforts were very expensive, and colonial governments opted for the cheaper measures.

In 1924, the PMO wrote in his annual report, "No definite progress with regard to the improvement of sanitation in Native reserves can be recorded." In fact, there were few improvements in the sanitary conditions in the reserves in all of the 1920s or 1930s. The situation had not improved by 1932, for example, when the PMO stated, "The year was even less satisfactory than usual" (KNA, EAP, Kenya Colony Annual Medical Report, 1932). Housing remained poor, and as much as the Kikuyu may have desired better shelter, lack of money and building supplies held them back. The colonial government had a difficult enough time in the 1920s and 1930s maintaining a potable water supply to the cities, let alone worrying about water for the rural reserves.

NUTRITION

The last factor sometimes cited as a reason for an increase in Kenya's population was improved nutrition. Again there is little evidence for improvement among rural Kikuyu between 1900 and 1945, in spite of an increase in agricultural production. Large amounts of surplus crops were grown for export from the Kikuyu reserves, not for local consumption. At the same time as the Kikuyu began to expand cultivation, the colonial government began to restrict the size of the reserves. Thus, deforestation occurred rapidly as farmers cut down the last stands of trees for land and fuel. Land shortage in the Kikuyu reserves meant that land had to be kept under cultivation almost constantly with very short fallow periods. The result of this demand on the soil was a decreasing crop yield (Dawson, 1978-1979; Fisher, 1964). Also, given deforestation and the hilly terrain of the highlands, the government was forced to mandate terracing of gardens in the 1920s to stop soil erosion (Dawson, 1978-1979). Furthermore, surpluses were not evenly distributed among the Kikuyu but favored wealthy landowners. Thus, many farmers experienced a decline in soil fertility, leading to smaller and smaller harvests, while perhaps also suffering from soil erosion. These conditions hardly led to improved nutrition.

In precolonial Kikuyu society, work was divided according to sex. Men and women each had separate tasks in the agricultural work cycle. Men usually were responsible for doing the heavy clearing of the field, the initial turning of the soil, and helping with the harvest. Women usually were responsible for planting, weeding, and harvesting. With the introduction of labor migration, men were often away at crucial points in the agricultural cycle. Women had to take up their jobs. During World War I, the district commissioner of Kiambu was sure that agricultural production had dropped drastically owing to the absence of so many Kikuyu men.

Some farmers began to devote more time and effort to growing cash crops at the expense of food in order to pay taxes. Maize became the most widely grown crop for sale, and by 1930 it was the major staple in the Kikuyu diet along with a variety of bean (*njahi*). These two crops became popular because they were less labor intensive than the other traditional and more nutritious grains and vegetables (Fisher, 1964; Dawson, 1978-1979). Given that the work force was depleted with the men gone to work on European farms, less labor-intensive crops were needed. Women's workloads increased; they had to care for both the cash crops and the family's food supply. Also, the clearing of forest and bush had eliminated the source of many traditional wild greens. The loss of these foods was critical since they contained many important nutrients not found in maize and beans.

During the 1910s the Kikuyu also lost traditional pasture lands that bordered the highlands when the government set up the rural reserves. The shortage of land wihin the reserves meant that pasture had to be kept to a minimum. Consequently, Kikuyu with large herds of livestock either became squatters on European farms or lent out their stock to the neighboring Kamba (Kershaw, 1972). Most Kikuyu, however, had to reduce their herds dramatically. Fisher's informants claimed that in the nineteenth century many men had herds of 100 or 200 goats and 60 to 100 head of cattle; in the twentieth century a wealthy man owned 20 to 30 goats and a few cows (Fisher, 1964). In 1978-1979, Kikuyu elders also claimed to have owned much larger herds of animals before the arrival of the Europeans (Dawson, 1978-1979).

The loss of livestock meant that meat and dairy products were eliminated from the diet. Many Kikuyu elders claimed that in the past they ate meat much more frequently and no longer had access to blood and milk (Dawson, 1978-1979). Fisher's informants claimed that this loss had led to a deterioration in the Kikuyu male physique. Those Kikuyu lucky enough to have cows could not afford to drink the milk, because it had to be sold for cash (Fisher, 1964).

By the late 1920s, medical officials reported concerns over the Kikuyu diet. In 1926, the Medical Research Council commissioned a study to investigate the physique and health of the Kikuyu and neighboring Maasai. The study revealed that the Kikuyu diet was seriously deficient in calcium, protein, and various vitamins, and too rich in carbohydrates. The scientific commission recommended that the Kikuyu increase consumption of milk, meat, and green vegetables.

MORTALITY BEFORE AND AFTER 1930

Clearly, the period 1890-1930 saw a shift in disease patterns, which adversely affected the Kikuyu. The population experienced a rise in both morbidity and mortality, which was the result of the socioeconomic changes outlined above. When the rising mortality of this period is combined with the natural disasters of the 1890s (famines, epizootics, and epidemics), the 1898-1900 famine-epidemic (25 percent population loss, a moderate estimate), the 1913 CSM epidemic (7 percent loss), an estimated 10 percent population loss for World War I, the 1918 famine, and the 1918 influenza epidemic, a reduction in the size of the population seems an inescapable consequence.

Yet, the mortality from the disasters mentioned above was both age and sex specific. The 1898-1900 famine and smallpox epidemic struck hardest at the very young and the old. In her family reconstitution among the Kiambu Kikuyu, Kershaw reported that many about-to-be and just-circumcised youths also died in the epidemic. The 1913 cerebrospinal meningitis epidemic killed many young men, and in lesser numbers adolescent women; young children suffered heavily as well. During World War I, young adult men died in significant numbers. The 1918 influenza epidemic struck hardest around the world at young adult ages. The evidence also suggests that the mortality among young males rose as the result of labor migration; they in turn posed a significant threat to their wives and children. Thus these disasters struck at the groups that were in or about to enter their prime reproductive years in the 1920s. This evidence suggests the 1930s as a starting date for any population growth.

The two changes that contributed to the reduction of mortality came with the achievement of a new ecological balance between humans and their parasites, and the ability of the colonial government to provide famine relief to the major population centers of Kenya. Precolonial Kikuyu society had a particular human and disease ecology. Colonial policies initially disrupted the ecological balance, which resulted in increased morbidity and mortality. Eventually in the 1930s, a new homeostasis was achieved for a number of diseases. For instance, plague ceased to be a problem in the Kikuyu reserves because a new balance was achieved among the wild-rodent population, correcting the initial advantage gained by the wild-rodent hosts of plague during the years of forest clearing and agricultural expansion. Overall, the 1930s saw a decrease in disease-related mortality, but not sufficiently large to account alone for substantial population growth and not as the result of colonial biomedical care.

The ability of the colonial government to combat famine was also important in shaping modern Kenya's population. The colonial transportation system provided the means to deliver large amounts of grain to most parts of Kenya. In 1918 and 1919, when the rains failed in central Kenya, a serious famine seemed imminent. Maize from other parts of the country and South Africa was brought by rail to Thika, where thousands of Kikuyu, Embu, and Meru traveled to get food. Kikuyu oral sources indicated that the drought was serious, but no one starved owing to the government famine relief efforts (Dawson, 1978-1979). Since this development, central Kenya has not experienced famine-related mortality on the scale of the 1898-1900 famine, when a substantial part of the population died of starvation or disease.

ANOTHER ANALYSIS:
A POSSIBLE CASE FOR HIGHER FERTILITY

Changes of the colonial era also appear to have had an important impact on Kikuyu fertility. The causal linkages between socioeconomic change and fertility are not entirely clear, and careful local research and attempts at family reconstitution need to be done. Nevertheless, since the reduction in mortality in the 1930s and 1940s alone cannot fully account for a surge in population, Kikuyu fertility must have changed. Land alienation and agricultural policies, colonial taxes, the ability of young men to earn money on European farms, and the spread of Christianity all affected Kikuyu institutions of circumcision and marriage. The results were a reduction in the male ages of marriage and circumcision, a disappearance of *nguiko* (a sanctioned premarital form of incomplete sexual intercourse), a probable rise in premarital sexual intercourse, a rise in monogamy, and a shortening of birth spacing.

The ability of young men to earn money by working for wages had numerous social and political ramifications. Formerly, a young man was dependent on his father and other *mbari* (lineage) elders for livestock for important ritual events, such as circumcision and marriage. Also, a young man and members of his *riika* (circumcision agemates) helped each other get a start on gathering livestock for bridewealth through cattle raiding. Colonial prohibition of raiding, however, weakened the cohesion of the riika. Colonial land policies eliminated traditional pastures and reduced or eliminated many Kikuyu herds, which thus eroded the elders' control of young men (Dawson, 1978-1979; Kershaw, 1972). Beginning in 1902, the colonial government imposed a series of hut and poll taxes, which could be paid only in cash. Elders with large compounds and many teenage sons were faced with finding relatively large sums of cash. They became dependent upon their sons for cash earned in the colonial economy. Therefore, sons could make new demands on their elders (Lambert, 1956).

The first demand would appear to have been a reduction in the age of male circumcision. In the nineteenth century, most Kikuyu males were not circumcised until they were at least 17 or 18 years old, and frequently not until 22 and possibly up to 25 (Leakey, [1933] 1979;

Kershaw, 1972; Dawson, 1978-1979). The rite was performed com-
munally and a bond developed between all initiated at the same
ceremony, members of the same riika. The rite marked the passage
from boyhood to becoming a warrior, and conferred upon the young
man the right to perform nguiko, a form of incomplete sexual intercourse, with initiated young women.

The age of circumcision dropped in the 1930s to 15 and by the 1950s
(and still today) to 13 or 14 years old. The formerly communal rite was
also restricted to the immediate family (Kershaw, 1972; Dawson,
1978-1979). Did this age change reflect the new colonial economy?
Many Kikuyu parents may have decided that "boys" should become
"men" sooner. There was little perceived risk in male teenagers working for Europeans (as opposed to being warriors); in any case, males
16 years and older had to pay the poll tax. Thus, if teenagers could be
adults they could better contribute to the homestead's budget and tax
burden. The decline in the age of circumcision also meant that, potentially, young males were sexually active at an earlier age.

Also, in the twentieth century, male circumcision became a family
ritual reflecting the decline of the riika. There was no longer a military
need to band together and the riika was no longer an important source
for acquiring bridewealth. Therefore, young men became more dependent on their mbari for bridewealth payments; the lineage, however,
had become more dependent upon the wage-earning ability of its
young men for tax payments. Thus, young men could use this
economic leverage to get elders to agree to earlier marriages. This
leverage was probably effective because young men could also
threaten to raise the sum themselves, removing all influence of the
mbari.

There was little change in the age of female circumcision. Kikuyu
custom implies that every girl should be circumcised before menarche.
The only significant question would be whether the age of menarche
has remained the same. The Routledges estimated that in 1910 most
girls were circumcised between 10 and 15 years of age, which roughly
corresponds to Fisher's study in the 1960s (Routledge and Routledge,
1910; Fisher, 1964). Leakey reported that most girls were circumcised
before age 12, but that in 1930 elders claimed that girls got their
menses earlier than in the past (Leakey, [1933] 1979). If Leakey's informants were correct in stating the age of menarche was lower, this
would have some demographic impact. Yet current thinking on
changes in the age of menarche in North America and Europe sees the
crucial factor to be improved nutrition, which in turn leads to an increase in body fat. The first thirty years of this century would hardly

appear to be a period of improved nutrition and there seems to be no corroborative evidence to support the testimony reported by Leakey. As noted above, male age of marriage declined in the twentieth century. In the precolonial era, men did not usually marry until their late twenties or early thirties, about ten years after circumcision. For the following three mariika—Mburu (circumcised 1886-1887), Ngigi (circa 1891), and Mutung'u (circa 1893)—Kershaw found the following pattern of marriage. In 1900 all members of Mburu were married; 20 percent were working towards a second wife. One third of Ngigi had married; no member of the Mutung'u riika had married (Kershaw, 1972). Yet, many men circumcised in the Njaramba riika (1913-1914) claimed that by 1917 and 1918 they were not only married, but some had children. All had worked on European farms, in Nairobi, or locally for the colonial government; some specifically stated that their reason for working was to raise cash for bridewealth (Dawson, 1978-1979). The age of marriage for males had clearly declined.

The evidence for changes in the age of female marriage is less clear. In the precolonial era, estimates ranged from 15 to 20 years (Routledge and Routledge, 1910; Kenyatta, [1938] 1965). Female age of marriage in 1977-1978 was 17.8 years, which suggests no decline (Faruqee, 1982). Nevertheless, the new demand by young men for wives may have meant that a higher percentage of women may have been married at a younger age. This change would have resulted in a lower average age at first pregnancy.

In twentieth-century Kikuyu society, there has also been a clear increase in the fraction of monogamous marriages. Again the causal factors and the impact of monogamy on fertility are not clear, but recent studies suggest that monogamous marriages are more fertile (Adadevoh, 1974; Faruqee, 1982; Newman and Lura, 1983). With a relatively balanced sex ratio, in the precolonial period the Kikuyu relied on the large age gap between spouses to provide the necessary pool of brides for polygamous marriages (Kenyatta, [1938] 1965; Leakey, [1933] 1979). The trend toward monogamy could be caused by a narrowing of the age difference and a rise in demand for wives by young men, both of which reduced the number of potential second wives. The colonial period also brought Christianity, which may have reinforced this trend. Another possible cause of increased monogamy may have been the shortage of land in the Kikuyu reserves. Every husband was obliged to provide his wife with a garden. As land grew increasingly scarce and expensive, the opportunities for acquiring a second wife decreased.

Another factor that may have encouraged monogamy was the inflation of bridewealth (Fisher, 1964; Ferraro, 1976; Kershaw, 1972). Also, the nature of the payments changed from beer and livestock to include cash. Thus monetization may also have accelerated changes in the riika and mbari mentioned above. The increase in bridewealth has two possible causes: (1) the rising demand by young men for first wives and the continued demand by wealthy men for multiple wives; and (2) the increased cultivation of cash crops. Since Kikuyu women do most of the agricultural work and large numbers of men are labor migrants, the value of female labor would appear to have risen significantly. The wife became almost entirely responsible for producing both food and cash crops. Thus, the parents' loss of a young woman's labor has risen in the twentieth century and may be reflected in the rise in bridewealth.

An unexplored aspect of Kikuyu fertility is that of possible changes in sexuality. For instance, premarital sexual relations were a serious offense, and the consequences were severe if one was caught. Nguiko was permitted between initiated young men and women as a means of courtship and probably to preclude full premarital intercourse. Any male caught trying to have complete intercourse with a young woman was liable to complete ostracism by young women and punishment by his male agemates. Similarly, if the young woman had full intercourse, she would be punished by her agemates, and the penalties for pregnancy were substantial (Kenyatta, [1938] 1965; Routledge and Routledge, 1910; Leakey, [1933] 1979). The riika enforced the ban and exacted the punishment. Yet, in the twentieth century the riika was on the decline, and by the 1920s had little influence. Premarital intercourse probably began to increase in the 1920s, and by 1931 Leakey reported there were "an ever increasing number of young girls who are pregnant before they are fully mature."

The observation of ritual periods of sexual abstinence could also have begun to decline. For instance, after the birth of a child, a husband was not to sleep with his wife or any other woman for a month. Several days after the birth, a purification ceremony was held for the mother, which had to be attended by several elders. The invited elders also had to abstain from sexual relations until the final purification rite was performed, usually one month after the birth. This requirement meant that agreeable elders were sometimes difficult to find. After ritual intercourse at the final purification rite, the husband was not permitted to sleep with his wife for several additional months

(Leakey, [1933] 1979). This prohibition did not pose a problem if the young man was still a warrior. He could still perform nguiko with initiated maidens or had the right to sleep with the wives of his agemates, viable options as long as the riika system remained in operation. What did a young husband do after the 1920s? Did elders continue their observance of abstinence? Finally, Kikuyu Christians would not likely observe traditional periods of abstinence.

Labor migration may also have affected sexual activity. First, males were away from their wives for long periods of time. In the cities, many men sought the company of prostitutes, which had obvious implications for the spread of sexually transmitted diseases. Men were allowed very short and very occasional home visits, usually at the discretion of the employer. Both situations—reduced contact between husband and wife and possible complications from sexually transmitted diseases—would appear to discourage any rise in fertility.

The last aspect of fertility that appears to have changed is birth spacing. In 1922 the PMO reported that surveys suggested that the average woman may have borne 6.8 children during her reproductive years. In 1977-1978 in Central Province, the average Kikuyu woman bore an average 8.6 children—a rate down from the 1969 estimate of 8.9 children. The reasons for this change can only be surmised. At present, Kikuyu women experience high rates of fertility throughout their reproductive years. This pattern may be the result of the need for help with the work of the homestead. As mentioned earlier, the absence of adult and teenage males meant that the work load of Kikuyu women had increased. The increase in monogamy meant that the average Kikuyu woman also lost access to the potential help of co-wives and their children. Mbari members could still be called on for help, but usually only for harvest, not daily work in the fields. Also, calls on cooperative labor had to be repaid. The only available relief would appear to be an increased number of children in the homestead (this general argument can be found in Gergory and Piché, 1982).

CONCLUSION

The evidence suggests that "commonsense" explanations of Kenyan demographic history are incorrect. The period 1890-1930 is clearly one of population decline due to increased mortality, the result of the integration of Kikuyu society into the colonial economy. The period 1930-1945 witnessed gradually accelerating population growth. Evidence does not support the idea that this growth stemmed from substantial reductions in mortality, resulting from improvements in sanitary conditions (especially water supplies), nutrition, or the introduction of Western biomedical care. Any reduction in mortality came from improved famine relief capabilities and the achievement of a colonial homeostasis between humans and their parasites.

Thus, population growth must also be the result of changing patterns of fertility. The new colonial society and economy had strong influence on important Kikuyu social institutions affecting fertility. The male age of marriage clearly declined, resulting in increasing monogamy; male age of circumcision declined, resulting in potentially earlier sexual activity. The riika or circumcision set lost its importance as a source of bridewealth, but also as a deterrent to premarital sex. Periods of abstinence may have begun to disappear. Finally, Kikuyu women appear to have shortened birth intervals, bearing more children than in the past. The new colonial economy may have forced this reproductive strategy.

Most demographic work has relied heavily on commonsense knowledge and a few colonial documents for discussing demographic history. The tentative arguments above concerning changing patterns of fertility demand exploration both in the archives and in the field. The data for the precolonial era are probably lost, but some early colonial populations possibly could be reconstructed. The results of these studies could significantly alter thinking about the origins of Kenya's staggering growth rate. If changing fertility has contributed heavily to population growth and is the result of socioeconomic change, then, rural information campaigns on birth control alone are unlikely to have a substantial impact on growth. Solutions will instead have to address not simply ignorance about birth control, but the rational causes that rural Kenyans have for high fertility.

PART V

SOUTHERN AFRICA: INTENSE PRESSURES
ON DEMOGRAPHIC VIABILITY

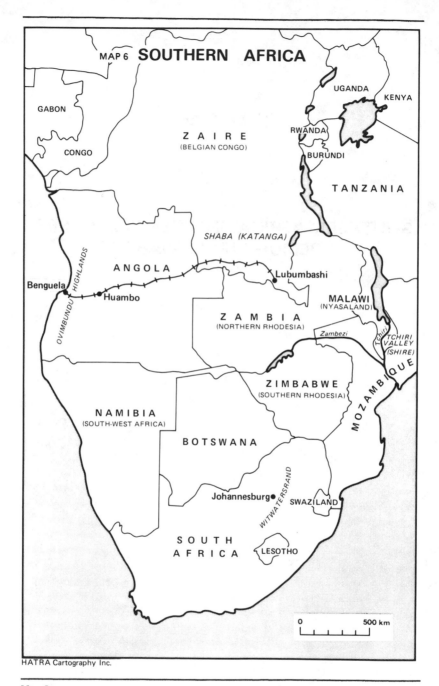

MAP 6 **SOUTHERN AFRICA**

GABON

CONGO

Z A I R E
(BELGIAN CONGO)

UGANDA

KENYA

RWANDA

BURUNDI

T A N Z A N I A

SHABA (KATANGA)

A N G O L A

Lubumbashi

Benguela

OVIMBUNDU HIGHLANDS

Huambo

MALAWI
(NYASALAND)

Z A M B I A
(NORTHERN RHODESIA)

Zambezi

Tchiri

TCHIRI
VALLEY
(SHIRE)

ZIMBABWE
(SOUTHERN RHODESIA)

M O Z A M B I Q U E

N A M I B I A
(SOUTH-WEST AFRICA)

B O T S W A N A

WITWATERSRAND

Johannesburg

SWAZILAND

**S O U T H
A F R I C A**

LESOTHO

0   500 km

HATRA Cartography Inc.

Map 6

220

14

DIMENSIONS OF CONFLICT
Emigrant Labor from Colonial Malawi
and Zambia, 1900-1945

JOEL W. GREGORY
ELIAS MANDALA

THE PROBLEM

Since the turn of the century the two faces of labor migration have become familiar to Africans. The hardship of life as a labor migrant is mirrored in the struggle of rural households to compensate for the loss of husbands, fathers, brothers, sons ... and occasionally a daughter. The circulation of labor between two spheres of production—one capitalist, the other noncapitalist—is a key characteristic of early development in Africa (Gregory and Piché, 1983).

Most early analyses of the necessity for capital to capture a part of the value of labor in order to accumulate and expand are inadequate, observers usually defending the European civilizing mission:

> The explosion of material civilisation has gotten the better of the black man's inertia. ... He wants money without which it would be necessary to resign himself to wallow in the misery from which his elders were never able to escape. He will therefore go to the white man, hundreds, even

Author's Note: We would like to thank M. Enoch T. Mvula for use of the songs he collected and for criticism of an earlier draft of this chapter. The Social Science Research Council and the American Council of Learned Societies provided valuable financial support for the research on which this chapter is based. Valuable comments were provided by Robert Allie, Sam Chipungu, Bruce Fetter, Danielle Gauvreau, Nancy Howell, and Victor Piché.

thousands of kilometers away, and he will force himself, because he cannot do otherwise, to work hard and strong like a white man [Guilleme, 1932: 41].

The scientific analysis of our academic elders, with its "developmentalist" bias is, for the most part, still unsatisfying:

Economic development ... has only been made possible through the availability of a large reservoir of cheap labour. But the supply of this labour has not always been constant. In spite of the conspicuous poverty of the tribal Africans and the apparent abundance of men with no calls on their time, the enterpreneur has not always been able to count on a steady and sufficient flow of labour for his needs. Wage labour was foreign to the tribesman of the late 19th century, and savored to him somewhat of slavery [Mitchell, 1961: 199].

Why *did* the African at the turn of the century regard labor as akin to slavery? This question suggests at least two others: (1) How were labor reservoirs created? (2) Why was the process so difficult?

More recent attempts to theorize about migration as a result of capital's need to accumulate on the basis of absolute value and to externalize the costs of labor reproduction have changed the terms of debate as set by neoclassical economics. They have not, however, helped us to understand how labor actually is generated within the domestic domain or how contradictions within the latter affect the ways in which capital extracts labor. Most analyses begin with Arrighi's (1973) formulation, in which migration is viewed as a mirror image of only one form of peasant production: agriculture. Unfortunately, they ignore the nonagricultural sector, which, as we shall demonstrate, was crucial for precolonial accumulation and shaped peasant responses to colonial pressures for labor migration.

Marxist analysis of these issues can benefit from a careful marshaling of demographic data. Statistics from the colonial period, despite defects, hold considerable potential for one crucial area of analysis: the changes in the intensity and the direction of migration, as part of the process of "freeing" labor from precapitalist social relations. Emigration from Malawi and Zambia, like that from Burkina Faso and its Sahelian neighbors, is an instructive example of the circulation of labor between the capitalist and noncapitalist spheres (see Map 6). It shows capital's successes as well as the considerable resistance of African peasants. We begin with an attempt to determine the scope of the phenomenon by analyzing one source of emigration statistics from

South Central Africa, Kuczynski's chapters on colonial Malawi and Zambia in his encyclopedic study of the demography of the colonial British empire (1949, vol. II: 424-474; 536-581; all further page references to this volume). We then attempt to relate the data to changes in the dynamic of peasant production and accumulation.

THE DATA

The demographic data are better for Malawi. Five censuses were taken during the first half of this century: 1911, 1921, 1926, 1931, and 1945. These data allowed Kuczynski to analyze the evolution of the population from the founding of the protectorate in 1891 and to discuss emigration in detail. Kuczynski's report may be supplemented by several other sources, including the Blue Books, the Medical Reports, and the Colonial Reports. But his 50-page study of emigration from Malawi also draws on a wide variety of other data: the debates of the Legislative Council, Labour Department statistics, and several ad hoc official studies of migrant labor. Finally, Kuczynski employs several Zimbabwean sources: data from the Rhodesian Chamber of Mines, the Southern Rhodesian Reports on Mines, and the 1911 and 1936 censuses.

For Zambia, the sources are more heterogenous, and even the census of 1950 was based on regional estimates. A so-called census took place in 1931, but, in effect, "it actually is the estimated figure of 1930 minus the estimated number of absentees in May 1931" (p. 409).

Kuczynski's description of the Zambian population is based on estimates made by colonial administrators during periodic village visits. These data, the quality of which may have deteriorated in the 1930s, were found in the Native Affairs Reports. Numerous other documents, however, furnish statistics: the British South Africa (BSA) Company Reports before 1924 (when Zambia was turned over to the Colonial Office for direct administration); the Colonial Reports from 1924, or the Blue Books; the Medical Reports; the Mines Department Reports; the Legislative Council Debates; various studies including the Pym Commission in the 1920s and the Rhodesia-Nyasaland Royal Commission in 1939; and reports on labor from colonial Zimbabwe and Zaire.

The population and migration data are critically presented by Kuczynski. The paucity of age data, particularly crucial for the demographer, is striking. Internal incoherence is identified. Progress in the quality of data collection, and occasional backsliding is demonstrated. Different sources are confronted. Kuczynski's personal estimates are noted. One concludes, after a careful reading, that the estimates are usually underestimates.

Kuczynski does not do three things that would have aided his analysis. First, he does not assemble in one place all the data he presents on migration. Second, he does not consider the difference between stock (the number of *migrants* in a given geographical unit at a given point in *time*) and flow (the number of *moves* from one unit to another during a given *period*). And third, he does not compare the data on stocks and flows with the number of people actually present, the population "at risk," in demographic terms. These three operations permit a more accurate appraisal of the effects of emigration.

ANALYSIS OF THE DATA

Population Size

Kuczynski's data on the size of the African population of Malawi and Zambia are presented in Tables 14.1 and 14.2.

Estimates for Malawi before the first census in 1921 fluctuate in an unlikely pattern (Table 14.1). The early figures (1897-1904) are substantially lower than those for the following seven years, when an upward adjustment seems to have been made, and when the population of Northern Angoniland was included for the first time (p. 631). The fluctuation undoubtedly also results from uneven local and regional estimates. These variations probably also reflect unstable economic conditions (see Part IV) coupled with uncertainty about the importance of immigration, especially from Mozambique (p. 631). An overestimate seems to appear in the 1916-1920 period, and in 1921 the superintendent of the census assumed that the natural increase of the population (births minus deaths) in the previous decade may actually have been negative, with growth coming from immigration (p. 633):

> In the period preceding the proclamation of the British Protectorate the native population was probably declining. During the fifty years of British administration there was a net immigration of several hundred thousands. In the first three decades births probably did not exceed deaths. In the last two decades there may have been a natural increase but it certainly was not large [p. 638].

From 1921 to 1945 Malawi's population showed a steady, although irregular, increase. Probably at least half of the increase between 1921 and 1931 was due to Lomwe and Sena immigration (p. 635). The sub-

TABLE 14.1
Malawi: Early Estimates of the African Population, 1897-1920; by Sex and/or Age Categories, 1921-1945

Year	Estimates	Year	Estimates	Year	Estimates
1897	687,752	1908	947,168	1915	1,088,057
1902	705,592	1909	996,166	1916	1,137,572
1903	736,719	1910	922,313	1917	1,137,266
1904	792,726	1911	969,183	1918	1,227,442
1905	923,500	1912	1,000,659	1919	1,215,976
1906	976,641	1913	1,020,537	1920	1,202,208
1907	927,355	1914	1,065,119		

Year	Less than 5 Years	5 to Marriage Age	Marriage Age	Totals
1921 census				
females	175,141	72,592	394,063	641,796
males	173,475	84,925	299,711	558,138
total	348,616	157,544	693,774	1,199,934
sex ratio	99.0	117.0	76.1	87.0
1926 census				
females	177,110	83,579	429,349	690,038
males	179,559	96,008	325,280	600,847
total	356,669	179,587	754,629	1,290,885
sex ratio	101.4	114.9	75.8	87.1
1931 census				
females	222,112	111,732	513,827	847,671
males	220,423	122,995	408,799	752,217
total	442,535	234,727	922,626	1,599,888
sex ratio	99.2	110.1	79.6	88.7

	1935 Estimate	1939 Estimate	1941 Estimate
Females	849,531	899,720	926,494
Males	750,545	776,880	786,398
Total	1,600,076	1,676,600	1,712,892
Sex ratio	88.3	86.3	84.9

	< 1 Year	1-4 Years	5-18 Years	Over 18	Totals	De jure
1945 census						
females	87,992	185,652	256,348	567,428	1,097,420	1,106,866
males	84,753	188,598	286,075	387,861	947,287	1,071,147
total	172,745	374,250	542,423	955,289	2,044,707	2,178,013
sex ratio	96.3	101.6	111.6	68.4	86.3	96.8

SOURCE: Kuczynski (1949: vol. II: 535, 586, 591).

stantial growth between the 1931 and 1945 census was "explained" by colonial officials in a variety of ways, with some credence given to the hypothesis that there was an undercount in 1931 (p. 637); this would mean that some of the earlier censuses were also undercounts.

Two characteristics of the colonial Malawi population merit attention. First, at adult ages, the sex ratio is predominantly feminine. This is probably the result of (1) the artificial aging of younger teenage females into the older age category (while younger males remain in the pre-adult age category, a common inaccuracy in nonliterate populations, when the average age of female marriage is less than the average age of male marriage), and (2) the selective emigration of adult males, while females remain behind in Malawi. The sex ratios indicate this: Females are 10 to 15 percent less numerous than males in the younger age category (selective "aging" of females *plus* selective emigration of males? See Chapter 15, this volume, by Heywood and Thornton). If these hypotheses are correct, then an emigration of at least 15 percent of the adult male population seems probable in 1921, 1926, and 1931; and of 25 percent in 1945. In other words, the overrepresentation of adult females is equal to the sum of their underrepresentation at younger ages *and* their overrepresentation in the adult nonemigrant population. For several reasons, this relationship is *very* approximate: (1) The young age category is smaller in absolute numbers and, therefore, 10 to 15 percent of this age group is smaller than 10 to 15 percent of the older category; (2) the emigration of adults does include a small fraction of females; (3) even in the absence of migration, "aging," and errors, the sex ratio at preadult and adult ages is not exactly equal to 100; and (4) there is no assurance that *all* the underrepresentation of males in the adult category is due to their emigration and the phenomenon of female "aging" (adult males, for example, may have been more undercounted than adult females, due to hut taxes, military service, and the dynamic of female-male relations in these societies).

A second characteristic of the colonial Malawi population is the major difference between the de facto and the de jure population in 1945, the first time this distinction was made. The resident population (de facto) was 133,000 people less than the legal population. This difference can, in large part, be interpreted as a minimum estimate of emigrant Malawians living in another territory in 1945. This de facto/ de jure difference was predominantly masculine: 124,000 males, 9,000 females.

For colonial Zambia the population data are subject to even greater caution. Based on noncensus estimates, Kuczynski's work permits the construction of the upper parts of Table 14.2. From 1907 until 1932,

TABLE 14.2
Zambia: Estimates of Total Population, 1907-1923; by Sex 1924-1934; by Sex and Age Categories, 1950 Census

Year	Population	Year	Population	Year	Population	Year	Population
1907	718,400	1912	824,756	1918	928,975	1921	999,876
1910	796,086	1914	875,000	1919	938,383	1922	1,001,062
1911	820,985	1916	884,000	1920	997,674	1923	1,052,193

Year	Children			Adults				Totals		
	Females	Males	Totals	Females	Males	Totals	Sex Ratio	Females	Males	Population
1924			422,210	384,593	299,731	684,324	77.9			1,106,534
1925			443,389	392,819	304,434	697,253	77.5			1,140,642
1926			474,121	412,137	312,802	724,939	75.9			1,199,063[a]
1927			496,382	420,832	320,272	741,104	76.1			1,237,486
1928			506,651	428,607	326,714	755,321	76.2			1,261,972
1929			519,516	444,780	334,355	779,135	75.2			1,298,651
1930-1931[b]	266,444	269,690	536,134	448,136	310,811	758,947	69.4	714,580	580,501	1,295,081
1930-1931[c]	266,967	270,252	537,219	448,493	345,517	794,010	77.0	715,460	615,769	1,331,229
1931			556,051	446,302	369,882	816,184	82.9			1,372,235
1932			562,725	445,408	374,572	819,980	84.1			1,382,705
1933			560,383	438,701	372,129	810,830	84.8			1,371,213
1934			561,304	436,292	368,829	805,121	84.5			1,366,425

1950 Census Data

Age	Female	Male	Totals	Sex Ratio
1 year	48,000	44,000	92,000	91.7
1 – puberty	332,000	356,000	688,000	107.2
Over puberty	562,000	474,000	1,036,000	84.3
Totals	942,000	874,000	1,816,000	92.8

SOURCES: Kuczynski (1949: vol. II, 406, 415-416, 418); Northern Rhodesia Census (30 May 1950). See United Nations (1956: 233).
a. Total is not equal to sum.
b. De Facto population.
c. De Jure population.

227

colonial estimates suggested a steady and sometimes rapid rate of growth (1 to 5 percent per year). A slight decline was indicated in the early 1930s, followed by obvious growth for at least some of the period between the last estimates in 1934 and the first census in 1950. Noting that the Department of Native Affairs "accepted every figure which showed a population increase but usually doubted the accuracy of figures which indicated a decrease," Kuczynski suggests that the decline for the 1930s might be the result of return migration to Portuguese West Africa and a slight overestimate in the late 1920s (p. 406).

Again, as for Malawi, the number of adult females was much greater than the number of adult males, in the years for which there were estimates by sex (1924-1934) and at the time of the first census (in 1950), reflecting the fact that labor migration was predominantly male. The femininity of these adult sex ratios (approximately the same as for Malawi for the 1920s) declines in the 1930s. Yet this decline is partially an artifact of the diminishing quality of the female population count (p. 406).

Emigration and Emigrants

For Malawi, the data suggest a considerable increase in emigration, particularly in the 1930s (see Table 14.3). From estimates of several thousand moves per year for the period around 1920, emigration (flow data) grows to several tens of thousands per annum for seven of the last years covered by the data (1938-1944). Furthermore, the estimates of emigrants (stock data) are consistent: Figures suggest that 20,000 to 75,000 were absent from Malawi in various years before 1932, with the range jumping to 90,000 to 140,000 for the years 1934 to 1945. As we shall see in the next major section of this chapter, this change reflects the opening of Malawian borders that had been closed to Rhodesian and South African labor recruitment from 1909 to the early 1930s. The principal destinations, therefore, for Malawi-born emigrants were, first, colonial Zimbabwe, and then South Africa.

For Zambia, on the other hand, a pattern of relative stability in migration flows and migrant stocks seems to exist from 1921 until 1943, with estimates of annual emigration varying between 20,000 and 40,000, and of emigrant stocks varying from 50,000 (see Table 14.4). Colonial Zimbabwe was the major destination for Zambian migrants; Shaba, Tanzania, and South Africa competed as alternative destinations.

SOURCE: Kuczynski (1949: volume 2, passim). For a detailed compilation, see Gregory (1982).
a. Employed males.
b. Underestimated.
c. Certificates of migration issued under Salisbury Tripartite Agreement.
d. Employed.
e. 25,000 of which in armed services.
f. 9,446 of which are females; 25,236 in armed services.
g. Kuczynski's estimate.

TABLE 14.3

Colonial Malawi: Emigration (Flow) and Emigrant (Stock) Data, Estimates from Kuczynski

Year	Flow	Stock	Year	Flow	Stock
1911	na	20,000[g]	1938	45,125[c]	113,500[d]
1920	6,099	20,000[a]	1939	39,760[c]	112,765[d]
1921	7,194[b]	60,000[g]	1940	38,924	101,800
1922	4,758[b]	na	1941	49,686	110,100
1925	na	30,000	1942	23,860[c]	na
1929	na	30,000-60,000	1943	32,995[c]	na
1930	na	30,000-40,000	1944	38,199[c]	141,986[e]
1934	na	120,000	1945	na	133,306[f]
1937	na	90,097[a]			

These figures may be underestimates. Large numbers of people crossed the boundaries of Malawi and Zambia without formally passing a border post, for reasons of convenience as well as for more explicitly political or economic motives. Furthermore, data collected on emigrants in the country of origin must rely on second-hand informants (Who is gone? Where are they? When did they leave?). Statistics gathered in the countries of immigration are compromised by imprecision of definition—who, for example, is a "resident" at the time of a census?—by the clandestine nature of some of this migration, and by the mobility of any migrant subpopulation. Finally, the fact that emigrants went to several countries means that estimates are based on data that are heterogeneous in terms of collection and tabulation.

Emigration and Emigrant Data Compared with the Total Population

Keeping these facts in mind, what can be deduced about the relative impact of emigration on the populations of Malawi and Zambia? In Table 14.5 indices are calculated to suggest the annual effect of emigration flows on the total population (index I) and on the adult male population (II), and the cumulative effect of the stock of absentees on the total population (III) and the adult male population (IV).

TABLE 14.4

Colonial Zambia: Emigration (Flow) and Emigrant (Stock) Data,
Estimates from Kuczynski

Year	Flow	Stock	Year	Flow	Stock
1921	na	50,000[e]	1932	25,139[b]	
1924	28,000[a]	na		24,260[c]	na
1926	na	50,000[e]		879[d]	
1927	42,539[b]		1933	21,293[b]	
	31,438[c]	na		21,010[c]	na
	11,101[d]			283[d]	
1928	36,875[b]	na	1934	31,572[bc]	na
	27,650[c]		1935	na	49,000[a]
	9,225[d]				75,000[e]
1929	42,450[b]		1936	na	51,212[a]
	33,741[c]	na	1937	na	67,776[a]
	8,709[d]				80,000[e]
1930	38,056[b]		1938	na	54,254[a]
	33,564[c]	na	1940	na	60,000[a]
	4,492[d]		1941	na	46,896[a]
1931	30,943[b]		1942	na	64,000[a]
	29,181[c]	na	1943	na	60,791[a]
	1,762[d]				

SOURCE: Kuczynski (1949: vol. II, passim); for a detailed compilation, see Gregory (1982).
a. Total laborers.
b. Total migration.
c. Independent migration.
d. Recruited laborers.
e. Employed, Kuczynski's estimate.

The annual impact of the outflow of emigrants (index I) ranges from 5 per 1000 in 1920 to nearly 30 per 1000 in 1940 for Malawi. In other words, for each 1000 people living in Malawi in 1940, approximately 30 left. In Zambia, the same index ranges from 16 to 34 per 1000 for the period 1924 to 1934. The index that estimates the impact of the outflow of emigrants on the adult male population (II) can be calculated for Zambia for the same period. If all emigrants in each of these years had been adult males, 57 to 133 of each 1,000 adult males would have emigrated. This suggests that emigration was having a considerable impact on the local population, especially on males of working age.

The third and fourth indices, emphasizing the cumulative impact of emigration, show that the stock of emigrants absent from Malawi varies between 20 and 50 per 1000 before 1932, and from 55 to 75 per 1000 in later years (index III). The equivalent rates are 30 to 55 per

TABLE 14.5
Some Emigration and Emigrant Statistics (per thousand), Malawi and Zambia 1911 to 1945

	Malawi				Zambia			
	Emigration		Emigrant		Emigration		Emigrant	
Year	I	II	III	IV	I	II	III	IV
1911			21					
1920	5		17[a]					
1921	6[b]	24[b]	50	200			50	
1924					25[a]	93[a]		
1926			23	92			42	160
1927					34	133		
1928					29	113		
1929			21-42[c]	80-160[d]	33	127		
1930					29	110	38	145
1931			19-47	73-183	23	84		
1932					18	67		
1933					16	57		
1934			75[e]		23	86		
1935							35-54[f]	131-200[f]
1936							36[a]	134[a]
1937			55[a,g]				47-55	174-206
1938	25[h]		68[h]				37[a]	137[a]
1939	24		67					
1940	23[i]		60				39[a]	147[a]
1941	29		64				30[a]	113[a]
1942	13[j]						40[a]	152[a]
1943	18[k]						38[a]	142[a]
1944	19[l]		72[l]					
1945			65	344				

Indices:

$$\text{I} \quad \frac{\text{flow}}{\text{total population}} \cdot .1000 \qquad\qquad \text{III} \quad \frac{\text{stock}}{\text{total population}} \cdot .1000$$

$$\text{II} \quad \frac{\text{flow}}{\text{adult male population}} \cdot .1000 \qquad\qquad \frac{\text{flow}}{\text{adult male population}} \cdot .1000$$

a. Employed males, or all employed, in numberator (n).
b. Recognized underestimate, n.
c. Denominator (d): 1,416,287; straight line extrapolation (sle).
d. d: 375,391, sle.
e. d: 1,600,029 sle.

(continued)

TABLE 14.5 (Continued)

f. Straight line extrapolation (sle) of denominator: Zambian population, 1935-1943, using 1934 data from Kuczynski and 1950 census:

Year	Adult Male	Total	Year	Adult Male	Total
1935	375,402	1,394,523	1940	408,267	1,535,016
1936	381,975	1,422,622	1941	414,840	1,563,114
1937	388,548	1,450,720	1942	421,413	1,591,212
1938	395,121	1,478,819	1943	427,986	1,619,311
1939	401,694	1,506,918			

g. d: 1,638,338, sle.
h. d: 1,657,469, sle.
i. d: 1,694,701, sle.
j. d: 1,795,846, sle.
k. d: 1,878,800, sle.
l. d: 1,961,753, sle.

1000 for Zambia, with no regular upward or downward movement between 1921 and 1943. When converted into the final index (IV), the proportion of the adult male population that would have been absent in any given year—if all emigrants had been adult males—varies from slightly under 100 to over 300 per 1000 for Malawi, and is concentrated between 130 and 200 per 1000 for Zambia. These proportions reinforce our conclusion: Emigration was indeed having a considerable quantitative impact on the population.

The indices, in fact, probably underestimate the effect of emigration. The numerators of these indices are possibly underevaluated more than the denominators. Kuczynski, for example, estimated that one-fifth of able-bodied males emigrated in 1931 from the Northern Province of Malawi (p. 560). And in 1937, the Bell Commission estimated that 20 percent of the "fit adult males" were employed outside of Malawi (p. 568). An independent study in 1939 revealed that 23 to 43 percent of all men were away from 110 villages in the Northern province (Read 1942, 618-619). Retrospective data suggest that the adult male absentee rate for the Lower Tchiri Valley varied between 22 percent and 35 percent for the 1909 to 1943 period (Garbett, 1977: Table 7). We have less corroborating evidence for Zambia, but at least one governor estimated in 1943 that only 30 percent of the able-bodied men were left in some native reserves (p. 469).

Malawi initially compensated for her temporary southward and southwesterly losses of emigrants with the settlement of immigrants from Mozambique (Chanock, 1977: 399). During the 1920s, immigration of the Lomwe and Sena reached several tens of thousands (pp. 537-542). By the end of the 1930s, however, Malawi was probably firmly established as a net exporter of labor. Zambia, despite its capacity to attract labor to the Copperbelt, was a substantial reservoir for Zimbabwe, and even for South Africa (Scott, 1954: 31).

THE STATE, FORMS OF PEASANT PRODUCTION, AND ACCUMULATION

This quantitative reconstruction of migration from colonial Malawi and Zambia is limited not only by the quality of the data, but also by the aggregate level of analysis. Malawi and Zambia are heterogeneous societies. The social organization of diverse groups was dramatically challenged by colonial capitalism; the challenge varied from one area to another, as did African response. In this section we provide a few examples of how the challenge and response contributed to the "freeing" of labor and thus to the generation of migration. In order for Malawian and Zambian societies to provide labor for South Central and Southern African capitalist development, a necessary readjustment in rural production and reproduction had to occur. The aggregate data on population and migration can do no more than point to areas of potential change in the communities that migrants left. They are silent on the dynamics of change: the mechanisms used during the colonial period to "free" labor, the nature of capitalist production, and the dynamics of rural resistance.

Mechanisms to Free Labor

The theory that assumes that labor flows naturally from areas of low productivity to those of high productivity underestimates the obstacles colonial Malawi or Zambia encountered in "freeing" labor from the noncapitalist sphere. Colonial states in both countries had to turn, very early, to the now classical litany of coercive measures: violence, taxation (beginning in 1892 in Malawi and 1900-1901 in Zambia), as well as land expropriation. Nearly 3.75 million acres, or over 15 percent of the country's arable land, were already taken away from peasants in Malawi by 1894 (Pachai, 1973: 100). The Africans who lost their land were forced to live on European estates as tenants under the notorious *thangata* or rent-labor system. Thangata was reinforced in 1901 by doubling the "hut" tax for all those who were unable to provide a certificate proving they had worked at least thirty days for a European (Kandawire, 1979: 110-115).

In 1909, to meet the labor requirements of the fledgling European estate economy, the state in Malawi banned the Rhodesian Native Labour Bureau (RNLB) and the Witwatersrand Native Labour Association (WENWLA), which had recruited labor for Zimbabwean and South African mines and agriculture since 1903 (Sanderson, 1961: 266-267). Thus, until the 1930s, when Malawi's borders were again opened to recruiters, Zambia became the labor reservoir for Zimbabwe and South Africa (see Tables 14.3 and 14.4). The British South Africa (BSA) Company, which ruled Zambia until 1924, used *chibaro*—a form of semi-servile labor based on raids in Zambian villages and the capture of migrants at ferry crossings and elsewhere—as a method of labor supply. The system was reinforced by vigorous prosecution of tardy taxpayers and the glorification of conditions in the mines.

State intervention constituted only one set of pressures affecting labor mobility. Banning the RNLB and WENWLA did not, for example, stop the integration of Malawi—along with Zambia—into the growing South Central African migratory networks during the 1910s and 1920s. The data in Table 14.5 attest eloquently to this fact. But the ability of the state to extract migrants and the impact of their extraction were determined in part by the nature of labor control and accumulation in the precapitalist economy (Berry, 1984).

Like any concept, primitive accumulation has to be handled with care. We need to specify the nature of productive resources available to a noncapitalist social order and to determine the mechanisms through which some groups appropriated these resources to the exclusion of others. Studies have tended to focus on agriculture, but the evidence from precolonial Malawi and Zambia cautions against restricting the analysis of rural accumulation to only one form of peasant production. Nonagricultural activities were historically as significant for precapitalist accumulation and labor control as agriculture. The nonagricultural sphere encompassed a wide range of activities, including the production and exchange of cotton cloth, iron tools, and salt, as well as hunting, fishing, cattle raising, and warfare. Although ultimately linked to agriculture, these activities had their own "logic," and, therefore, their own significance for accumulation and migration during the colonial era.

Production within the nonagricultural sector was associated more with male than with female labor. Hunting and warfare, for example, were exclusively male activities. Moreover, whereas all female or male elders enjoyed rights with respect to the distribution of agricultural land, control of nonagricultural resources such as iron deposits was the privilege of dominant classes and families to whom direct producers were usually obliged to give part of their product. Finally, most nonagricultural products were polyvalent. In addition to being use values, they circulated within the prestige and long-distance exchange networks, fetching women and slaves, among other things. This sphere was intimately linked to accumulation in precolonial Malawi and Zambia, while agricultural production was for the most part confined to meeting subsistence needs (see Mandala, 1983: 24-31; Beach, 1977: 37-65).

Nonagricultural production and exchange hence provides a strategic entry point for the analysis of what has been rather vaguely described as the "destruction of the cycle of simple reproduction of the domestic economy" (Berman, 1984: 408-409). In Malawi and Zambia the initial break was primarily accomplished through the destruction of nonagricultural production. The process involved the substitution of locally manufactured goods such as cloth, tools, or salt for foreign imports. Colonial control also meant the end of the rights of the dominant classes to conduct raiding or warfare. In some areas, such as northeastern Zambia and northern Malawi, these same groups also lost part of their productive resources to the colonial conquerors. The BSA Company looted the cattle of the Bemba and Ngoni, which, with the rinderpest epidemic, drastically reduced cattle holdings (Vail, 1983). Shortfalls in food production in early colonial Malawi and Zambia were part of a deeper social crisis, a crisis in precapitalist accumulation that ultimately limited the effectiveness of colonial measures to curb male emigration from Malawi during the first two decades of this century.

Routinizing Migration and African Struggles to Resist

Some communities resolved the crisis by routinizing migration. This option appears to have been determined by the historical relation of accumulation to both agricultural *and* nonagricultural production. Two broad types of relations come to mind. The first is best exemplified by the Ngoni economies of northern Malawi and northeastern Zambia: Agriculture had been subordinated to the nonagricultural sphere from the perspectives of both accumulation and the social division of labor. The position of dominant classes had rested on the systematic withdrawal of male labor from agriculture for use within the critical branches of the nonagricultural sector, particularly cattle raising and warfare.

When colonial conquest put an end to raiding and warfare, Ngoni aristocrats found themselves without an established alternative to the earlier process of accumulation. Whereas other dominant groups with alternatives resisted recruiters, the Ngoni instead cooperated in the hope of using part of the earnings of their male dependents to reconstitute their basis of power. Dependents welcomed wage labor as a source of cash with which to acquire cattle and women independently, removed from the control of their Ngoni masters. The result was that emigration from northern Malawi and eastern Zambia acquired a logic specific to an Ngoni male world, relatively unaffected by changes in colonial policy or in female-dominated agriculture (see Vail, 1983: 200-250).

In most societies in precolonial Malawi or Zambia, however, agriculture was not as completely subordinated to the nonagricultural sphere. The distinction between the two was limited primarily to the greater relevance of nonagricultural production within the exchange sphere. One group of elders or class often controlled labor within the two sectors. This pattern of labor control and accumulation prevailed in some class societies, such as the Lozi (Van Horn, 1977), as well as in most kin-organized societies, especially those in which a matrilineal ideology was dominant (Poewe, 1981; Mandala, 1983). Agriculture was as much a male domain as it was female. Yet gender was significant to the extent that male and female labor were associated with different stages of agricultural production and different branches of nonagricultural production. The products of some of these branches, such as salt in precolonial Malawi, were completely controlled by women (Mandala, 1983). This gave them a voice in intercommunity public relations as well as access to servile and youth labor, for the most part deployed within agriculture.

Capital met greater resistance in appropriating the male labor released from the nonagricultural sector in such societies. Unlike their Ngoni and, to some extent, Bemba counterparts, the Lozi aristocracy vigorously contested the rise of a labor market among the subordinated classes. Even after the BSA Company halted raiding, there were other precapitalist forms of production to which such labor could be put. These included cattle raising—before the outbreak of bovine pleuro-pneumonia killed the herds in 1915—and, more significantly, Lewanika's agricultural scheme, a colonial sequel to precolonial canal construction. The aristocracy eased its hold over dependent and servile labor only after a series of disasters struck the agricultural economy in the late 1920s and 1930s (Van Horn, 1977: 156-166).

The Lozi pattern of resistance was repeated in most kin-organized, nonclass groups of Malawi and Zambia, although at a later date. It took a long time before these societies recovered from the initial capitalist colonial attack, mainly because the assault on the nonagricultural sector directly affected the agricultural economy. Partial recovery was possible only from the mid-1920s, after the epidemics and the massive labor conscriptions of the war had come to an end (Mandala, 1983: 118-144). This set the stage for resistance to migration, a reaction that was characteristically spearheaded by women, as the following song illustrates.

Amuna anga musabvutika	My husband, don't worry
Ndi kundisiya ndekha	Don't leave me alone
Kuti mupite ku Joni.	Don't go to Joni [Johannesburg]
Kaya ndi zobvala	Since you need clothes,
Kaya ndi ndalama	Since you need money for the "hut" tax,
Zolipira msonkho	I will brew beer
Ndingofulula mowa.	We will sell the beer
Tigulitse, mubvale	We will buy cloth
Kaya ndi msonkho tikhome	And pay the "hut" tax
Zopita ku Goli'zi ndiyc ai.	Don't go to the slavery (of the gold mines).[1]

Beer brewing was but one alternative to migration. Another strategy took the form of commodity agriculture, which became the new arena of domestic struggle and accumulation. In Zambia the rise of commodity production as an alternative to migration was encouraged by a new colonial policy. The beginning of copper production in the late 1920s forced the government to ban the activities of labor recruiters for the Katanga and South African mines in 1931 and 1933, respectively (Chauncey, 1981: 137). Not only did the mines require large amounts of labor, but, owing to the poor performance of the European estate sector, the state had to turn to peasants for maize to feed the miners. The southern province and the area along the railway emerged as centers of peasant maize production by the early 1930s (Muntemba, 1982; Wright, 1983). Commodity production in Malawi, on the other hand, witnessed the rise of peasant tobacco and cotton agriculture in the central region and the Lower Tchiri valley, respectively (Chanock, 1972).

These changes partly explain why European employers in Zambia tried now to stabilize part of their labor force (Chauncey, 1981). Cash crop agriculture drastically reduced the rate of emigration from the affected areas (Mandala, 1983: 196; Wright, 1983: 78). The data in Tables 14.3 to 14.5 suggest similar national trends. Emigration flows from Zambia fell from 50,000 in 1921 to 21,293 in 1933—a drop of more than 50 percent—that also reflected the growing importance of the internal copperbelt labor market. The decline in emigrant stocks from Malawi from 60,000 in 1921 to between 30,000 and 40,000 in 1931 is perhaps a better indication of the strength of the rural economy, because no labor market similar to the copperbelt evolved within the country during this period. In taking measures to stabilize labor, capitalists in Zambia were responding not only to competition from the south (Chauncey, 1981: 136-137), but also to changes in the peasant sector.

It would be false to assume a mechanical one-to-one relationship between the performance of the agricultural economy and migration. Other studies of eastern Zambia and other parts of colonial Africa have shown how relatively prosperous rural economies could furnish substantial numbers of migrants (Kitching, 1980; Van Donge, 1984). Beyond the maize, tobacco, and cotton were several struggles that shaped both commodity production and migration.

The crucial variable in these struggles was the control of labor. As elsewhere in Africa, in Malawi and Zambia commodity production was heavily dependent on labor. Even where the plough was adopted, as in the Mazabuka area, it remained a form of piecemeal technology that never undermined the importance of the noncapitalist channels of labor recruitment. As Muntemba (1982) and Wright (1983) have demonstrated, the story of maize production in Zambia is the story of how men exploited the labor of their wives and how they usurped women's prerogatives to the labor of their male juniors. In the Lower Tchiri valley, on the other hand, where women managed to delay patriarchal economic power until the 1940s, the burden of commodity production fell primarily on the young, particularly boys (Mandala, 1982). Elders manipulated every existing channel of youth labor recruitment, such as the *nomi* organizations and the *chikamwini* brideservice, to underwrite accumulation.

The new system of labor control engendered several types of conflict that ultimately affected migration. The manipulation of traditional forms of youth labor recruitment strained otherwise harmonious relations between village elders and government officials. When labor shortages threatened the European estate sector in the Tchiri valley in the 1920s, government officials joined missionaries in condemning the chikamwini and nomi. Missionaries singled out the nomi for promoting "promiscuity" among the young and for undermining school work. The more mundane administrators confronted elders on terms understood by all: The nomi sheltered tax defaulters and potential recruits (Mandala, 1983: 170-174).

While this confrontation should not disguise the similarity of interests between two dominant social groups with respect to the exploitation of youth labor, it is important to note its existence. It explains, in part, why Malawian teenage males were systematically underrepresented in government censuses (see the second major section of this chapter). In addition to being the more stable segment of the young population in predominantly matrilineal rural Malawi, female teenagers did not have to be defended against capitalist production. The contest between peasant and capitalist accumulation focused on able-bodied young males. The debate over brideservice and the nomi serves as a reminder that, given the choice, colonial agents would support capitalist over peasant accumulation; they thus become unconscious allies of the youth in their struggles for freedom from the fetters of rural oppression (Mandala, 1982).

CONCLUSION

This account of change in colonial Malawi and Zambia implies a new interpretation of the relationship between agriculture and migration from the 1930s. The rise-and-fall hypothesis is inadequate, as many writers have recently observed (Cooper, 1981; Ranger, 1978). The history of maize production in Zambia and of tobacco in Malawi does not reinforce the image of peasant agriculture suddenly collapsing before the onslaught of the state in the 1930s. Moreover, even where production did decline in the 1930s, as in the Lower Tchiri valley, male emigration, supported at this time by the state, only aggravated the situation. The dynamics of the process are to be found principally in the contradictory development between the forces and relations of agricultural production. In particular, the lack of structural change in the productive forces led, ironically, to serious changes—real and perceived—in the ecosystem.

These transformations helped to forge seemingly unusual alliances between dominant colonial and African groups. Falling agricultural productivity from the late 1930s made it more difficult for elders to rely upon agriculture as a source of accumulation. Like the Ngoni before them, elders in the valley began to look to migration as a more reliable base for accumulation (Mandala, 1982).

The substantial quantitative impact of emigration on rural Malawi and Zambia (see Table 14.5)—in the absence of mortality decline (see Chapter 13, by Dawson, and Chapter 12, by Turshen)—suggests that pressures on African fertility were probably intensified. We can hypothesize (see Gregory and Piché, 1981) that there would have been a double demand for reproducing labor: the rapidly changing peasant economy and the expanding capitalist sphere. The struggle for the control of this labor created or intensified conflicts within African societies—between women and men and between elders and youth—and between Africans and their European colonizers.

It is not surprising that the biggest losers in the emerging pattern of labor control were new wives, who found themselves at a double disadvantage: They were both young and female. They lost their work partners. Young men took advantage of their newly won "freedom" to deny women one of the most fundamental aspects of the marriage contract: the wife's right to the agricultural labor of the husband, particularly for opening new fields. Another pounding song from Malawi echoes with the resentment of a generation of dispossessed women:

Amuna wanji	What husband is he
Wochoka pososa?	Who emigrates when people are preparing fields?
Amuna wanji	What husband is he
Wochok pososa?	Who emigrates when people are preparing fields?
Adzadya telelini	He will eat his terylene (garment)
Adzadya telelini	He will eat his terylene (garment).
Amuna wanji	What husband is he
Adzadya telelini.	He will eat his tyrelene (garment) (upon his return).

NOTES

1. This song and the one appearing at the end of the chapter were recorded in Central Malawi by E. T. Mvula as part of a major study on oral poetry and socioeconomic change (see Mvula, 1982: 31-55).

15

DEMOGRAPHY, PRODUCTION, AND LABOR
Central Angola, 1890-1950

LINDA HEYWOOD
JOHN K. THORNTON

Vital statistics, age structures, population change, and life expectancy data all reveal the human clement in colonial history because they create a portrait of the "average person." Africans often fared reasonably well initially in the colonial period, if they could avoid dispossession. But when dispossession did occur, the results could be devastating. Colonial statistics on the Ovimbundu of the highlands of central Angola provide insights into the way policies and opportunities altered their lives (see Map 6).

DEMOGRAPHIC DATA FOR THE HIGHLANDS

All estimates or censuses of the highland population relied on statistics collected for fiscal purposes; thus their utility here depends largely on how closely fiscal information relates to our own interests.

During and after the Portuguese conquest of the highlands (roughly the period of 1890-1915), the household ("hut" or *cubata*) replaced the village as the fiscal unit. This was linked to Portuguese plans to institute a household tax, although there was a parallel attempt to count people or at least adults. Estimates for a few districts in 1906 and 1908 arc broken down into adults and cubatas (Centro de Documentação e Investigação [hereafter CDIH] 103/3/1904-1909). The long-range plans of the Portuguese were to develop a labor pool on the highlands (whose exact size and composition would need to be known), although their first concern was to generate revenue through a household tax

(Boletim Oficial da Colonia de Angola [hereafter BO], #42, 20 October 1906; A Defesa de Angola [hereafter Defesa], 11 December 1907). By 1914 the counts were age and sex specific, and the reports and summaries broke population down into irregular age categories (up to 7, 7-14, 14-20, and then by ten-year intervals) (CDIH 68/Balilundo 1/32, 1914), and by 1918 into regular age groups of ten years (CDIH 24/11/1917; CDIH 77/8/Estatísica Geral, 1981). The 1920s saw a further and final evolution: Detailed registers listed the entire population by name and exact age, including family groupings, assessment of landholdings (almost always 2 hectares per household—the legal limit), counts of stock, and residence in villages. Possession of abundant documentation does not ensure that the data are accurate, however; we must assess the means by which this information was obtained. We have relatively little information on how the early enumerations were conducted. From what we do know, the initial procedure involved responses from leaders of the small local political units (*sobados*) who were supposed to gather and count all the people in their areas. Then the names of all heads of sobados and villages, along with their population, ages, marriage patterns, land they worked, and livestock they kept, were set down in large registers. These sobados under "traditional" authorities were then connected to the administration through posts usually headed by Portuguese officials (*chefes*).

For example, in 1916, the administration of Huambo had four posts besides the seat. Two of these posts had four sobados. The chefe of one post was able to put on his tax rolls 1014 households in the smallest sobado and 6682 households in the largest, figures that suggest an attempt actually was made to count houses and people (CDIH 24/Huambo 35/1, 1916).

THE 1918-1925 ENUMERATIONS

In 1918 the tax was changed from households to persons, and the administration shifted its attention from assessments of houses to assessments of people in various age groups. This enumeration and subsequent ones to 1925 represented the first systematic attempt to assess the labor pool, and were tied to plans (still in an embryonic stage) to formulate a general labor policy. As such, they provide us with the most detailed and useful set of demographic data available for Angola until the 1940 census. They thus deserve special analysis as a baseline for examining later demographic change.

We can identify several sources of error. The 1922 enumeration, for example, showed a tendency toward clustering at rounded ages (CDIH 11/Huambo 23/Recensamento, 1923); hence people aged 20, 30, 40, and so on are proportionately more numerous than those, say, 41 or 57. Likewise, there is a tendency to place girls in age categories according to the occurrence of puberty more than according to chronological age. Both tendencies are found widely in African demographic material and are what might be termed "honest mistakes" (Van de Walle, 1968: 143-150).

The 1922 census also exhibits what might be termed less-than-honest mistakes, linked to desires of local officials to maximize revenue. There are suspiciously large numbers of men in the youngest adult age categories and suspiciously few in the oldest child categories, suggesting the "aging" of boys in an attempt to maximize the number of people eligible for forced labor, contract work, or tax payment (American Board of Mission Archives, Cambridge, Massachusetts; Series West Central African Mission [hereafter ABC], Reports 1, Bailundo Station Reports, 1925-1926). Such deceptions did indeed take place in Angola: Missionaries mention the occasional dishonest inscribing of children as adults (ABC 23a/390/1 May 1926: 5), and one public scandal of 1924 involved a party of laborers shipped to the coast who were mostly children (CDIH 33/Huambo 2/77/1 May 1925; CDIH 11/Huambo 23/17 January 1924). A similar deception took place at the line that divided adults eligible for labor from the elderly, for once again one finds suspiciously large numbers of men aged 50 (the last of the eligible ages) and remarkably low numbers of older men (ABC 23a/390/1 May 1926: 5).

As a result, the census cannot be taken as a literal description of the size or structure of the population. However, the inability to measure fertility, dependency ratios, or death rates precisely does not necessarily decrease its value as widely descriptive—once we make allowances for known sources of error or misrepresentation.

Some Examples

Table 15.1 summarizes the age and sex structure extracted from a 1918 report on the population of five districts in the central highlands (Huambo, Sambo, Lepi, Quipeio, and Cuima). Given that even a cursory glance at the columns showing proportions reveals that male and female populations were substantially different, it is appropriate to examine the age-specific sex ratios (men per 100 women) in the last column.

TABLE 15.1
Age and Sex Distribution, Huambo, 1918

| Age | Males | | Females | | Sex Ratios |
	Proportion Age x	Proportion Under Age x	Proportion Age x	Proportion Under Age x	
Under 10	20.5	20.5	18.7	18.7	99.5
10-20[a]	22.2	42.7	21.5	40.2	93.8
20-30	20.8	63.5	25.3	65.5	74.6
30-40	21.3	84.4	19.8	85.3	97.4
40-50	10.4	95.2	9.2	94.5	104.1
50-60	2.6	7.8	3.0	7.5	78.6
60-70	1.3	99.1	1.4	98.9	82.1
70-80	0.6	99.7	0.9	99.8	62.3
80-90	0.1	99.8	0.1	99.9	0.2

a. The census takers placed people in these age categories, even though people aged 20, 30, 40, and so on were technically placed in two groups. In all probability, of course, the categories were 0-9, 10-19, and so on, or 0-10, 11-20, and so on.

Perhaps the most distinctive feature of the raw data is that they do not form the familiar age pyramid of a model life table. Children under 10 are fewer than older age groups until ages 40 to 50. For males, the age group 30 to 40 is also larger than the group 20 to 30, and for females the 20 to 30 group is the largest age category of all. In short, there is a marked "bulge" in age distribution between 10 and 40, most pronounced in the 30 to 40 age group for males and in the 20 to 30 age group for females.

Some of the bulge may be explained by official desires to maximize the age group eligible for taxation and forced labor, but probably not all. First of all, this manipulation would be relevant only in the 10 to 20 versus the 20 to 30 age groups, but would not effect the 30 to 40 or older groups, which are also quite large. Moreover, such distortions would normally not apply to females, who were not then eligible for forced labor. (After 1918 women *were* required to work, mostly building roads ABC 23/514/3 April 1920; in 1919, for example, local sobas accused the chefe of Arma of "mistreatment, violence and extortion," noting that he ordered women, some of whom were pregnant, to Huambo to work as forced laborers [CDIH 76/Bailundo 1/1919]). However, females as well as males show the "bulge." We assume, therefore, that the unusually large number of people in these age groups had a historic cause, and was not simply a product of zealous census takers.

HISTORY AND DEMOGRAPHY IN CENTRAL ANGOLA

A better way to explain the unusual sex and age distribution of the 1918 data is to place them in their historical context. Similar age-sex distributions may result from different causes. In the absence of better numeric data, our analysis relies on an interpretation of the probable demographic impact of various events that were known to have taken place within the lifetimes of the people counted in 1918.

The bulge in age groups 20 to 50 might have several causes—an increase in mortality of young children; events that interrupted fertility, leading to fewer births; and/or recent migration of young adults without children. This last cause seems to be the one that produced the 1918 distribution, for one of the most significant patterns of the nineteenth century was the great influx of slaves to the highlands. The midnineteenth century, which brought official abolition of the Atlantic slave trade, did not bring an end to the inmigration of slaves in the central highlands. Ovimbundu active in a variety of "legitimate" trades involving ivory, wax, and rubber often used profits to acquire slaves, who in turn made it possible for traders to found towns, purchase political titles, acquire followers, and generally increase production (Heywood, 1984: ch. 4). Since many of these slaves were female, the tendency of the population to grow through natural increase was probably enhanced as well, although it should be noted that many of these females were involved in polygamous marriages that may have showed potential growth (Caminho de Ferro de Benguela, hereafter CFB; Relatório as Serviços de Exploração, hereafter Exploração).

A survey of the few decades before Portuguese conquest reveals an expanding population with great potential for productive development, deeply involved in trade. Long-distance trade involved what people called "rich products." Short-distance commerce in grain and vegetables, or "poor products," linked the rich agricultural lands of the highlands to the agriculturally poor coastal towns, especially Benguela. Both trades involved substantial numbers of people (Heywood, 1984: ch. 8).

This caravan commerce often entailed considerable risk, and probably increased mortality, especially among adult males, although toward the end of the century females increasingly followed the trading parties and were exposed to similar dangers (Heywood, 1984: ch. 6). Yet increased mortality was probably not sufficient to offset the effects of the influx of slaves. The caravan trade also contributed to the spread of disease, a result of the large numbers of people who circulated between the interior and the coast; several smallpox epidemics swept the plateau in the last decade of the nineteenth century. But despite these negative factors, mortality was probably not pronounced enough to offset the growth that resulted from the influx of women of childbearing age.

The same may be said for wars, which on the whole were in decline as the population turned from slave and cattle raiding to commerce, refusing at times to take part in conflict that interfered with commerce (Heywood, 1984). Even the Portuguese wars of conquest from 1890 to 1906 were short and relatively bloodless, save for a few sharp engagements (Heywood, 1984).

Although the highlands were generally well watered, occasional droughts might have had a demographic impact, although famine-induced deaths were probably few. One administrator noted that 1000 people died in a drought in his district in 1915, 2.5 per thousand (CDIH 103/Huambo 13/7 January 1916). Drought still may explain some of the features of the 1918 population. A drought struck southern and central Angola in 1915 as Portuguese troops and their Ovimbundu porters were invading the German colony of Southwest Africa (modern Namibia), resulting in the deaths of thousands of porters. Correspondence from the governor-general himself reassured the minister of colonies in 1916 that reports of up to 50,000 deaths were exaggerated (Arquivo Histórico Ultramarino [hereafter AHU] 2/6/706, 31 March 1916). However, the negative impact of this drought may have been partially offset by inmigration of people to the fairly secure highlands from the drought-prone south and east. Many of these people accepted slave status to escape starvation (CDIH 73/3 Relatório Sambo, 1938). The combination of male losses in the south and the immigration of young women made childless by the drought may also be factors contributing to the age and sex distribution of 1918.

Thus immigration and, to a lesser degree, mortality in disasters can probably account for the peculiar structure of the highlands population in 1918. The age group under age 40, the oldest in the "bulge," would have been born after 1878, while the youngest of the 10 to 20 age group, the last of the disproportionately large cohorts, would have been born in 1908 and shortly before. Portuguese administration in eastern Angola and the highlands would have tended to slow the migration of slaves to the highlands (although not as much as propaganda on the end of the internal slave trade would suggest; the trade was still going on in the late 1920s if not beyond) (ABC 2/70/Bell, 7 January 1926).

The influx of females may explain the apparent dearth of males in the age group 20 to 30 (sex ratio, 74.6 males for 100 females), although the ratios in older age groups ought to be equally unbalanced and are not. In part this is probably due to the absence of males in the last years of long-distance rubber trade. Although this trade was greatly damaged by the competition from Asian plantations in the early twentieth century, World War I gave a renewed impetus to the collection of wild rubber (Estatística Comercial, 1916: 107-195). Moreover, men in this age group would be most likely to flee tax assessors. They were accustomed to moving freely about the district and beyond, and networks that supported mobility were well developed. Finally, men of this age group would have been particularly hit by the 1915-1916 famine; their depletion may well reflect this demographic catastrophe. For example, a report for Chitembe noted that of a total of 3000 Africans who had died of hunger during the drought, 60 percent were men and only 25 percent women (even though women outnumbered men in the population at large); only 15 percent of the dead were children (CDIH 103/Huambo 13/1 February 1916).

Whatever its causes, the demographic perspective for the central highlands suggested by the age and sex distribution of 1920 was encouraging. The labor force was large, and the dependent population, both young and old, was proportionately reduced by the bulge in able-bodied age groups. Although theoretically such a blessing might have later become a burden when this group became too old to work and joined the dependent population, the impact would be muted by high mortality after age 50.

In addition, the population was not dense. Figures recorded by the 1918 assessments ranged from 4.6 people per square kilometer for Cuima district to 11.2 people per square for Quipeio, the most densely populated (CDIH 75/2/Huambo, 1918). Calculations in relation to the amount of arable land reveal differences from one district to another: When their considerable mountain wastelands are subtracted, densities in Samba and Cuima ran to around 5 people per square kilometer. The more open country of Quipeio and Lepi counted 11 people per square kilometer. The terrain of Huambo, with 7 people per square kilometer, lay between the extremes. The fact that there was no land shortage is partially confirmed by the 1922 survey, which shows every household working 2 hectares of land.

Moreover, the people of the early 1920s were fairly wealthy. The 1922 survey shows that virtually all households had some small stock. Larger stock, especially cattle, were much rarer and tended to be concentrated in the hands of the richest people. Much of this stock was lost to Portuguese raiding and tax collection after 1905; the wars of conquest were as much rustling expeditions as military conflicts (Heywood, 1984: ch. 8).

Long-range Portuguese policy, almost from the conquest, was to make the central highlands a center for white colonization. In its more grandiose moments, the plan conceived of white farmers owning the land and working it with the labor of Ovimbundu smallholders in a model similar to that of other colonies in East and South Africa (Heywood, 1984). However, long before such a scheme could be put in place, the area needed to yield revenue, and in products that had a better future (and over which the government could exercise more control) than wild rubber or wax. The production and export of maize and, to a lesser degree, beans and wheat served this purpose.

The Ovimbundu had long exported foodstuffs to coastal towns, and were quite capable of redirecting energy devoted to trading and carrying to farming. When the Benguela Railway Company, originally meant to carry copper from Katanga and Northern Rhodesia to the Atlantic coast, reached the highlands in 1911, it provided an ideal transportation outlet for maize. In the two decades before the railroad began to carry copper, maize shipments provided the bulk of tonnage. This dovetailed with the colonial government's interest in revenue. Moreover, protestant missionaries provided technical assistance in the belief that a farming population would be an ideal Christian community. The result was a major boom in maize exports. By 1920 maize became the major revenue earner for the central highlands (and indeed was second in value only to coffee for the whole colony) (Estatística Comercial, 1920: 167-195). At the same time, the central highlands, with its large population, provided the Angolan government with the bulk of its tax revenues (CFB, 1920: 12).

The colonial government, however, saw Ovimbundu maize growing as only temporary, and continued to dream of white settlers dominating the agricultural life of the colony. Land grants provided for Portuguese to settle and begin to farm in the highlands, but it was impossible for them to compete with African maize producers, even when land laws and marketing arrangements heavily favored the colonists (BO 37/15 September 1930: 603-604). Failing to compete in agriculture, most Portuguese concentrated on retailing consumer goods in exchange for agricultural products.

By the mid-1920s travelers in the highlands noted a well-established pattern—African maize growers, some fairly prosperous, and a significant number of white settlers who depended largely on the purchase of peasant produce. But the declaration of the "Estado Novo" by Antonio Salazar in Portugal in 1927 brought policies that would eventually alter this situation. Policies that would turn Angola into a "corporate state" modeled on Fascist Italy lagged behind similar developments in Portugal. Nonetheless, the establishment of a centralized banking system in 1927 (União dos Bancos Ultramarinos [hereafter UBU] Benguela, 1927: 13) and a marketing board in 1933 to monopolize purchase of African agricultural production and to maintain low prices successfully redistributed profits away from peasants in favor of the state and large exporters (BO 39/30 September 1933: 775-778).

THE END OF AFRICAN PROSPERITY: DEMOGRAPHIC REFLECTIONS

However unfavorable these developments might have been to the Ovimbundu peasants, they did not change the basic structure of production or of population. Small family holdings still produced maize for export and indeed remained somewhat prosperous. The more successful peasant farmers obtained plows and even carts, and adopted more modern agricultural techniques thanks to missionary encouragement of Christian smallholders (ABC Reports 1930-1939/2/76/Currie Institute, 1933; ABC Letters 1930-1939/2/497/4 September 1939: 2). Only when the export economy in the highlands began to turn from maize did the colonial government begin to realize its original plans of settler-dominated agriculture fed by Ovimbundu labor.

The shift in favor of large-scale enterprise, and the simultaneous requirement for a larger labor pool, weakened the peasant economy. This was especially true as production shifted to plantation crops such as sugar and sisal (Estatística Comercial, 1932: 125-140). No one envisioned the elimination of maize farmers because their contribution to domestic consumption allowed employers to save on wage bills. More important, however, the majority of Portuguese still engaged in retailing, and their interests in local production and trade certainly prevented the government from eliminating peasant production altogether. The most significant demographic impact resulted from the erosion of an independent peasantry and an increase in migrant labor. The resulting absence of males undermined Ovimbundu subsistence farming.

Unfortunately, we cannot trace the demographic effects of these policies in detail, for the period that followed 1925 did not generate the type of data that allowed us to examine the situation in 1918. Demographic assessments of the Ovimbundu from 1925 to 1950 reflected both the changing economy and government policies and attitudes. It is clear that the primary purpose of the annual *recensamentos* conducted by local administrators after 1930 was to ascertain the size and structure of the male labor pool. Instead of the regular age groups of the censuses of 1914 to 1925, the population was now divided into three age groups: 12 and under, 13 to 18, and "adult" (by sex). The purpose was to get an idea of the present and immediately forecastable labor force.

An examination of the figures of a large number of these censuses between 1935 and 1945 reveals similarities (CDIH 33/22/3). First of all, males seem to outnumber females greatly, and the numbers in the 13 to 18 group and adult groups are unusually large, at least when we compare them to the earlier census. This gap, however, unlike the earlier distortions of the age pyramid, is probably a product of census-taking methodology and not the result of demographic history. Second, reports of village visits mention that a large percentage of people (mostly women) were absent in the fields or hiding to avoid payment of taxes; their numbers were only estimated (CDIH, Relatório Anual, Bailundo). Finally, the wild fluctuations in the number of women and children among regions suggests that they were counted carelessly.

The most telling demonstration of probable distortions in the annual recensamentos between 1935 and 1950 can be shown by comparing the age and sex data in the 1940 administrative recensamento for the *Posto* of Mungo (Huambo district) with data from the 1940 census, which was methodologically more correct. The 1940 administrative data listed 9,011 adult males over 18 (both able-bodied and disabled), while the census found 7,864 in the same age category. On the other hand, while the census found 8,140 male children under 12, the administration found only 6,627. The same problem appears in comparing the male and female populations. Whereas the administration counted 8,023 females over age 18 (as against 9,011 males), the census found 12,676 females in the same group (CDIH 103/Bailundo: Província de Angola, 1941: vol. 3, 244). Most posts reported equally great discrepancies. The same tendency seems to have continued for the whole period, as can be judged by comparing the 1947 administrative report on population and the 1950 census (Província de Angola, 1951: vol. 3, 234; CDIH 78/Huambo 3/10 Recensamento, 31 December 1947). As a guide to the numbers of males in age groups

TABLE 15.2
Age and Sex Distribution, Huambo, 1940

	Males		Females		
Age	Proportion Age x	Proportion Under Age x	Proportion Age x	Proportion Under Age x	Sex Ratios
Under 10	34.3	34.3	29.3	29.3	98.3
10-19	24.7	59.0	20.6	49.9	101.7
20-29	13.4	72.4	16.3	66.2	68.8
30-39	12.0	84.4	14.2	80.4	71.1
40-49	7.5	91.9	9.9	90.3	63.5
50-59	3.7	95.6	4.4	94.7	70.7
60-69	2.3	97.9	2.9	97.6	67.8
70-79	1.2	99.1	1.2	98.8	86.6
over 80	0.9	100.00	1.0	99.8	79.2

vulnerable to labor recruitment, the administrative assessments are probably reasonably accurate, but as an indication of the overall demography of the highlands, they are not particularly useful.

The 1940 Census

In contrast to the recensamentos, a great deal of information can be gleaned about the demographic evolution of the Ovimbundu under twenty years of colonial rule by an examination of the results of the First General Census of Population in 1940. Unlike the administrative reports, the 1940 enumeration was conducted according to the norms of census taking, and attempted to assess accurately the size and composition of the total population, and not just the labor force. Table 15.2 shows the population structure of Huambo district in 1940 (Provincia de Angola, 1941: vol. 3, 234), presented in the same age groups as in 1918. Although district borders changed slightly, in its demographic characteristics it is substantially the same population.

Perhaps the most visible change is the disappearance of the bulge in the adult age groups of the 1910s, and the appearance of a more "normal" pyramidal age structure. Most of the advantages of a low dependency ratio have disappeared. Such would be the expected outcome of fairly high rates of natural increase, which would produce a younger population. And the population structure suggested by the 1918 census would tend to promote a rapid growth rate, despite fairly low fertility. Polygamy seems as exceptional in the 1940s as earlier, being largely restricted to chiefs, who benefited from expansion in agriculture, and who could use the extra labor. One enumeration shows that of a total of 127 such persons, 46 had between 2 and 7 wives. Those with only 1 wife usually fell in the youngest age category—presumably as they gained status they would increase their households (CDIH 33/19/26 Registro biografico, Huambo, 1946). This correlation between age and economic position did not differ much from that of the nineteenth century.

Dependency ratios did change, however. In 1918 a working population (males and females aged 15-60) of 75,066 was looking after a dependent population (males and females aged 0-14 and over 60) of 37,029, giving a very favorable ratio of 49.3 dependents for every 100 workers. In 1940, however, the situation had gone from favorable to quite unfavorable, with the census finding 269,636 dependent people for a working population of 271,712, or 99.2 dependents per 100 workers.

A second fact emerges from the age-specific sex ratios, for it is immediately obvious that in all groups over age 20, males are decidedly less numerous than females, and often substantially so. The same tendency was noted for 1918, but primarily in older age groups. Indeed, in 1918 the 30 to 50 age group had a more or less balanced sex ratio. It seems likely that the forced and migrant labor systems of the colonial government account for some of the change.

The impact of male migration on population structure can be gauged by examining migration statistics from the *Concelho* of Bailundo, a subunit of Huambo district. An administrative report of 1949 giving retrospective data on contract workers noted that in the census year of 1940, 4,019 workers were contracted for labor elsewhere (CDIH 25/31/13, 24 April 1949). Examining the 20 to 50 age group (prime ages of recruitment) in the 1940 census reveals that women outnumbered men by 27,143 (Província de Angola, 1940: vol. 3, 240). While this discrepancy covers only about 15 percent of the total missing males, one must remember that recruitment was usually for more than one year (often up to three), and the overall recruitment for 1938 to 1940 totaled 9,520. There was, moreover, unofficial (and officially discouraged) migration across colonial borders to Northern Rhodesia, South Africa, and the Belgian Congo.

Male-specific mortality may also have contributed to the differences. First of all, mortality among migrants, perhaps as much as 150 to 200 per thousand, affected the entire age group. In addition to mortality resulting from contract labor, especially high among migrants who left for the different climatic regime of the coast, there was the mortality among those engaged in shorter-range projects in the highlands. Although not migrants as far as census taking was concerned, their deaths might account for some of the missing men.

Workers on local farms, especially poorly funded farms run by Portuguese, rarely received their full rations of food or clothing (in a climate that could be quite cold), and were often seriously mistreated. A fairly objective German observer, Adolf Jessen (1933: 210-211), who crossed the highlands in 1931, noted that workers were poorly treated, and that even the well-capitalized companies fell short in supplying rations. North American missionaries in the 1940s also were shocked by the conditions faced by Ovimbundu workers. This led to poor health in Ovimbundu males. An official report from Mungo (Bailundo) in 1938 noted that often as many as half of potential labor recruits were rejected because of poor health; it also noted that the Ovimbundu had formerly been regarded as the "flower of the blacks" (CDIH 24/16/6, 1938). These factors are not quantifiable, but taken together they go a long way toward explaining the striking absence of males in Ovimbundu society in 1940.

The absence of males, along with population growth, contributed to the unfavorable dependency ratios calculated from the 1940 census. It adds another dimension to dependency as well, for it means that additional burdens fell on women; if our observations about male health are correct, even those who were available were less capable than they might otherwise have been.

The impact of the final implementation of the "Estado Novo" in the highlands is clearly shown in labor statistics compiled by the administrator of Bailundo in 1949 from records for the period from 1935 to 1948. He noted not only a dramatic rise in labor recruitment after 1945, but the increasing use of force. In 1935 some 1,680 recruits (all volunteers) were contracted for labor; although we do not know the size of the labor pool in 1935, it totaled 50,000 in 1948 (surely more than in 1935). In 1948, on the other hand, 8,497 men were recruited, or about 17 percent of the 50,764 males of working age (CDIH 25/31/13, 24 April 1949). Although such large-scale recruitment may have affected agricultural production, local administrators might have tried to blunt its impact by focusing on the people less valuable in agriculture, especially young, even underaged, males (CDIH 25/31/27, 22 February 1949).

CONCLUSION

Unlike the rosy picture that one might paint of the evolution of the Ovimbundu in 1918, the Ovimbundu in 1940 faced an uncertain future. Colonial policies that undermined maize growing and demanded migrant laborers in numbers double or even triple pre-1940 levels were to have a devastating effect in the decade that followed. The 1950s saw the Ovimbundu transformed from a quite independent, even prosperous, farming peasantry to a migrant labor reserve, used in every corner of Angola and even exported to Atlantic islands such as São Tomé. The effects of this change may be seen in the age-sex structure of 1950, which shows all the features of the 1940 census, but in worse measure. Colonial policy had thus transformed a potentially productive and healthy population into a hopeless pool of migrant workers.

16

CAPITAL, STATE, AND THE AFRICAN POPULATION OF JOHANNESBURG, 1921-1980

MICHAEL P. PROCTOR

Johannesburg has, for many decades, been recognized as the dominant economic center of southern Africa (see Map 6) comprising the largest concentration of people and capitalist enterprise in the subcontinent. As Johannesburg changed from mining camp to metropolis, so the African population[1] altered from one dominated by men to one increasingly characterized by settled families. This essay consists of a discussion of the change in the structure of the African population of Johannesburg in two parts: The first identifies trends through an examination of census data, and the second attempts to explain these trends.

THE AFRICAN POPULATION OF JOHANNESBURG 1921-1980

Although it has been state policy to conduct national censuses every ten years, this has occurred only since 1960; earlier comprehensive national censuses were taken in 1921, 1936, 1946, and 1951. Although official census data are viewed skeptically by many academics, they are useful in confirming or questioning aspects of theory (Simkins, 1983). It is not my intention to regard the census figures as absolutes: Underenumeration is acknowledged. Rather, the broader evolution of the population, as depicted by the censuses, is my chief concern.

The structure of the African population of Johannesburg has changed dramatically since the city's establishment in 1886. Age and

Author's Note: Thanks go to Gordon Pirie and Charles van Onselen for comments on earlier drafts and to Wendy Job, who prepared the figures.

TABLE 16.1
The Age/Sex Structure of the African Population
of Johannesburg, 1921-1980

	1921	1936	1946	Year 1951	1960	1970	1980
Population							
male[a]	104,783	168,130	247,275	277,533	350,831	429,636	548,170
female[a]	13,570	60,992	139,900	187,733	298,202	390,070	491,672
Sex ratio	772	276	178	148	118	110	111
Percentage under 15							
males	4	9	13	17	27	30	25
females	25	27	26	29	34	34	28
Percentage 15-54							
males	95[b]	89	83	79	68	63	66
females	73[b]	70	69	67	61	60	64
15-54 as percentage of total population							
males	84[b]	65	53	47	37	33	35
females	8[b]	19	25	27	28	28	30
both sexes	93[b]	84	78	74	65	61	65
Annual rate of increase	—	4.5	5.4	3.7	3.8	2.4	2.4

SOURCE: Population censuses, Government Printer, Pretoria.
a. Includes those of uncertain age.
b. Ages 15-50.

sex data for 1921 indicate a large predominance of men, 89 percent of the African population, 95 percent of whom were between the ages of 15 and 50. This predominance, which was probably even higher during the previous three decades, declines in every subsequent intercensal period until 1960, after which the proportion of men to women fluctuates slightly (see Table 16.1 and Figure 16.1). From constituting just over nine-tenths of the African population in 1921, the proportion of working-age African men declined to one-half by 1946 and to one-third by 1970. Preliminary figures for 1980 reveal that the proportion of men between the ages of 15 and 54 has increased, reversing the trend of almost a century. This alteration has not meant a reduction in the proportion of women of the same age group; rather, the proportion of children of each sex has diminished, indicating either lower fertility levels or an increase in the number of adult migrants in the city.

The age/sex structure of the Johannesburg African population has altered from one dominated by working-age men who, with working-age women, constituted 93 percent of the total population in 1921, to a structure that increasingly showed a rise in the proportion of both women and children under 15 (Figure 16.1). The 1970 data (Figure 16.1e) exhibit many of the characteristics of a settled, more permanent population. The 1970 pyramid also reveals that the male migrant laborer population is still present, although not in as significant numbers as in previous decades.

Although registration of births has been required by law for some decades, fertility data for the African population are scant and the census is not sufficiently accurate. Studies of urban African fertility (Unterhalter, 1955; Verster, 1965; Lotter, 1977) indicate that fertility has remained high: 44.4 per thousand in 1953, 37.5 per thousand in 1963, although a minority of African women with longer formal education have tended to exhibit lower fertility. Mortality rates, especially for infants, are equally difficult to determine, but remain particularly high for the African population.

The increase in the proportion of children under 15 and in the proportion of women over successive census periods is an indication of the increase in the number of people living under family conditions in Johannesburg. This dramatic shift, from a predominance of working-age men to a more "normal" population structure, is the result of forces that include the changing nature of capitalist enterprise in Johannesburg, changing legislation by the state to control the movement and settlement of Africans, and the attempts of African people to control the quality and direction of their lives. These forces are discussed below within two broad periods: the segregationist period before 1946, and the apartheid period between 1946 and 1980. The discussion begins with the legislative background to labor coercion and the migrant labor system, which has been vital for the particular form of the South Africa economy.

THE CREATION OF THE MIGRANT LABOR SYSTEM

Extraeconomic forms of coercing people into wage labor in southern Africa date back to the early 1800s (Legassick, 1975). Rural African men were proletarianized and encouraged to remain in wage employment by vagrancy laws, taxes (Rex, 1974), and regulations regarding employment contracts. Pass laws in the mid-1890s were partly framed by mine owners (Kahn, 1949) in an attempt to reduce desertions, but they were not always successful: 14,000 miners

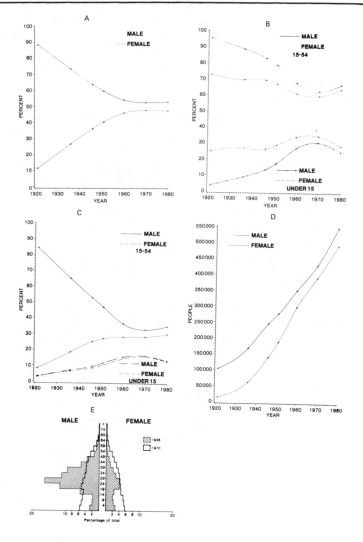

SOURCE: Population censuses, Government Printer, Pretoria.
a. Sex structure.
b. Proportion of sex under 15 and 15-54.
c. Proportion of total under 15 and 15-54, by sex.
d. African population growth in Johannesburg.
e. African age/sex structure, 1936 and 1970.

Figure 16.1   Demography of Johannesburg's African Population, 1921-1980

deserted from 33 mines in six months of 1897 (Kahn, 1949), an indication that wages and state regulations were insufficient to induce men to remain working and living under the conditions that then existed. The foundation of the migrant labor system that provided cheap labor to the mining industry was the existence of noncapitalist economies in the rural areas of Southern Africa. This largely agricultural sector, often of a peasant nature and a threat to early settler agriculture (Bundy, 1972), was one of the reasons for the imposition of extraeconomic pressure on men of working age to enter wage employment. This ensured that the major site of the reproduction of the African population, and thus the residence of African families, would be the rural areas and later the reserves. The necessity to coerce Africans to work on the mines and white farms contradicts theories that the backwardness of rural economies (Houghton, 1971) obliged Africans to seek wage employment (Wolpe, 1972; Legassick, 1975). Labor supply remained a problem for mine owners, however; between 1890 and 1910 most additional labor for the mines was recruited from Portuguese East Africa, and between 1902 and 1906 Chinese labor was indentured (Legassick, 1975).

Perhaps the most important legislation for the future of the migrant labor system was the Natives' Land Act (number 27 of 1913), which scheduled areas in which only Africans were allowed to purchase land. Although stated in terms of segregation of racial groups, the act ensured that wealthy Africans could not repurchase land owned by whites, but also that Africans would retain access, through the reserves and the African redistributive economies, to subsistence means of production, the cornerstone of the migrant labor system (Wolpe, 1972). The act also prohibited the practice of "farming on the half," or sharecropping, and although it did not prescribe eviction of such workers from white farms, it effectively restricted their access to independent production and forced many into the employ of white farmers (Wolpe, 1972; Plaatje, 1982).

Stated somewhat crudely, a supply of labor cheaper than would otherwise have been possible was facilitated by both the 1913 Natives' Land Act and its consequences for African access to means of production, and by migrant housing conditions in Johannesburg and other urban areas. The reserves allowed the extraction of increased surplus value from labor on the mines because part of the cost of reproducing the labor force was borne by the workers' families (Wolpe, 1972; Legassick, 1975; Erwin and Webster, 1978). Proletarianization in the country was thus structured by the existence of the noncapitalist sector, later limited to the reserves (Erwin and Webster, 1978; de Villiers,

1979b). Between 1900 and 1930 the surplus production of reserve areas dropped to sub-subsistence (Legassick, 1975), although the reserves continued to provide social services such as the care of children and of the aged. Urban compound and hostel accommodation, through the provision of basic material needs for the existence of migrant laborers, brought (and still afford) a high degree of "rationality," as economies of scale could be achieved in what would otherwise be an individual worker's spending pattern (Rex, 1974). A further advantage of the compound system was the control exercised by management that inhibited the emergence of major worker organizations (Rex, 1974).

1921-1946: Segregation

Legislation to complement the 1913 Natives' Land Act was enacted in 1923 after being delayed by World War I (Hellmann, 1949; Davenport, 1969). The Native (Urban Areas) Act (number 21 of 1923) appeared as a relatively mild bill in 1918: It contemplated freehold tenure for Africans in locations,[2] as well as the removal of the main causes of African objections to pass laws. But a select committee deleted these clauses as the result of pressure by members of Parliament who also opposed trading and other urban rights for Africans (Davenport, 1969). The act thus broadly followed the earlier Stallard Commission principles (Report of the Local Government Commission, 1921), which held that Africans were only temporarily resident in "white" areas and were to return to the reserves once they no longer ministered to the needs of the white population (Davenport, 1969). Sections of the act required the establishment of separate locations for African residence, the creation of a Native Revenue Account separate from that into which white rates and taxes were paid, and the regulation of beer brewing and African representation to the local authority (Davenport, 1969; Beavon, 1981). The act placed more emphasis on segregation than on influx control, ensuring that Africans were contained in easily controlled areas away from white centers (Lacey, 1981). As a result, legal African accommodation in Johannesburg would largely be limited to the bleak rows of mass-produced houses and hostels "provided" by the municipality 15 to 20 kilometers to the southwest.

Johannesburg adopted the Native (Urban Areas) Act regulations in 1924 (Davenport, 1969) at a time when the African population was characterized by men of working age, although the number of women *entering* the city was growing and, in fact, exceeded that of men.

Johannesburg was still dominated by the mining industry, although engineering and other mine-related enterprises were increasingly important. African urban life in Johannesburg continued with little alteration over the next decade: overcrowded inner-city slum yards and multiracial suburbs. Migrants stayed with families in these areas to avoid compound or hostel accommodation. Settlements also existed in the hills south of the city (Simkins, 1983), probably comprising families unable to secure accommodation in Johannesburg, and who found living near the city preferable to living in the reserves or on white farms. In 1933 the government proclaimed Johannesburg white, except for the African freehold areas west of the city (Sophiatown and surrounds). This proclamation made 43,000 Africans illegal residents in Johannesburg, and subject to eviction. When evicted, most moved to the relative freedom of the freehold townships as opposed to the municipal locations. A further attraction of the freehold areas was their proximity to the city; Johannesburg's location (present-day Soweto) was 15 to 20 kilometers away. Eventually, however, the townships became excessively overcrowded, so that by 1938 some 90 percent had moved to locations, compared to 12 percent in the early 1930s (Morris, 1980).

During the interwar years African women, who had little access to cash wages in the rural areas, increasingly migrated to urban areas, entering domestic employment; their income supplemented that of men and made urban family life sustainable (Freund, 1985). As much of the influx-control legislation was not rigidly applied in Johannesburg, and travel permits were not required by women, amendments were made to the Native (Urban Areas) Act and additional legislation was enacted. In 1930 the Native (Urban Areas) Act was amended and required that women obtain a certificate of approval to enter an urban area; access was made conditional on employment and accommodation (de Villiers, 1979b), and local authorities were given powers to remove unemployed Africans (Hellman, 1949). This put increased pressure on people in towns surrounding Johannesburg, and some moved to the city, where regulations were not as effectively enforced. Attempts also were made to halt the movement of labor from white farms to urban centers: The Native Service Contract Act (number 24 of 1932) required that Africans not living in a location produce a document signed by the owner of the land on which they lived before being employed elsewhere (Kahn, 1949). Penalties for farm labor desertions were increased, and families became collectively responsible for work on farms (Kahn, 1949). These acts were not popular in the cities because they limited the mobility of labor. By 1937, only eleven towns had made use of the 1930 legislation. It became compulsory in 200 urban areas in that year (including Johannesburg; Kahn, 1949) in an attempt to stem the immigration of African women and to ensure that African families remained in the reserves or on white farms.

By 1937 the major structures that have made Africans a more exploitable stratum of the working class had been created. Farming and mining interests, once in conflict, now cooperated to exploit African labor, although secondary industry continued to pay relatively higher wages than the other sectors (Lacey, 1981). Influx-control regulations were not strictly enforced in Johannesburg, positively influencing the boom in secondary industry that occurred in the twelve years after 1933, enhancing the predominance of African men in the industrial work force (Freund, 1985). In 1942 influx-control measures were relaxed as the need for labor in urban areas during the war years grew (Kahn, 1949: Morris, 1980). In order to reduce the hardship associated with carrying a pass for some Africans, pass exemptions (passes, nonetheless) were issued to those Africans of "good character." By the end of 1946 23,500 such exemptions had been issued in Johannesburg (Kahn, 1949), constituting 46 percent of all such exemptions in the Union and an indication of the number of "formally" educated Africans resident in Johannesburg. These exemptions eased conditions for a privileged minority who were largely part of what was then identified as a "conservative" middle class (Hellmann, 1949), many of whom lived in settled family units.

During the 1920s and 1930s the state had not only involved itself in the control of the labor force, but also helped turn the economy away from being simply externally oriented (Erwin and Webster, 1978). World War I stimulated the growth of secondary industry, which was later protected by the Customs Tariff and Excise Duties Amendment Act (number 36 of 1925; Stent, 1948). This altered the form of dependence of the South African economy on the industrial core and, although it promoted a more indigenous process of accumulation (Saul and Gelb, 1981), was not contrary to the interests of the center's capitalists (Erwin and Webster, 1978). The 1940s saw greater state attention to the systematic planning of the economy, especially with regard to secondary industry (Legassick, 1974), which was concentrated at the three major ports and around Johannesburg (Stent, 1948), and benefited from the state policy of import substitution.

As Johannesburg grew, so did the number of families; but the African population remained dominated by migrant men until the 1940s. This segment of the labor force, often from outside the Union (Stent, 1948), was somewhat cyclical, unlike that of the 1950s and

1960s. During the latter half of the 1940s, "foreign" labor was removed from urban domestic employment, often to white farms, and replaced by African women. With the decline of mining activity in Johannesburg, the number of migrant men employed in this industry declined.

Population growth in Johannesburg led to an acute housing shortage from 1943, although African accommodation had been in short supply for some time and was an impediment to permanent residence. This situation was exacerbated by a Johannesburg City Council decision not to construct any new houses during 1943 and 1944 (Morris, 1980). In response to overcrowding and long waiting lists, and in an attempt to reduce costs associated with living in the urban area, squatter movements developed, drawn largely from subtenants of the municipal location (Stadler, 1979; Morris, 1980). During 1946, for example, a large group of squatters organized their own police force, levied taxes, and reserved sites for the erection of stores; the municipality provided temporary rudimentary water and sewerage facilities. The municipality broke the power of this squatter leadership by creating an alternative approved area under its control, implicitly acknowledging that its housing provision in terms of the Native (Urban Areas) Act was inadequate. Prior to moving to the new site, all squatters were "screened": Of the 8861 families processed, 90 percent were living in the area legally (Hellmann, 1949).

The growing number of African families, their demands on available infrastructure, the housing policy of the Johannesburg Council, and the squatter movements provoked debate in the mid-1940s over the responsibilities of both the Council and the employers of labor. The Council maintained that Africans did not earn wages that allowed them to pay economic rents, and that through the Council the local community was subsidizing industries whose employees lived in municipal locations (Hellman, 1949). Johannesburg, along with other local authorities, was dissatisfied with the scheme under which it shared the loss on financing subeconomic housing construction with the central state—a dissatisfaction that limited its provision of housing. In an effort to generate revenue for housing construction the Council operated a beer monopoly from 1937, although African representatives opposed this practice as a concealed tax. In the 1940s, African workers replaced whites in the construction of African housing to reduce the cost of the wage bill (Hellmann, 1949). Despite these measures, by 1948 the Native Revenue account had a deficit of several hundred thousand pounds that had to be balanced by the (white) General Revenue Account (de Villiers, 1979a).

1946-1980: Apartheid

Partially prompted by the crisis surrounding African urban housing following the war, the government appointed a committee to examine influx control. The Fagan Report (Report of the Native Laws Commission, 1946-1948), although toying with scrapping influx control provisions, supported migrant labor and differentiation between races (Legassick, 1974; Saul and Gelb, 1981). Hence the accession to power of the National Party in 1948 and the development of its apartheid policies did not initially bring a dramatic alteration from earlier years (Legassick, 1974; Saul and Gelb, 1981). The Nationalists responded to the crisis by tightening influx control, facilitating labor allocation through national labor bureaus, and promoting Afrikaner capital (Saul and Gelb, 1981) and secondary industry (Legassick, 1974). The industrial wage bill was reduced through the floating of the color bar with white union approval (Legassick, 1974) in an attempt to increase the ratio of African workers to whites. White workers filled the growing number of skilled and supervisory positions and the consumer market expanded, further promoting industry. Although this crisis was resolved, the foundation was laid for its resurgence in the 1970s (Saul and Gelb, 1981).

African wages in the postwar period fell as the demand for labor decreased. Labor unrest increased as did unionization (Saul and Gelb, 1981): African mineworkers struck in 1946 during a period when strikes by Africans were illegal (Legassick, 1974). The estimated 40,000 largely male "illegal" foreign Africans in Johannesburg in 1946 (Hellman, 1949) were probably also responsible for undercutting wages. The influx of "illegal" or unqualified workers was a problem that the state confronted in 1946 with emergency powers restricting the travel of unemployed Africans by train on certain lines (Hellman, 1949). In 1949, the registration of contracts with the state, and subsequently with local authorities, attempted to ensure that only "legal" workers were employed in municipal areas. This, together with the closing of the Reef to African influx, reduced even further the legal security of the majority of the urban population of the Witwatersrand. Johannesburg remained something of a refuge for Africans unable to live in nearby towns (Simkins, 1983).

In the early 1950s, new legislation attempted to assist local authorities in financing housing and services in locations; the Bantu Building Workers Act (number 27 of 1951) confirmed the use of Africans for the construction of housing, and the Bantu Services Levy Act (number 64 of 1952) required all employers of African labor who resided in locations to contribute to a central fund. Site and service schemes were introduced in Johannesburg in 1954 and squatter areas gradually cleared. In 1956 mining capital negotiated a loan for the Johannesburg City Council that allowed the construction of 14,000 new houses and additional slum clearance (Hlophe, 1977). The proportion of Africans living under family conditions in Johannesburg increased to 53 percent, 8 percent above the national average in urban areas (Simkins, 1983), and significantly above the proportions in the towns to the east and west. The western freehold townships, once something of a refuge from the municipal locations, were demolished between 1955 and 1963 and their residents settled in the locations they had previously avoided (Proctor, 1979). Restrictions also were extended to limit the number of workers staying in segregated quarters atop buildings in the "white" city and in domestic workers' rooms in the suburbs, reducing the opportunities for casual employment. Along with the boom in the construction of family housing in locations went further segregation; in 1951 separate housing areas for different ethnic groups was introduced (Pirié, 1984), accompanied by the beginning of devolution of political power in the reserves to Africans themselves (Rex, 1974). This marked a change in the dominant ideology, which now perceived the country's population as a number of minorities (Legassick, 1974). Consolidation of African residential areas was accompanied by the introduction of Section 10(1)(a), (b), and (c) "rights," which gave those who qualified more security because their legal presence in urban areas was no longer dependent on employment (Davenport, 1969). However, pass regulations were extended to women by the Black (Abolition of Passes and Coordination of Documents) Act (number 67 of 1952); such action had been discussed before, but not attempted on a national scale.

The major concern of the new central government during the 1950s was the reduction of the dependence of urban industry on migrant labor by the promotion of a stable urban population and an urban labor preference policy (Posel, 1984), supplemented by the expansion in family accommodation and the legislation of residence rights. The urban labor preference policy complemented the government's border industry policy, which encouraged capital-intensive manufacture in urban centers and labor-intensive production in areas bordering on the reserves. The need for semiskilled and skilled settled labor by secondary industry clashed with the need for migrant labor in mining and farming; the government's border industry policy exacerbated this contradiction (Legassick, 1974).

Organized commerce and industry were known to work outside the labor policy and employ cheaper migrant labor, an indication of less harmony between state and capital than existed before 1948 (Freund, 1985). Something of a reversal occurred in the 1960s when the state, concerned by the anomaly of the Section 10(1) rights, reduced the security earlier given to urban Africans by applying sections allowing the removal of "idle and undesirable" Africans to those with "permanent" residence rights (Davenport, 1969; Posel, 1984). The government intended all Africans to have temporary status while commerce and industry increasingly employed settled Africans in skilled and semiskilled positions (Posel, 1984). The earlier promotion of settled urban labor was perhaps encouraged by the *relatively* large number of openings for African workers. For example, two Africans entered industrial employment for every white between 1949-1950 and 1953-1954 (Pursell, 1968). The subsequent decrease in employment opportunities—only one African gained employment in industry for every two whites between 1958-1959 and 1961-1962 (Pursell, 1968)—and the increase in African urban unemployment may have encouraged the state to reassert its control by reducing the security of the African population in urban areas, allowing the unemployed to be removed to "homeland" areas.

After concern following the Sharpeville killings subsided, most of the 1960s witnessed an expansion of the economy, with large sums of foreign investment fueling the boom (Saul and Gelb, 1981). However, African unemployment remained high, increasing by 118 percent above 1953-1958 levels (Pursell, 1968); the number of employment opportunities open to Africans also decreased. Partly as a result, the 1960s showed a reduction in the trend toward African families in Johannesburg and a stabilization in the sex ratio, with slight male dominance.

Fewer houses were built after 1958 (Morris, 1980), and the Black Laws Amendment Act (number 76 of 1963) further increased restrictions on temporary African residents in white areas (Morris, 1980). To ensure that African families without a male head did not remain in urban areas, African women were barred from Johannesburg house waiting lists in 1967 (Morris, 1980). In June 1968, similar regulations made housing permits for men under 21 years of age conditional on continued employment (Morris, 1980). The policy of 30-year leasehold was withdrawn in 1968 with the intention that all location housing would be rented. Urban residence rights contained in the Native (Urban Areas) Act were also undermined (Davenport, 1969; Posel, 1984). Both further decreased the security of the urban African population. In an attempt to prevent the employment of unqualified labor and thus inhibit immigration, the Physical Planning and Utilisation of Resources Act (number 88 of 1967) placed the responsibility for employing legal workers on employers and not on municipalities or the African workers (Legassick, 1974).

With the intention of making labor allocation and the regulation of African urban life more "efficient," the central state assumed the duties of the local authorities in 1971 through the creation of 21 Bantu Affairs Administration Boards with jurisdictions larger than those of local governments. The boards inaugurated direct central government intervention in the running of African locations and thus highly visible involvement in the reproduction and management of the urban African population. Subsequent African opposition, often violent, has encouraged the devolution of control of visible services onto African Community Councils.

Government policy returned to the promotion of a stable and permanent urban African population during the 1970s and 1980s, partly because of the increasingly evident contradictions of racial capitalism. These contradictions include the relatively small size of the white consumer market, the high rate of African unemployment, and the shortage of skilled labor (Davies, 1979; Saul and Gelb, 1981). Attempts to deal with this crisis included expanding the consumer market to include part of the African population employed in skilled positions. This policy may well exacerbate unemployment and raise the cost of imported technology (Saul and Gelb, 1981). The reintroduction of leasehold for a 99-year period has also encouraged the entrenchment of an elite within the African population—a well-defined class of semiskilled, skilled, and managerial workers needed by the increasingly sophisticated industrial and commercial operations in Johannesburg. In addition to these measures, some restrictions placed earlier on African businesspeople have been reduced in an attempt to allow the emergence of a trader/consumer class. African entrepreneurs are no longer restricted with regard to the size and number of businesses they may own, but are still limited to areas defined as African by the Group Areas Act (number 41 of 1950) (Morris, 1980).

Monopoly capital, through the Urban Foundation, has lobbied the government in an attempt to relax certain restrictions as well, especially those limiting Africans in skilled and managerial positions. Its major undertakings have been limited to Johannesburg and other large urban areas: Examples include an electrification project began in Soweto early in the 1980s, and modern family houses that will be made available to the minority of Africans who can afford them. Such developments have not benefited the majority of the urban African population. The structures of apartheid embodied in segregationist legislation continue to allow control of the African working class, relocating the surplus population to the African "homelands" where half now live in "urban" areas that have few employment opportunities (Freund, 1984). Contrary to the situation that prevailed earlier in the century, families in such areas, where no significant agriculture is permitted, are now often assisted materially by those working in "white" urban areas.

CONCLUSION

The evolution of the urban African population of Johannesburg has been largely determined by the changing nature of the local economy on the Reef. Once dominated by mining and its demand for cheap labor power, Johannesburg is now the center of commerce and an important site of secondary industry. The increasingly modern manufacturing sector has, while continuing to employ migrants, also needed more skilled and semiskilled labor than can be supplied by the white population (Davies, 1979; Posel, 1984). The employment of Africans in these positions has exacerbated unemployment and the high cost of imported technology (Saul and Gelb, 1981), but has enlarged the consumer market and created a permanent and relatively advantaged African population in Johannesburg. State and capital have, largely through control and manipulation of African labor (the more exploitable section of the working class), been influential in shaping Johannesburg's African population structure. But by forming squatter and community organizations, by willfully disobeying laws, by striking, and by popular violence, this population has expressed its demands and influenced its own form. The 1976 uprisings, the labor unrest, and the continued violence in the urban areas during the 1980s indicate that the African population will increasingly decide on the circumstances under which it is willing to live in South Africa.

NOTES

1. Here the word "African" denotes people the South African government calls "Black"; "Black" denotes those classified "Black," "Indian," or "Coloured" by the South African state.

2. The term "location" denotes an African dormitory area or "township" that has little of the infrastructure or amenities found in a white suburb.

PART VI

CONCLUSION

17

TOWARD A HISTORICAL SOCIOLOGY
OF POPULATION IN ZAÏRE
Proposals for the Analysis of
the Demographic Regime

Knowledge and understanding of the reconstitution of human population often takes two routes that are needlessly compartmentalized: demometrics and population history. The first, faithful to the positivist tradition, refuses to go beyond the recording and formalized manipulation of observable demographic behavior; the second, in contrast, frequently takes the avenue of conceptual history, and from its lofty perch tends to forget reality. Along with the other contributors to this volume (who are in other ways better qualified for the task and also call on quantification), I want to contribute to a historical sociology of African population (Wallerstein, 1977).[1] It seems to me unthinkable to separate phenomena that are biological, such as childbirth or mortality, from the social and cultural or the political and economic. In a time when a discipline as "rational" as Western medicine integrates the social dimensions of disease in its treatment, it seems impossible to separate so-called demographic phenomena from the history of the family, sexual relations, class relations, and so on. Total analysis is a dangerous ambition in the social sciences because it often leads to dilettantism and ignorance, and yet blind specialization is still more costly, because it implies an absence of social relevance.[2]

271

ARE HIGH BIRTHRATES "AUTHENTICALLY" AFRICAN?

To speak of a demographic regime characteristic of Africa, even if one refers only to precolonial sub-Saharan Africa, is not only an abuse of language, but proof of our ignorance of the past. Several contributors to this volume insist that nothing suggests that high fertility is anything more than an imaginary "African" trait (Mudimbe, 1984; Vansina, 1985). The notion of a demographic regime characterized by a high birthrate to compensate for a high morbidity rate and a limited ability to extract resources from the environment is but a reflection of the old image of a hostile Africa. At present the empirical data necessary to document the variety of African demographic regimes and their transformation are limited. However, historical information is ample enough to reject the idea of stagnation; the readiness of local institutions to manipulate the demographic regime is beginning to be documented. As with the myth of the "African as tribal being," or that of the antiquity of lineage relations, the proposition that associates "Africanity" and conservatism (Africa as a museum of natural history) was produced by the convergence of hypotheses based on the Western image of how Africans should be, supported by the political and social interests of privileged local informants, chiefs, and notables, installed by and integrated into the colonial administrations (Vansina, 1981; W. MacGaffey, 1983, 1985; Jewsiewicki, 1981a). The same convergence seems to be the basis for the apparent empirical proof (which exists only by extrapolation of the experience of the Occident) for the orientation of African social values toward maximal natality. Hence, an anachronism legitimizes a selection of facts whose historicity confers political meaning in conformity with the Western paradigm. African political actors, subjected to numerous surveys and participating actively in the game of power, have quickly grasped the role played by this historical discourse.

Having children was not always a dominant social value, as shown by the following example. In southern Africa, the groups that would become the Zulu experienced great economic prosperity in the second half of the eighteenth century. A half century of heavy and regular rainfall favored the adoption of corn, a major technological innovation. Growth of the population seems attributable not only to the direct effects of this economic change, but also to the gradual adaptation of social norms surrounding reproduction. Oral tradition speaks of a "relaxing of customs," which seems to indicate a lowering of the socially acceptable age of procreation. Expansion in cattle-holding and the agricultural transition, however, rendered local societies more vulnerable to a shift in climate at the outset of the nineteenth century. The breakdown of the agricultural base (corn has a higher yield than millet, but is much more fragile in the face of drought) led to increased reliance on herding and hunting. The overgrazing of pasture already undermined by drought and increased social conflict (over inequal access to cattle) emphasized the importance of controlling resources. A gap appeared between the available food resources and the high birthrate, the social heritage of prosperity. It was in this context that Shaka gave form to a social revolution: holding in common of the patrimony (cattle and pastureland),[3] temporary separation of units of reproduction from units of production and consumption, and political unification. The reform of military regiments endowed with cattle herds but living outside of the villages that constituted the units of production and reproduction permitted control of the birthrate (Marks, 1967; Smith, 1970; Guy, 1980; Omer-Cooper, 1966).

The Zulu case is not unique. The regiment is a form of social control, and even as an armed band, is quite widespread in Central Africa in the nineteenth century (Lloyd, 1978). But it is necessary to take into consideration the demographic regulation that was a feature of such state-directed socioeconomic intervention. It is in this perspective, and also in comparison with European demographic behavior, that changes in kinship and access to property and inheritance must be examined (to wit, the integration or not of "foreigners," the possibility of reproduction outside legal norms where access to property and inheritance is somewhat open). In addition, it is necessary to pay attention to the way that changes in political norms of descent that govern the processes of segmentation, concentration, migration, and so forth affected the demographic regime. Certain institutions, such as age-sets, allowed some control over the social mechanisms of reproduction. And apart from these examples, revolutions that undoubtedly affected demographic behavior would also include the West African *jihads,* the Chokwe and Ovimbundu migration/invasions, and the Sudanese-Egyptian penetration of Central Africa that put a slave-based economy in place (Vansina, 1982, 1983; Keim, 1979; Cordell, 1983b, 1985a; Jewsiewicki and Mumbanza mwa Bawele, 1981).

Finally, the hypothesis that slaves in Africa generally reproduced themselves at very low rates or not at all (Meillassoux, in press), suggests that political regulation of the social status of dependents was another way to manipulate socioeconomic and demographic behavior. The economy, whether it was based on slave raiding or on agricultural production using slave labor, would, in a regional perspective, have encouraged the attaching of high social value to childbirth, both among societies from which slaves were extracted and among those who received large numbers of captives (Meillassoux, 1983c). Insofar as both receiving and sending societies did not wish to lose their identities either through assimilation by other groups (including their own slaves) or through extinction, birthrates must have been pushed to the maximum; this is particularly so since a large part of the population— very large in nineteenth-century West Africa, for example—was excluded from reproduction. May we not suppose that the suppression of slavery generalized high rates of reproduction, formerly the "privilege" of free persons?

Modes of Reproduction and Modes of Production: Reflections on the Equatorial Basin

A relatively recent domestication of the ecological system of the equatorial forest imposed a particular demographic regime and probably explains why we find a great variety of forms of personal dependence, but almost no slavery, defined in terms of a mode of production (Harms, 1981, 1983b). Recent research shows that dispersed settlement patterns limited the adverse impact of pathogenic factors (Feierman, 1984). In the face of segmentation—indispensable, given that pathogenic factors limited population concentrations—and in the face of the small size of the fundamental social unit (the lineage), the assimilation of foreigners and the absorption of local groups weakened for one reason or another was the primary demographic process (Van Leynseele, 1979; Mumbanza mwa Bawele, 1980). The economic and social conversion of dependents into a distinct slave class hence was impossible because it would lead to the loss of their reproductive potential. Childbirth, because it was not a "privilege" of free persons, seems to have been less socially appreciated. Individual status depended especially on the ability to attract a group of dependents of whatever origin, which placed greater value on adults than children.

Beyond this, what we know now about the societies of the basin at the end of the nineteenth century goes so far as to suggest the hypothesis that the biological reproduction of the group was particularly the function of social dependents and not "big/men persons." The behavior of wives as "big persons" (Vansina, 1983)[4] confirms this model of personal success: They often had few children. If verified, this hypothesis will explain why *twa* women (pygmoids) enjoyed a reputation for being fertile among equatorial farmers (*ntu*). This reputation, apparently confirmed by some surveys in the colonial era, stemmed not

from any physical difference or lower incidence of sexually transmitted disease, but rather from their status in ntu society.

The low birthrate of these regions—so much decried—could well
be a demographic regime from the nineteenth century that favored
assimilation and made physical reproduction a function of dependents; the large "harems" of big men open to their juniors suggest
such a situation. Colonization, which directed efforts to controlling
migration, however, made this form of reproduction very important
until about 1930, particularly in marginally administered regions
heavily hit by epidemics. The combined effects of forced labor until
about 1910, and of the rapid spread of pathogenic factors until about
1940, intensified the drop in endogenous reproduction, a trend accentuated by migration toward marginal zones. Given the minimal penetration of wage labor and a monetarized economy, the earlier model
of social reproduction seems thus to have maintained itself in the face
of the model associated with Christian ideology (Mumbanza mwa Bawele, 1980).[5] After the "liberation" of the region from rubber collection, the earlier patterns of social advancement associated with "big
men" continued, profiting from the short copal boom of the 1920s.

The beginning of a gradual shift to reproduction within a "family"
production/reproduction unit began only toward the end of the 1940s
in the central basin (a generation after Bas-Zaïre, for example;
ADRAE, n.d.), at a time when commercial agriculture had become
more important in the economy and rural revenue had risen significantly (Sabakinu, 1981). Wage labor also became more widespread
(again, a generation later than in Bas-Zaire or Kasai; J. MacGaffey,
1983; Lux, 1971, 1972). In this context, social values gradually began
to shift toward a more individualistic and male-dominated model.
Colonial industrialization excluded women from wage labor, while
limited access to the monetary economy and exclusion from positions
of political authority further undermined their economic autonomy.
However, the impact of Kinshasa on demographic behavior in the central basin becomes statistically evident only after independence
(Tabutin, 1978; Sala-Diakanda, 1980; Sala-Diakanda and Lohlé-Tart,
1983).

WAGE LABOR, GENDER, AND CHILDBIRTH:
BIOLOGY OR POWER RELATIONS?

The demographic model of very high fertility is not an
"instinctive" reaction to high mortality. It results from the reorganization of power relations within colonial society reinforced by the im-

position of a complex of values by the dominant class. Colonial transformation initially produced radical social mobility, raising groups such as slaves from their inferior status. Internal stratification by class was replaced by external stratification by race (Jewsiewicki, 1984). By imposing wage relations as the dominant form of social relations *between* the races, a colonial mode of expression of class relations that benefited the colonizer, the possibility of wage labor penetrating socioeconomic relations *within* the society of the colonized was seriously limited. The perception of wage laborers as the slaves of the whites is obvious evidence of this fact; it is not a product of "false consciousness" and, in fact, reinforced socioeconomic factors that made it impossible for wage labor to reproduce itself "naturally" until the 1940s.

Furthermore, the adoption of money as a mediating agent of power relations produced a double restructuring of society, according to gender and according to "genealogical" age. It is important to remember that the colonial authorities acknowledged only male representatives of the local authorities, whom they then individualized. Until the 1940s the dominated society was largely masculine and characterized by individualized authority, expressed by the ideology (most often Christian) of modernization. The myth of gerontocracy in primitive societies, the place accorded history in legitimizing social relations, and the role played by veterans of various colonial services (veterans, workers, and so on) in "reconstituting" indigenous authority within colonial administrations accentuated and generalized precolonial distinctions between elders and juniors. This distinction meshed with the initial use of young men as temporary wage laborers. In the absence of economic and social autonomy, the position of women consequently began to be based solely on reproductive capacity. At the same time, women, as potential spouses, became objects of new kinds of conflict between elders placed in positions within "traditional" structures of authority (but generally outside the monetary economy), and juniors who, as wage laborers, made money—the importance of which for political relations was on the increase. And so it is impossible to explain the rise of a demographic regime of high fertility without demonstrating its socioeconomic necessity.

It seems to me possible to do this through reference to two processes. First, in the wake of World War I, actions by the colonial administrations gravely intensified food crises, while at the same time reducing the quality of the average village diet by generalizing cassava, marginalizing hunting, and expanding commercialized fishing. If demographic "accidents" obliterating entire groups became less probable, average levels of village morbidity probably increased through the 1950s when it first became possible to speak of real progress in public health. Beginning in the 1920s and 1930s, high rates of infant mortality, along with fairly high life expectancy after the age of 5 years, probably become the first "objective" components of a high-fertility regime. Second, a growing demand for male labor for colonial industry supplemented local labor demands (generally compensated by little money or none at all) for building infrastructure and maintaining roads, constructing local administrative buildings, and commercial agriculture. Contrary to administrative regulations, women and children provided most of the labor for such projects because responsibility for their execution was, indirectly and illegally, but very efficiently, placed on local chiefs. These burdens grew during the 1940s (Jewsiewicki, 1983). In such a situation high fertility in the villages was a necessity.

After World War II, and especially in the 1950s, a regime thus took shape emphasizing biological reproduction in the villages, followed by childhood and adolescence (social reproduction) in the city. The policy of urban labor stabilization, greater access to medical care and education, and especially expansion in family allocations for fostering children explain the transfer of a large number of young children (boys, in particular) from the countryside to the city. Interrupted between 1959 and 1966, this trend lasted until the present economic crisis, reinforcing the model of a very large family. It can be understood only in the context of a socioeconomic space that unifies the urban and rural spheres. This picture contrasts markedly with the statistical image—a product of the failure to distinguish between children actually born in the city and those sent there to be fostered—which suggests that urban fertility is much higher than in rural areas. Because social identity and social consciousness continued to be rooted in colonial village structure, high fertility remained a central value. We should also underscore how important it is to preserve access to patrimony as a guarantee against major urban upheavals (such as the political disruptions of 1959-1965, or the periodic economic crises that began with the depression of the 1930s).

The colonial village model of high fertility is reinforced as much by the total economic dependence of women, who receive no compensation in the city, other than that associated with their reproductive role, as by the transfer of some children to the city in search of formal education. It should also be recalled that the dominant colonial society worked very hard to impose the model of the "fertile woman," which was also advantageous for local authorities who controlled girls and young women, sources of bridewealth and bases of dependency relationships with younger men.[6]

CONCLUSION

This essay grows out of long acquaintance with the past of societies in Zaire; as yet it is not supported by detailed research. In any case, the administrative documents available for study of the phenomenon are of limited usefulness, given their narrow perspective (as I have demonstrated elsewhere). To carry out research successfully—and the first step has already been taken with an initial collection of personal life narratives—we must begin with recollections of the transformation of units of reproduction, production, and consumption, and use them as guides to reinterpret the statistical data. The reconstitution of families and patrimony may find inspiration in the historical sociology of population in Europe, with the difference that in Africa we cannot assume that a single institution organized reproduction, production, and consumption. We must begin with the premise that reproduction (which is to say childbirth, morbidity, mortality, migration, and socialization) is not a uniquely biological phenomenon, or a discrete structural unit of a mode of production, but rather the central component in the strategies of basic social units confronted with the vagaries of individual action and the norms of larger groups. Personal life histories and accounts of earlier social practice seem to me to be the only key to these dimensions of the past, although not a magic wand.

NOTES

1. In the absence of a global term to label a discipline that has as its aim the overall comprehension of social phenomena through time and space, I use this disgraceful neologism, which refers as much to the *rapprochment* between history and sociology (see Abrams, 1982; Skocpol, 1984) as to that between history and anthropology (see especially the new journal *History and Anthropology*), or to that between anthropology and sociology suggested by ethnomethodology (Leiter, 1980). It is important not to confuse the above with the "ethnodisciplines," such as ethnohistory. Also see the biographical approach implied in "people's history."

2. I consciously assume responsibility for dilettantism by proposing these incomplete reflections. Originally they were to be part of a larger research project with two Zairois colleagues who specialize in contemporary socioeconomic history of the central Zairois basin and Bas-Zaïre. Unfortunately, lack of resources made this joint project impossible. Hence I present myself as a Lone Ranger.

3. The concept of "patrimony" includes access to the means of production politically controlled by the group, as well as access to the sociopolitical and ideological means of controlling human labor and its product. These two aspects cannot be separated. Furthermore, it is in terms of access to patrimony that one can define social status: slave, client, junior, and so on (see Jewsiewicki, 1981b; Dupré, 1985).

4. Vansina's 1983 essay allows us to grasp the importance of his current research, which inspires me here. I appreciate the information he has provided me about unpublished work.

5. Apart from this 1980 work, I am drawing on an article in progress that was not completed in time for this collection. I wish to thank Mumbanza mwa Bawele for sending me the partial text.

6. The alternative model that is appearing today is in keeping with a group whose higher educational levels are a major characteristic, but whose most important trait is its elevated socioeconomic status. The latter has led to a break with the model of group identity and group solidarity. Those Zairois, called "whites" (*mindele*), who have taken up the position of the former colonizer are forsaking the unified rural-urban sphere and integrating themselves entirely in the capitalist sector, as a bourgeoisie in the broad sense of the word.

References

I. ARCHIVES

ABCFM. American Board of Foreign Missions Archives (Cambridge). Series: West Central African Mission. Missionary Correspondence cited as ABC, followed by series letters, volume and document numbers; or series documents and reports, volume and document numbers.

ADGRST. Archives de la Direction Générale de la Recherche Scientifique et Technologique (Ouagadougou).

ADRAE. Enquêtes sur les revenus des indigènes, Archives de la Direction régionale des affaires économiques, Mbandaka (Zaire).

AHU. Arquivo Histórico Ultramarino, Direcção Geral das Colonias (Lisbon). Citations in following order: repartição number, room number, carton number, document number, date.

ANCI. Archives nationales de la Côte d'Ivoire (Abidjan).

ANF-MI. Archives nationales de France, Service des microfilms (Paris).

ANF-SOM (Aix-en-Provence). Archives nationales de France, Section d'Outre-Mer, Aix-en-Provence, Afrique équatoriale française, Série D, s/série 4[3]D, Oubangui-Chari.

ANF-SOM (Paris). Archives nationales de France, Section d'Outre-Mer.

ANM. Archives nationales du Mali, Série 5D51, Census data, 1905-1913.

ANN. Archives nationales du Niger (Niamey).

ANS. Archives nationales du Sénégal (Dakar).

ASSC (Marseille). Archives du Service de santé colonial, Institut de medécine tropicale, Service de santé des armées.

CDIH. Centro de Documentação e Investigação Histórica (Luanda). Citations in following order: shelf number, box or folder number, document number, date.

KNA. Kenya National Archives (Nairobi).

PRO-CO. Public Records Office, Colonial Office (Kew Gardens, Great Britain).

UBU. União dos Bancos Ultramarinos. Archives include records of the Banco de Angola (Lisbon).

II. BOOKS, ARTICLES, THESES, REPORTS

Abadie, M. (1927) La colonie du Niger. Paris: Société d'éditions géographiques, maritimes et coloniales.

Abrams, Philipe. (1982) Historical Sociology. London: Open Book.

Adadevoh, B. Kwaku (ed.). (1974) Sub-Fertility and Infertility in Africa. Ibadan: Caxton Press.

Afrique occidentale fraçaise, Gouverneur-Général. (1954) Pluviométrie, 1920-1949; Haute-Volta. Dakar: Service météorologique.

Akinjogbin, I. A. (1967) Dahomey and Its Neighbors, 1708-1818. Cambridge: Cambridge University Press.

Ali, Taisier, and Jay O'Brien. (1984) "Labor, community and protest in Sudanese agriculture," pp. 205-238 in Jonathan Barker (ed.) The Politics of Agriculture in Tropical Africa. Beverly Hills, CA: Sage.

Amin, Samir. (1972) "L'Afrique sous-peuplée." Développement et civilisations 47-48: 59-67.

Amin, Samir. (1974a) "Le capitalisme et la rente foncière (la domination du capitalisme sur l'agriculture)," in Samir Amin and Kostas Vergopoulos (eds.) La question paysanne et le capitalisme. Paris: Maspero.

Amin, Samir (ed.) (1974b) Modern Migrations in Western Africa. London: Oxford University Press.

Amin, Samir. (1976) Unequal Development. New York: Monthly Review Press.

Amin, Samir, and Catherine Coquery-Vidrovitch. (1969) Histoire économique du Congo, 1889-1960. Paris: Anthropos.

Ampene, E. (1967) "Obuasi and its miners." Ghana Journal of Sociology 2: 73-80.

Ancey, Gérard. (1983) Monnaie et structures d'exploitations en pays Mossi. Paris: ORSTOM.

Anderson, T. Farnsworth. (1930) "Report on an investigation of health conditions on farms in Trans-Nzoia, with special reference to malaria." Kenya and East Africa Medical Journal 6: 274-308.

Angola, Provincia. (1941) Censo Geral da População, 1940 (12 vols.). Luanda: Author.

Angola, Provincia. (1951) Censo Geral da População, 1950 (12 vols.). Luanda: Author.

Anonymous. (1928) Tarikh Arbab hadha al-balad al-musamma Kano.

Anstey, Roger. (1975) The Atlantic Slave Trade and British Abolition. Cambridge: Cambridge University Press.

Arrighi, Giovanni. (1973) "Labor supplies in historical perspective: a study of the proletarianization of the African peasantry in Rhodesia," pp. 180-234 in Giovanni Arrighi and John Saul (eds.) Essays on the Political Economy of Africa. New York: Monthly Review Press.

Asiwaju, A. I. (1976) "Migration as revolt: the example of Ivory Coast and Upper Volta before 1945." Journal of African History 18: 555-576.

Austen, Ralph. (1979) "The trans-Sahara slave trade: A tentative census," pp. 23-74 in H. Gemery and Jan Hogendorn (eds.) The Uncommon Market. New York: Academic Press.

Azevedo, Mario Joaquim. (1976) "Sara demographic instability as a consequence of French colonial policy in Chad (1890-1940)." Ph.D. dissertation, Duke University.

Azevedo, Mario Joaquim. (1981) "The human price of development: the Brazzaville railroad and the Sara of Chad." African Studies Review 24: 1-20.

Baier, Stephen B. (1980) An Economic History of Central Niger. Oxford: Clarendon.

Balandier, Georges. (1971) Sociologie actuelle de l'Afrique noire: dynamique sociale en Afrique centrale. Paris: Presses Universitaires de France.

Barth, Heinrich. (1965) Travels and Discoveries in Northern and Central Africa (3 vols.). London: Frank Cass.

Beach, E. (1977) "The Shona economy: branches of production," pp. 37-65 in Robin Palmer and Neil Parsons (eds.) The Roots of Rural Poverty in Central and Southern Africa. Berkeley: University of California Press.

Bean, Richard Nelson. (1975) The British Trans-Atlantic Slave Trade. New York: Arno.

Beauminy, A. de. (1918-1919) "Le Mossi au point de vue économique." Revue de géographie commerciale de Bordeaux 44: 13-16, 52-55.

Beauvilain, A. (1977) Les Peul du Dallo Bosso. Niamey: Institut de recherches en sciences humaines.

Beavon, Keith S.O. (1981) "Black townships in South Africa: terra incognita for urban geographers." South African Geographical Journal 64: 3-20.

Becker, Gary S. (1960) "An economic analysis of fertility," pp. 209-231 in National Bureau of Economic Research (eds.) Demographic and Economic Change in Developed Countries. Princeton, NJ: Princeton University Press.

Berg, Elliot. (1965) "The economics of the migrant labor system," pp. 160-181 in Hilda Kuper (ed.) Urbanization and Migration in West Africa. Berkeley: University of California Press.

Berman, Bruce. (1984) "The concept of 'articulation' and the political economy of colonialism." Canadian Journal of African Studies 18: 407-414.

Berry, Sara. (1984) "The food crisis and agrarian change in Africa." African Studies Review 27: 59-112.

Bezy, F. (1957) Problèmes structurels de l'économie congolaise. Paris: Nauwelaerts.

Bezy, F., J.-P. Peemans, and J. M. Wautelet. (1981) Accumulation et sous-développement au Zaïre, 1960-1980. Louvain-la-neuve: Presses Universitaires de Louvain.

Birmingham, David. (1966) Trade and Conflict in Angola. Oxford: Clarendon.

Boute, Joseph, and Léon de Saint-Moulin. (1981) "Zaire," in L'évaluation des effectifs des populations africaines. Paris: Groupe de Démographie Africaine.

Boutillier, J. L. (1968) "Les captifs en A.O.F. (1903-1905)." Bulletin de l'IFAN 30: 514-535.

Bovill, E. W. (1964) Missions to the Niger. Cambridge: Cambridge University Press.

Brass, William, et al. (1968) The Demography of Tropical Africa. Princeton, NJ: Princeton University Press.

Bundy, Colin. (1972) "The emergence and decline of a South African peasantry." African Affairs 71: 369-388.

Burnet, Macfarlane, and David O. White. (1972) Natural History of Infectious Disease. Cambridge: Cambridge University Press.

Burnham, Philip. (1975) "'Regroupement' and mobile societies: two Cameroon cases." Journal of African History 16: 577-594.

Burnham, Philip. (1980) Opportunity and Constraint in a Savanna Society. New York: Academic Press.

Cahiers de l'ORSTOM. (1975) "Migrations sénégalaises. 1. Le bassin arachidier; 2. La vallée du Sénégal." 12: 1-208.

Cain, Mead T. (1977) "The economic activities of children in a village in Bangladesh." Population and Development Review 3: 201-227.

Caldwell, John C. (1976) "Toward a restatement of demographic transition theory." Population and Development Review 2: 321-366.

Caldwell, John C. (1981) "The mechanisms of demographic change in historical perspective." Population Studies 35: 5-27.

Caldwell, John C. (1982) Theory of Fertility Decline. New York: Academic Press.

Canadian Journal of African Studies. (1985) "Modes of production: The African challenge." (Special issue) 19: 1-174.

Cantrelle, Pierre (ed.). (1974) Population in African Development. Dolhain, Belgium: Ordina Editions.

Capelle, E. (1948) La cité indigène de Léopoldville. Léopoldville and Elisabethville: CESA-CEPSI.

Cattier, F. (1906) Etude sur la situation de l'Etat Indépendant du Congo. Paris: Larcier et Pédone.

Chanock, Martin. (1972) "The political economy of independent agriculture in Nyasaland: the Great War to the Great Depression." Journal of Social Science (Malawi) 1.

Chanock, Martin. (1977) "Agricultural change and continuity in Malawi," pp. 396-409 in Robin Palmer and Neil Parsons (eds.) Roots of Rural Poverty in Central and Southern Africa. Berkeley: University of California Press.

Chapman, A. M., and A. M. Jacquard. (1972) "Un isolat d'Amérique centrale: les Indiens Jicaques du Honduras." Génétique et Population 60: 163-185.

Charentré, André, et al. (1972) "Un 'isolat' du sud Sahara: les Kel Kummer." Population 27: 769-804.

Charles, V. (1948) "Le mal démographique de Léopoldville." Zaïre: 897-901.

Charpentier, Claude. (1952) "Avec les Peuls de la subdivision de Djénné." Mémoire, Centre des hautes études sur l'Afrique et l'Asie modernes, Paris.

Chauncey, G. (1981) "The locus of reproduction: women's labour in the Zambian copperbelt, 1927-1953." Journal of Southern African Studies 7: 135-164.

Chrétien, Jean-Pierre. (1978) "Des sédentaires devenus migrants—les motifs des départs des Burundais et Rwandais vers l'Ouganda (1920-1960)." Cultures et développement 10.

Clapperton, H. (1966) Journal of a Second Expedition into the Interior of Africa from the Bight of Benin to Soccatoo. London: Frank Cass.

Coale, Ansley J., and Edgar M. Hoover. (1958) Population Growth and Economic Development in Low-Income Countries: A Case Study of India's Prospects. Princeton, NJ: Princeton University Press.

Colvin, Lucie G. [ed.] (1981) The Uprooted of the Western Sahel: Migrants Quest for Cash in the Senegambia. New York: Praeger.

Comité d'information Sahel. (1975) Qui se nourrit de la famine en Afrique? Paris: Maspero.

Cooper, Frederick. (1981) "Peasants, capitalists, and historians: a review article." Journal of Southern African Studies 9: 285-314.

Coquery-Vidrovitch, Catherine. (1972) Le Congo au temps des grandes compagnies concessionnaires, 1898-1930. Paris: Mouton.

Coquery-Vidrovitch, Catherine. (1976) "L'Afrique coloniale française et la crise de 1930: crise structurelle et génèse du sous-développement." Revue française d'histoire d'outre-mer 63, 232-233: 386-424.

Coquery-Vidrovitch, Catherine. (1978) "Research on an African mode of production," pp. 261-288 in David Seddon (ed.) Relations of Production. London: Frank Cass.

Cordell, Dennis D. (1979) "Blood partnership in theory and practice: The expansion of Muslim power in Dar al-Kuti." Journal of African History 20: 379-394.

Cordell, Dennis D. (1983a) "Low fertility in Africa." Presented at the meeting of the Canadian Association of African Studies, Québec.

Cordell, Dennis D. (1983b) "The savanna belt of North Central Africa," pp. 30-74 in David Birmingham and Phyllis M. Martin (eds.) History of Central Africa, Vol. 1. London: Longman.

Cordell, Dennis D. (1985a) Dar al-Kuti and the Last Years of the Trans-Saharan Slave Trade. Madison: University of Wisconsin Press.

Cordell, Dennis D. (1985b) "The pursuit of the real: modes of production and history." Canadian Journal of African Studies 19: 58-63.

Cordell, Dennis D. (1985c) "La sous-fécondité et l'histoire en Centrafrique." Presented to the département de démographie, Université de Montréal.

Cordell, Dennis D., and Joel W. Gregory. (1980) "Historical demography and demographic history in Africa: theoretical and methodological considerations." Canadian Journal of African Studies 14: 389-416.

Cordell, Dennis D., and Joel W. Gregory. (1982) "Labour reservoirs and population: French colonial strategies in Koudougou, Upper Volta, 1914-1939." Journal of African History 23: 205-224.

Cordell, Dennis D., Joel W. Gregory, and Victor Piché. (in press) "The demographic reproduction of health and disease in Africa," in Steven Feierman and John Janzen (eds.) The Social Origins of Health and Disease in Africa (tentative title). Submitted to University of California Press.

Cornet, J. (1948) La bataille du rail—la construction du chemin de fer de Matadi au Stanley-Pool. Brussels: Cuypers.

Coulibaly, Sidiki P. (1978) "Les migrations voltaïques: les origines, les motifs et les perceptions des politiques." Ph.D. dissertation, Université de Montréal.

Coupland, Reginald. (1938) East Africa and Its Invaders from the Earliest Times to the Death of Seyyid Said in 1856. Oxford: Clarendon.

Critique de l'économie politique. (1981) "Le travail des femmes." (Special issue) nouvelle série 17.

Curtin, Philip D. (1969) The Atlantic Slave Trade: A Census. Madison: University of Wisconsin Press.

Curtin, Philip D. (1975) Economic Trade in Precolonial Africa: Senegambia in the Era of the Slave Trade. Madison: University of Wisconsin Press.

Daigre, R. P. (1947) Oubangui-Chari: témoignage sur son évolution. Issoudun: Dillen et Cie.

D'Almeida-Topor, Hélene. (1973) "Les populations dahoméennes et le recrutement militaire pendant la première guerre mondiale." Revue française d'histoire d'outre-mer 60: 196-241.

Davenport, Rodney. (1969) "African townsmen? South African natives (urban areas) legislation through the years." African Affairs 68: 95-109.

David, Philippe. (1980) Les Navétanes: Histoire des migrants saisonniers de l'arachide en Sénégambie des origines à nos jours. Dakar: Nouvelles Editions Africaines.

Davies, Robert. (1979) "Capital restructuring and the modification of the racial division of labour in South Africa." Journal of Southern African Studies 5: 181-198.

Davis, Kingsley, and Judith Blake. (1956) "Social structure and fertility: An analytical framework. Economic Development and Cultural Change 4: 211-235.

Davis, Shelby C. (1970) Reservoirs of Men: A History of the Black Troops of French West Africa. Westport, CT: Greenwood. (1934)

Dawson, Marc H. (1978-1979) "Murang'a District historical texts: interviews collected between 1978 and 1979 in Murang'a District, Kenya. (unpublished)

Dawson, Marc H. (1979) "Smallpox in Kenya, 1880-1920." Social Science and Medicine 13B: 245-250.

Dawson, Marc H. (1981a) "Disease and population decline of the Kikuyu of Kenya," pp. 121-138 in Christopher Fyfe and David McMaster (eds.) African Historical Demography, Vol. 2. Edinburgh: University of Edinburgh, Centre for African Studies.

Dawson, Marc H. (1981b) "The 1920s yaws eradication campaign in Kenya." Presented at the annual meeting of the African Studies Association (USA), Bloomington, IN.

Dawson, Marc H. (1983) "Socio-economic and epidemiological change in Kenya: 1880-1925." Ph.D. dissertation, University of Wisconsin—Madison.

DeGaudemar, Jean-Paul. (1976) Mobilité du travail et accumulation du capital. Paris: Maspero.

Delobsom, D.A.A. (1932) L'empire du Mogho-Naba: coutumes des Mossi de la Haute-Volta. Paris: Domat-Montchrestien.

Demunter, P. (1975) Masses rurales et luttes politiques au Zaïre—le processus de politisation des masses rurales au Bas-Zaïre. Paris: Anthropos.

Denis, J. (1956) "Léopoldville: étude de géographie urbaine et sociale." Zaïre 10: 563-611.

Derman, William. (1973) Serfs, Peasants, and Socialists. Berkeley: University of California Press.

Derriennic, H. (1977) Famines et dominations en Afrique noire: paysans et éleveurs du Sahel sous le joug. Paris: Harmattan.

de Villiers, Richard. (1979a) "The state, capital and labour allocation: the Johannesburg municipality, 1948-1962." Africa Perspective 12: 20-39.

de Villiers, Richard. (1979b) "The pass-laws: allocation and control (1760-1979)." South African Labour Bulletin 5: 87-104.

Dhanis, A. (1953) "Recrutements de main-d'oeuvre chez les Bakaya." Zaïre 7.

Dublin, Louis I., and Alfred J. Lotka. (1925) "On the true rate of natural increase, as exemplified by the population of the United States, 1920." Journal of the American Statistical Association 20: 305-339.

Dubois, J. P. (1975) "Les Serer et la question des Terres Neuves au Sénégal." Cahiers de l'ORSTOM 12: 81-120.

Dubourg, J. (1957) "La vie des paysans Mossi: le village de Taghalla," Cahiers d'Outre-Mer 40: 285-324.

Duc de Castries. (1960) Les rencontres de Stanley—Essai historique. Paris: France-Empire.

Duchac, Réné. (1974) La sociologie des migrations aux Etats-Unis. The Hague: Mouton.

Dumett, Raymond. (1979) "Precolonial gold-mining and the state in the Akan region: with a critique of the Terray hypothesis." Research in Economic Anthropology 2: 37-68.

Dunn, Richard. (1972) Sugar and Slaves: The Rise of the Planter Class in the English West Indies 1624-1713. Chapel Hill: University of North Carolina Press.

Dupré, Georges. (1982) Un ordre et sa destruction. Paris: ORSTOM.

Dupré, Georges. (1985) Naissances d'une société: espace et historicité chez les Beémbé du Congo. Paris: ORSTOM.

Dupré, Georges, and Pierre-Philippe Rey. (1978) "Reflections on the relevance of a theory of the history of exchange," pp. 171-208 in David Sedon (ed.) Relations of Production. London: Frank Cass.

Dupriez, H. (1980) Paysans d'Afrique noire. Nivelles: Terre et vie.

Easterlin, Richard. (1968) Population, Labor Force, and Long Swings in Economic Growth: The American Experience. New York: National Bureau of Economic Research.

Echenberg, Myron J. (1975) "Paying the blood tax: military conscription in French West Africa, 1914-1929." Canadian Journal of African Studies 9: 171-192.

Echenberg, Myron J. (1980) "Les migrations militaires en Afrique occidentale française." Canadian Journal of African Studies 14: 429-450.

Eltis, David. (1977) "The export of slaves from Afirca, 1821-1843." Journal of Economic History 37: 409-433.

Eltis, David. (in press) Economic Growth and Coercion: The Ending of the Atlantic Slave Trade.

Engels, Frederick. (1948) The Origin of the Family, Private Property, and the State in the Light of the Researches of Lewis H. Morgan. Moscow: Progress. (1884)

Erwin, Alec, and Eddie Webster. (1978) "Ideology and capitalism in South Africa," pp. 91-107 in L. Schlemmer and Eddie Webster (eds.) Change, Reform and Economic Growth in South Africa. Johannesburg: Ravan.

Eynikel, H. (1984) Congo-Belge—Portrait d'une société coloniale. Paris and Gembloux: Duculot.

Fage, J. D. (1969) "Slavery and the slave trade in the context of West African History." Journal of African History 10: 393-404.

Faris, James C. (1975) "Social evolution, population, and production," pp. 235-271 in S. Polgar (ed.) Population, Ecology, and Social Evolution. The Hague: Mouton.

Faruqee, Rashid. (1982) "Fertility and its trend in Kenya." Rural Africana 14: 25-48.

Feierman, Steven. (1984) "The social origins of health and healing in Africa." Presented at the annual meeting of the African Studies Association (USA), 25-28 October, Los Angeles.

Ferraro, Gary. (1976) "Changing patterns of bridewealth among the Kikuyu of East Africa," in W. Arens (ed.) A Century of Change in Eastern Africa. The Hague: Mouton.

Finley, Moses. (1968) "Slavery," pp. 307-313 in International Encyclopedia of the Social Sciences, Vol. 14. New York: Free Press.

Finley, Moses. (1980) Ancient Slavery and Modern Ideology. New York: Viking.

Fisher, Joan. (1964) The Anatomy of Kikuyu Domesticity and Husbandry. London: Department of Technical Coooperation.

Fourneau, Alfred. (1904) "Deux années dans la région du Tchad," L'Afrique française 15: 121-124.

France, Ministère de la Guerre. (1925-1942) Statistique médicale de l'Armée métropolitaine et de l'Armée coloniale (vol. L, 1919-1920, to LXVIII, 1938). Paris: Author.

France, Ministère des Colonies. (1922) Annuaire de l'A.O.F., 1917-1921. Paris: Author.

Frank, Odile. (1983) Infertility in Sub-Saharan Africa (Center for Policy Studies, working paper 97). New York: Population Council.

Freund, Bill. (1981) Capital and Labour in Nigerian Tin Mines. London: Longman.

Freund, Bill. (1984) "Forced resettlement and the political economy of South Africa." Review of African Political Economy 29: 49-63.

Freund, Bill. (1985) "The social character of secondary industry in South Africa." Presented to the African Studies Institute seminar, Witwatersrand.

Frisch, Rose E. (1978) "Population, food intake, and fertility." Science 199: 22-30.

Fuglestad, F. (1974) "La grande famine de 1931 dans l'Ouest nigérien: reflexions autour d'une catastrophe naturelle." Revue française d'histoire d'Outre-Mer 61, 222: 18-33.

Fugelstad, F. (1983) A History of Niger, 1850-1960. Cambridge: Cambridge University Press.

Gado, B. (1980) Le Zarmatarey: contribution à l'histoire des populations d'entre Niger et Dallol Mawri. Niamey: Institut de recherches en sciences humaines.

Galal-el-din, Mohamed el Awad. (1975) The Human Factor in the Rahad Project Area. Khartoum: Ministry of Agriculture, Food, and Natural Resources.

Gallais, Jean. (1967) Le delta intérieur du Niger (2 vols.). Dakar: Institut Fondamental de l'Afrique Noire.

Garbett, G. K. (1977) "Labour migration and development in the Lower Shire Valley, Malawi, in historical perspective." Presented to a seminar on Migration and Rural Development in Tropical Africa, Afrikastudiecentrum, November, Leiden.

Gervais, Raymond. (1982) "Les conséquences démographiques de la secheresse au Sahel: le cas du Niger." M.Sc. thesis, Université de Montréal.

Gnampa, N. (1980) "L'organisation sociale du travail agricole dans la société traditionelle mossi." Master's thesis, ESECJ, Lomé.

Godelier, Maurice. (1978) "The concept of the 'Asiatic Mode of Production' and Marxist models of social evolution," pp. 209-257 in David Seddon (ed.) Relations of Production. London: Frank Cass.

Goody, Jack. (1969) "Economy and feudalism in Africa." Economic History Review 22: 393-405.

Gopalan, C., and A. Nadamuni Naidu. (1972) "Nutrition and fertility." Lancet 18: 1077-1079.

Goutalier, R. (1979) "Au début du 20e siècle: un problème vital pour les pays et protectorats du Tchad: l'établissement de la route de ravitaillement," pp. 133-153 in Groupement d'intérêt scientifique "Sciences humaines sur l'aire mediterranéenne" (eds.) Recherches sahariennes. Paris: CNRS.

Greenhalgh, P. (1974) "An economic history of the Ghanaian diamond industry, 1919-1973." Ph.D. dissertation, University of Birmingham.

Gregory, Joel W. (1975) "Les migrations des hommes de Niamey." Population et famille 35: 127-137.

Gregory, Joel W. (1982) "Emigrant labor from Nyasaland and northern Rhodesia, 1900-1945." Presented at the annual meeting of the Canadian Association of African Studies, May, Toronto.

Gregory, Joel W., Dennis D. Cordell, and Raymond Gervais. (1984) African Historical Demography: A Multidisciplinary Bibliography. Los Angeles: Crossroads Press.

Gregory, Joel W., and Victor Piche. (1978) "African migration and peripheral capitalism." African Perspectives 1: 37-50.

Gregory, Joel W., and Victor Piché. (1981) The Demographic Process of Peripheral Capitalism. Montréal: Centre for Developing Area Studies, McGill University. (working paper 29)

Gregory, Joel W., and Victor Piché. (1982) "African population: reproduction for whom?" Daedalus 111: 179-209.

Gregory, Joel W., and Victor Piché. (1983) "African return migration: past, present and future." Contemporary Marxism 7: 169-183.

Gregory, Joel W., and Victor Piché. (1985) "Mode de production et régime démographique." Canadian Journal of African Studies 19: 73-79.

Gruenbaum, Ellen. (1979) Patterns of Family Living: A Case Study of Two Villages on the Rahad River. Khartoum: Development Studies and Research Centre.

Guibbert, Jean. (1949) "Le coton en Oubangui-Chari." Mémoire, Centre des hautes études sur l'Afrique et l'Asie modernes, Paris.

Guillème, Monsignor. (1932) "Simples notes sur l'émigration des indigènes de l'Afrique centrale vers les villes industrielles." Africa 5: 49-49.

Guillemin, R. (1956) "L'évolution de l'agriculture autochtone dans les savanes de l'Oubangui." L'Agronomie tropicale 11: 39-61.

Gulliver, P. H. (1955) Labour Migration in a Rural Economy. Kampala: East African Institute of Social Research.

Guy, Jeff. (1980) "Ecological factors in the rise of Shaka and the Zulu Kingdom," pp. 102-119 in Shula Marks and A. Atmore (eds.) Economy and Society in Pre-Industrial South Africa. London: Longman.

Hammam, Mahmoud. (1983) "The rise and fall of the emirate of Muri (Hammarawa), c. 1812-1903." Ph.D. dissertation, Ahmadu Bello University.

Harms, Robert. (1981) River of Wealth, River of Sorrow: the Central Zaire Basin in the Era of the Slave and Ivory Trade. 1500-1891. New Haven, CT: Yale University Press.

Harms, Robert. (1983a) "Choice and political economy in precolonial Africa: a game theory approach." Presented at the annual meeting of the American Historical Association, San Francisco.

Harms, Robert. (1983b) "Sustaining the system: trading towns along the Middle Zaire," pp. 95-110 in Claire Robertson and Martin Klein (eds.) Women and Slavery in Africa. Madison: University of Wisconsin Press.

Hellmann, Ellen. (1949) "Urban areas," pp. 229-247 in E. Hellmann (ed.) Handbook on Race Relations in South Africa. Cape Town: Oxford University Press.

Henin, R., and Bertil Egero. (1972) 1967 Population Census of Tanzania: A Demographic Analysis. Dar es Salaam: Bureau of Resource Assessment and Land Use Planning, University of Dar es Salaam. (Research paper 19)

Hesling, X. (1923) "Report to the President of the Republic." Journal Officiel de la Haute-Volta: 5-6, 113-114.

Herz, Barbara Knapp. (1974) "Demographic pressure and economic change: the case of Kenyan land reforms." Ph.D. dissertation, Yale University.

Heywood, Linda. (1984) "Production, trade and power: the political economy of Central Angola, 1859-1930." Ph.D. dissertation, Columbia University.

Hill, Allan, Sara Randall, and Oriel Sullivan. (1982) "The mortality and fertility of farmers and pastoralists in Central Mali, 1950-1981." London: Centre for Population Studies, London School of Hygiene and Tropical Medicine.

History and Anthropology. (1984) Paris: Harwood Academic Publisher.

Hlophe, Stephen S. (1977) "The crisis of urban living under apartheid condition: a socio-economic analysis of Soweto." Journal of Southern African Affairs 2: 343-356.

Hopkins, Anthony G. (1973) An Economic History of West Africa. London: Longman.

Hopkins, Keith. (1978) Conquerers and Slaves. Cambridge: Cambridge University Press.

Horton, Robin. (1972-1974) "Stateless societies in the history of West Africa," Vol. 1, pp. 78-119 in J. F. Ajayi and Michael Crowder (eds.) History of West Africa. London: Longman.

Houghton, D. Hobart. (1971) "Economic Development, 1865-1965," Vol. 2, pp. 1-48 in Monica Wilson and Leonard Thompson (eds.) The Oxford History of South Africa. London: Oxford University Press.

Howell, Nancy. (1979) The Demography of the Dobe !Kung. New York: Academic Press.

Huybrechts, et al. (1980) Du Congo au Zaïre, 1960-1980. Essai de bilan. Brussels: CRISP.

Illife, John. (1979) A Modern History of Tanzania. Cambridge: Cambridge University Press.

Imoru, Imam. (1973) "The lands of the Hausa people: K'asashen Hausawa," in "Nineteenth-century Hausaland, being a description by Imam Imoru of the land, economy, and society of his people," by D. E. Ferguson. Ph.D. dissertation, University of California at Los Angeles.

Infor-Congo, I and II. (1959) Le Congo Belge. Brussels: Ministère des Colonies.

Inikori, Joseph E. (1982) "Introduction," pp. 13-60 in Joseph E. Inikori (ed.) Forced Migration. London: Hutchison.

Inikori, Joseph E. (1984) "Slave trade, slavery and the development of industrial capitalism in England in the eighteenth century: a reassessment." Presented at the Conference on Capitalism and Slavery in the British West Indies: The Contribution of Eric Williams, May 21-25, Bellagio, Italy.

Institut National de la Statistique et des Etudes Economiques (INSEE). (1964) Enquête démographique en République centrafricaine, 1959-1960: résultats définitifs. Paris: Ministère de la Coopération and INSEE.

Izard, Michel. (1970) Introduction à l'histoire des royaumes Mossi (2 vols.). Paris: CNRS/CVRS.

Izard-Heritier, Françoise and Michel Izard. (1959) Les Mossi du Yatenga: Etude de la vie économique et sociale. Bordeaux: Institut des sciences humaines appliquées.

Janvry, Alain de. (1981) The Agrarian Question and Reformism in Latin America. Baltimore: Johns Hopkins University Press.

Jessen, Adolph. (1933) Reisen und Forschungen im Hochland Angolas. Leipzig.

Jewsiewicki, Bogumil. (1981a) "L'état et l'accumulation primitive coloniale: la formation du mode de production coloniale au Zaire." Revue française d'histoire d'outremer 68.

Jewsiewicki, Bogumil. (1981b) "Lineage mode of production: social inequalities in Equatorial Central Africa," pp. 93-113 in Donald Crummey and C. C. Stewart (eds.) Modes of Production in Africa. Beverly Hills, CA: Sage.

Jewsiewicki, Bogumil. (1983) "Modernisation ou destruction du village africain: l'économie politique de la 'modernisation agricole' au Congo-Belge." Les Cahiers du CEDAF 5.

Jewsiewicki, Bogumil [ed.] (1984) L'état Independant du Congo, Congo belge, République Démocratique du Congo, Republique du Zaïre. Québec: Safi Press.

Jewsiewicki, Bogumil, and Mumbanza mwa Bawele. (1981) "The social context of slavery in Equatorial Africa during the 19th and 20th centuries," in Paul E. Lovejoy (ed.) the Ideology of Slavery in Africa. Beverly Hills, CA: Sage.

Jewsiewicki, Bogumil, and David Newberry (eds.). (1985) African Historiographies. Beverly Hills, CA: Sage.

Kaboré, G. V. (1966) Organisation politique traditionnelle et évolution politique des Mossi de Ouagadougou. Paris: CNRS/CVRS.

Kagan, Noreen. (1978) "African settlement in the Johannesburg area, 1903-1923." Master's thesis, University of the Witswatersrand.

Kahn, Ellison. (1949) "The pass laws," pp. 275-291 in E. Hellmann (ed.) Handbook on Race Relations in South Africa. Cape Town: Oxford University Press.

Kandawire, J.A. Kamchitere. (1979) Thangata: Forced Labour or Reciprocal Assistance? Blantyre: Research and Publications Committee, University of Malawi.

Kay, G. B. (1972) The Political Economy of Colonialism in Ghana: A Collection of Documents and Statistics, 1900-1960. Cambridge: Cambridge University Press.

Keim, Curtis. (1979) "Precolonial Mangbetu rule: political and economic factors in nineteenth-century Mangbetu history." Ph.D. dissertation, Indiana University.

Keita, T. (1978) "Quelques aspects de l'immigration interne à l'Afrique: L'exemple de trois villages de l'Ouest du Niger." Mémoire de maîtrise, Université de Paris VIII.

Kenyatta, Jomo. (1965) Facing Mount Kenya (1938). New York: Vintage.

Kershaw, Greet. (1972) "The land and people: A study of Kikuyu social organization in historical perspective." Ph.D. dissertation, University of Chicago.

Kimba, I. (1981) Guerres et sociétés: les populations du "Niger" occidentale au XIXe siècle et leurs réactions face à la colonisation (1896-1906). Niamey: Institut de recherches en sciences humaines.

Kitching, Gavin. (1980) Class and Economic Change in Kenya: The Making of an African Petite-Bourgeoisie. New Haven, CT: Yale University Press.

Kitching, Gavin. (1983) "Proto-industrialization and demographic change: a thesis and some possible African implications." Journal of African History 24: 221-240.

Kjekshus, Helge. (1977) Ecology Control and Economic Development in East African History. London: Heinemann.

Klein, Martin A. (1983a) "From slave to sharecropper in the French Soudan: an effort at controlled social change." Itinerario 6.

Klein, Martin A. (1983b) "Women in slavery in the western Soudan," pp. 67-92 in Claire Robertson and Martin A. Klein (eds.) Women and Slavery in Africa. Madison: University of Wisconsin Press.

Klein, Martin A., and Paul E. Lovejoy. (1979) "Slavery in West Africa," in H. A. Gemery and J. S. Hogendorn (eds.) The Uncommon Market: Essays in the Economic History of the Atlantic Slave Trade. New York: Academic Press.

Klein, Martin, and Richard Roberts. (1981) "The Banamba Slave exodus of 1905 and the decline of slavery in the western Soudan." Journal of African History 21: 375-394.

Kohler, Jean-Marie. (1971) Activités agricoles et changements sociaux dans l'Ouest Mossi (Haute-Volta). Paris: ORSTOM.

Koyptoff, Igor. (1979) "Comment on Lovejoy." Historical Reflexions 6.

Kuczynski, Robert Rene. (1949) Demographic Survey of the British Colonial Empire. London: Oxford University Press.

Lacey, Marian. (1981) Working for Boroko. Johannesburg: Ravan Press.

Lacombe, Bernard. (1970) Fakao (Sénégal). Dépouillement de registres paroissiaux et enquête démographique rétrospective. Méthodologie et résultats. Paris: ORSTOM.

Lake, L. A., and E.H.S.N. Touré. (1984) L'expansion du bassin arachidier. Sénégal 1954-1979. Dakar: I.F.A.N.

Lallemand, Suzanne. (1977) Une famille mossi. Ouagadougou: CVRS.

Lamal, F. (1954) "L'exode massif des hommes adultes vers Léopoldville—Les Basku du territoire de Feshi." Zaïre 8.

Lambert, H. E. (1956) Kikuyu Social and Political Institutions. London: Oxford University Press for the International Africa Institute.

Lasalle-Séré, R. (1929) Le recrutement de l'Armée noire. Paris: Librairie Moderne de Droit et de Jurisprudence.

Leakey, L.S.B. (1931) "The Kikuyu problem of the initiation of girls." Journal of the Royal Anthropological Institute 61: 277-285.

Leakey, L.S.B. (1979) The Southern Kikuyu Before 1903 (vols. 1-3) (1933). London: Academic Press.

Legassick, Martin. (1974) "Legislation, ideology, and economy in post-1948 South Africa." Journal of Southern African Studies 1: 5-35.

Legassick, Martin. (1975) "South Africa: forced labour, industrialization, and racial differentiation," pp. 229-270 in R. Harris (ed.) The Political Economy of Africa. New York: John Wiley.

Leiter, K. (1980) A Primer on Ethnomethodology. Oxford: Oxford University Press.

Levine, David. (1977) Family Formation in the Age of Nascent Capitalism. New York: Academic Press.

Lloyd, David T. (1978) "The precolonial economic history of the Avongara-Azande, c. 1750-1916." Ph.D. dissertation, University of California at Los Angeles.

Lotter, J. M. (1977) "The effect of urbanization and education on the fertility of Blacks in South Africa." Humanitas 4: 21-28.

Lovejoy, Paul E. (ed.). (1981) The Ideology of Slavery in Africa. Beverly Hills, CA: Sage.

Lovejoy, Paul E. (1982) "The volume of the Atlantic slave trade: a Synthesis." Journal of African History 23: 473-501.

Lovejoy, Paul E. (1983) Transformations in Slavery. Cambridge: Cambridge University Press.

Lukoki, M. (1984) De l'Etat Indépendant du Congo à la République du Zaïre—l'économie zaïroise aux prises avec les structures coloniales traditionnelles. Mayidi: Publications du Grand Séminaire.

Lututala, Mumpasi. (1982) "La mobilité de la population dans l'Ouest du Zaire avant 1975: un essai d'analyse." Master's thesis, Université de Montréal.

Lux, André. (1958) "Migrations, accroissement et urbanisation de la population congolaise de Luluabourg." Zaïre 7.

Lux, André. (1961) Le marché de travail en Afrique noire. Louvain and Paris: Nauwelaerts.

Lux, André. (1966) "Industrialisation et dynamique des tensions raciales et sociales dans l'ancien Congo-Belge." Anthropologica 8: 291-314.

Lux, André. (1971) "The network of visits between Yombe rural wage-earners and their kinsfolk in western Zaire." Africa 41: 109-128.

Lux, André. (1972) "Gift exchange and income redistribution between Yombe rural wage-earners and their kinsfolk in western Zaire," Africa 42: 173-191.

MacGaffey, Janet. (1983) "The effect of rural-urban ties, kinship, and marriage on household structure in a Kongo village." Canadian Journal of African Studies 17: 69-84.

MacGaffey, Wyatt. (1983) "Lineage structure, marriage, and the family amongst the Central Bantu." Journal of African History 24: 173-187.

MacGaffey, Wyatt. (1985) "On the moderate usefulness of modes of production." Canadian Journal of African Studies 19: 51-57.

Mahadi, Abdullahi. (1982) "The state and the economy: the Sarauta System and its roles in shaping the society and economy of Kano, with particular reference to the eighteenth and the nineteenth centuries." Ph.D. dissertation, Ahmadu Bello University.

Mahadi, Abdullahi. (1983) "Population growth and urbanisation process in Kasar Kano in the nineteenth century." Presented at the meeting of the Historical Society of Nigeria, 1-6 March, Ilorin, Nigeria.

Makwala, J. (1966-1967) "Les conséquences de l'exode pour le millieu rural du Congo et spécialement du Bas-Congo." Thesis for the licence, Université Libre de Bruxelles.

Mamdani, Mahmood. (1971) The Myth of Population Control. New York: Monthly Review Press.

Mandala, Elias. (1982) "Peasant cotton agriculture, gender, and inter-generational relationships: the Lower Tchiri (Shire) Valley of Malawi, 1906-1940. African Studies Review, 25: 27-44.

Mandala, Elias. (1983) "Capitalism, ecology, and society: the Lower Tchiri (Shire) Valley of Malawi, 1860-1960." Ph.D. dissertation, University of Minnesota.

Mangin, Charles. (1910) La Force noire. Paris: Hachette.

Mangin, Charles. (1920) Comment finit la guerre. Paris: Plon.

Manning, Patrick. (1981) "The enslavement of Africans: a demographic model." Canadian Journal of African Studies 15: 499-526.

Manning, Patrick. (1982) Slavery, Colonialism and Economic Growth in Dahomey, 1640-1960. Cambridge: Cambridge University Press.

Manning, Patrick. (1985) "The impact of slave exports on the population of the western coast of Africa, 1700-1850." Presented at the annual meeting of the Canadian Association of African Studies, Montréal.

Manning, Patrick, and William S. Griffiths. (1985) "Slave exports and African demography: a recursive simulation." (unpublished)

Marchal, Jean-Yves. (1983) Yatenga, nord Haute-Volta: La dynamique d'un espace rural soudano-sahélien. Paris: ORSTOM.

Marks, Shula. (1967) "The rise of the Zulu kingdom," pp. 85-91 in Roland Oliver (ed.) The Middle Age of African History. Oxford: Oxford University Press.

Martin, Phyllis M. (1972) The External Trade of the Loango Coast, 1576-1870. Oxford: Clarendon Press.

Marx, Karl. (1954) Capital. Moscow: Progress Publishers.

Marx, Karl. (1976) Capital, Volume 1. New York: Vintage Books.

Mason, Michael. (1969) "Population density and 'slave raiding'—the case of the Middle Belt of Nigeria." Journal of African History 10: 551-564.

Mason, Michael. (1978) "Working on the railway: Forced labor in northern Nigeria, 1907-1912," pp. 56-79 in Peter E. W. Gutkind, Robin Cohen, and Jean Copans (eds.) African Labor History. Beverly Hills, CA: Sage.

Matson, A. T. (1957) "The history of malaria in Nandi." East African Medical Journal 34: 431-441.

Mbodj, Mohamed. (1978) "Un exemple de l'économie coloniale, le Sine-Saloum (Sénégal), de 1887 à 1940. Culture arachidière et mutations sociales." Thesis, 3e cycle, Université de Paris, VII.

Mbodj, Mohamed. (1981) "Le Sine-Saloum et l'arachide, 1887-1940," pp. 139-154 in Catherine Coquery-Vidrovitch (ed.) Sociétés paysannes du Tiers-Monde. Lille: Presses Universitaires de Lille.

Mbumba, N. (198?) Kinshasa 1881-1981, 100 ans après Stanley: problèmes et avenir d'une ville. Kinshasa: Collection U.7.

Meek, C. K. (1925) The Northern Tribes of Nigeria. London: Oxford University Press.

Meek, Ronald (1971) "Malthus—yesterday and today: an introductory essay," pp. 3-49 in Ronald Meek (ed.) Marx and Engels and the Population Bomb. Berkeley, CA: Ramparts Press.

Meillassoux, Claude. (1972) "From reproduction to production." Economy and Society 1: 93-105.

Meillassoux, Claude. (1975a) "Etat et conditions des esclaves à Gumbu (Mali) au XIXe siècle," in L'esclavage en Afrique précoloniale. Paris: Maspero.

Meillassoux, Claude. (1975b) Femmes, greniers et capitaux. Paris: Maspero.

Meillassoux, Claude. (1978) "Correspondance." Economie et Société 7: 321-331.

Meillassoux, Claude. (1983a) "The economic bases of demographic reproduction: from the domestic mode of production to wage-earning." Journal of Peasant Studies 11: 50-61.

Meillassoux, Claude. (1983b) "Economie politique de la capture." Presented at the annual meeting of the American Historical Association, San Francisco.

Meillassoux, Claude. (1983c) "Female slavery," pp. 49-66 in Claire Robertson and Martin A. Klein (eds.) Women and Slavery in Africa. Madison: University of Wisconsin Press.

Meillassoux, Claude. (in press) Le ventre de fer et d'argent: sur la reproduction des esclaves. Paris: Maspero.

Mendelsohn, Isaac. (1949) Slavery in the Ancient Near East. New York: Oxford University Press.

Merlier, M. (1962) Le Congo—de la colonisation belge à l'indépendance. Paris: Maspero.

Mesnil, J. (1970) Connaissance du milieu et vulgarisation agricole: le cas de l'opération Centre-Mossi (9 volumes). Paris: SATEC.

Metge, P. (1966a) Le peuplement du Sénégal (2 volumes). Dakar: Ministère du Plan, du Développement et de l'Aménagement du Territoire.

Metge, P. (1966b) "Politiques migratoires: les migrations et la transformation de la société rurale traditionnelle au Sénégal" and "Les villes et l'avenement d'une société moderne au Sénégal et en Afrique de l'ouest" in M. Petit-Pont (ed.). Structures traditionnelles et développement. Paris: Eyrolles.

Michel, Marc. (1982) L'appel à l'Afrique: contributions et réactions à l'effort de guerre en A.O.F., 1914-1919. Paris: Editions de la Sorbonne.

Miers, Suzanne, and Igor Kopytoff [eds] (1977) Slavery in Africa. Madison: University of Wisconsin Press.

Miers, Suzanne, Igor Kopytoff, and Richard Roberts [eds.] (in press) The Ending of Slavery in Africa. Madison: University of Wisconsin Press.

Miller, Joseph C. (1975) "Legal Portuguese slaving from Angola: some preliminary indications of volume and direction, 1760-1830." Revue française d'histoire d'outremer 226-227: 135-174.

Miller, Joseph C. (1983) "The paradoxes of impoverishment in the Atlantic Zone," vol. 1, pp. 118-159 in David Birmingham and Phyllis M. Martin (eds.) The History of Central Africa. London: Longman.

Mitchell, J. Clyde (1961) "Wage labour and African population movements in Central Africa," pp. 193-248 in Kenneth M. Barbour and R. Mansell Prothero (eds.) Essays on African Population. London: Routledge and Kegan Paul.

Mkundunge, G. L. (1973) "The Ukaguru environment: traditional and recent responses to food shortages." Journal of the Geographical Association of Tanzania 8: 63-85.

Monteil, P. L. (1895) De Saint-Louis à Tripoli par le Lac Tchad. Paris: Ancienne Librairie Bailliere et Cie.

Morris, Pauline (1980) Soweto. Johannesburg: Urban Foundation.

Mott, Frank L., and Susan H. Mott. (1980) "Kenya's record population growth: a dilemma of development." Population Bulletin 35 (3).

Mudimbe, V. Y. (1984) "African gnosis: philisophy and the order of knowledge. Presented at the annual meeting of the African Studies Association (USA), 25-28 October, Los Angeles.

Mumbanza mwa Bawele. (1980) "Histoire des peuples riverains de l'entre Zaïre-Ubangi, c. 1700-1930: évolution sociale et économique." Ph.D. dissertation, Université nationale du Zaïre, Lubumbashi.

Mulambu, M. (1971) "La révolte des Bapende (mai-septembre 1931)—Etude d'un mouvement de resistance des populations rurales congolaises à la colonisation." Zaïre-Afrique 53: 115-136.

Mulambu, M. (1974) "Cultures obligatoires et colonisation dans l'ex-Congo-Belge." Les Cahiers du CADEF 6.

Muntemba, Maud. (1982) "Women and agricultural change in the railway region of Zambia: dispossession and counterstrategies, 1930-1970," pp. 83-103 in Edna Bay (ed.) Women and Work in Africa. Boulder, CO: Westview.

Mvula, E.S.T. (1982) "The Pounding Song as a Vehicle for Social Consciousness." Outlook: A Journal of Language, Literature and Culture 1: 31-55.

Newman, James L., and Russell Lura. (1983) "Fertility control in Africa." Geographical Review 73: 396-406.

Ngondo a Pitshandenge. (1974) "Evolution et caracteristiques de la croissance démographique en République du Zaïre—de la colonisation belge à nos jours." Minithesis for Master's degree, Université Catholique de Louvain.

Ngondo a Pitshandenge. (1979) "Une recherche au pays des Yaka en 1977: les statistiques collectées et leur analyse critique." Louvain-la-neuve: département de démographie, Université Catholique de Louvain. (working paper 64)

Niger, Ministère du développement rural and the International Bank for Reconstruction and Development (World Bank). (1978) "Projet de développement rural du département de Dosso. I. Rapport de la mission de préparation complementaire." (mimeo)

Niger, Service départemental du plan. (n.d.) "Note sur l'enquête sur les migrations dans le département de Dosso," Document no. 169/232. Dosso. (mimeo)

Nikolinakos, Mario. (1975) "Notes toward a general theory of migration in late capitalism. Race and Class 17: 5-17.

Northrup, David. (1978) Trade Without Rulers. Oxford: Clarendon Press.

Notestein, Frank W. (1945) "Population: the long view," in T. Schultz (ed.) Food for the World. Chicago: University of Chicago Press.

O'Brien, Jay. (1980) "Agricultural labor and development in the Sudan." Ph.D. dissertation, University of Connecticut.

O'Brien, Jay. (1983) "The formation of the agricultural labor force in Sudan." Review of African Political Economy 26: 15-34.

O'Brien, Jay. (1984) "The political economy of semi-prolaterianisation under colonialism: Sudan 1925-1950," pp. 121-147 in Barry Munslow and H. Finch (eds.) Proletarianisation in the Third World. London: Croom Helm.

Olivier de Sardan, Jean-Pierre. (1973) "Esclavage d'échange et captivité familiale chez lez Songhay-Zerma." Journal de la société des africanistes 53: 151-167.

Olivier de Sardan, Jean-Pierre. (1975) "Captifs ruraux et esclaves imperiaux du Songhay," pp. 99-134 in Claude Meillassoux (ed.) L'Esclavage en Afrique précoloniale. Paris: Maspero.

Olivier de Sardan, Jean-Pierre. (1984) Les sociétés songhay et zarma (Niger-Mali). Paris: Karthala.

Omer-Cooper, J. D. (1966) The Zulu Aftermath: A Nineteenth-Century Revolution in Bantu Africa. London: Longman.

Pachai, B. (1973) Malawi: The History of the Nation. London: Longman.

Painter, Thomas M. (1984) "From warriors to migrants: The historiography of early Zarma migrations revisited." Presented at the annual meeting of the African Studies Association (USA), Los Angeles.

Painter, Thomas M. (1985) "Peasant migration and rural transformations in Niger: a study of incorporation within a West African capitalist regional economy, c. 1875 to c. 1982." Ph.D. dissertation, State University of New York, Binghamton.

Paillier, G. (1978) Géographie générale de la Haute-Volta. Limoges: Université de Limoges.

Patterson, K. David. (1975) The Northern Gabon Coast to 1875. Oxford: Clarendon Press.

Patterson, Orlando. (1983) Slavery and Social Death. Cambridge: Harvard University Press.

Pelissier, P. (1966) Les paysans du Sénégal. Saint-Yrieix: Abregue.

Périé, J. and M. Sellier. (1950) "Histoire des populations du cercle de Dosso (Niger)." Bulletin de l'IFAN 12, série B, 4: 1015-1074.

Pirie, Gordon H. (1984) "Ethno-linguistic zoning in South African black townships." Area 16: 291-298.

Plaatje, Sol T. (1982) Native Life in South Africa. Johannesburg: Ravan.

Poewe, K. (1981) Matrilinear Ideology: Male-Female Dynamics in Luapula, Zambia. London: Academic Press.

Pollet, Eric, and Grace Winter. (1971) La société Soninké (Dyahuna, Mali). Brussels: Université Libre.

Poncet, Yves. (1974) "La sécheresse en Afrique sahélienne: une étude micro-régionale en République du Niger, la région des Dallols." (Document no. CD/SDD/293.) Paris: OCDE, Centre de développement. (mimeo)

Posel, Deborah. (1984) "'Providing for the Legitimate Labour Requirements of Employers': secondary industry, commerce, and the state in South Africa during the

1950s and 1960s." Presented to the African Studies Institute seminar, University of the Witwatersrand, Johannesburg.

Prioul, Christian. (1981) Entre Oubangui et Chari vers 1890. Paris: Société d'ethnographie et Laboratoire d'ethnologie et de sociologie comparative, Université de Paris X.

Proctor, Andre. (1979) "Class struggle, segregation, and the city: a history of Sophiatown, 1905-1940," pp. 49-89 in B. Bozzoli (ed.) Labour, Towhships and Protest. Johannesburg: Ravan.

Pursell, Donald E. (1968) "Bantu real wages and employment opportunities in South Africa." South African Journal of Economics 36: 87-97.

Ranger, Terrance. (1978) "Growing from the roots: reflections on peasant research in Central and Southern Africa." Journal of Southern African Studies 5: 99-133.

Rash, Y. (1972) "Un éstablissement colonial sans histoires: les premières années françaises au Niger, 1897-1906." Thèse de 3e cycle, Université de Paris, I.

Read, Margaret. (1942) "Migrant labour in Africa and its effects on tribal life." International Labour Review 45: 605-631.

Reinhard, P. R., A. Armengaud, and Jacques Dupâquier. (1968). Histoire générale de la population mondiale. Paris: Montchrestien.

Remy, Gérard. (1972) Donsin: les structures agraires d'un village Mossi de la région de Nobéré (cercle de Manga). Paris and Ouagadougou: CNRS/CVRS.

Retel-Laurentin, Anne. (1974) Infécondité en Afrique noire: maladies et conséquences. Paris: Masson et Cie.

Rex, John. (1974) "The compound, the reserve and the urban location: the essential institutions of Southern African Labour exploitation." South African Labour Bulletin 1: 4-17.

Rey, Pierre-Philippe. (1975) "L'esclavage lignager chez les tsangui, les punu et les kuni du Congo-Brazzaville: sa place dans le système d'ensemble des rapports de production," pp. 509-528 in Claude Meillassoux (ed.) L'Esclavage en Afrique précoloniale. Paris: Maspero.

Rey, Pierre-Phillippe. (1976) Capitalisme négrier: la marche des paysans vers le prolétariat. Paris: Maspero.

Rey, Pierre-Philippe. (1978) Les alliances de classes. Paris: Maspero.

Richard-Molard, Jacques. (1951) Hommage à Jacques Richard-Molard. Paris: Présence africaine.

Roberts, D. F., and R.E.S. Tanner (1959) "A demographic study in an area of low fertility in Northeast Tanganyika." Population Studies 13: 61-80.

Roberts, Richard (1981) "Ideology, slavery, and social formation: the evolution of Maraka slavery in the Middle Niger Valley," pp. 171-199 in Paul E. Lovejoy (ed.) The Ideology of Slavery in Africa. Beverly Hills, CA: Sage.

Roberts, Richard, and Martin Klein. (1981) "The Banamba slave exodus of 1905 and the decline of slavery in western Sudan." Journal of African History 21: 375-394.

Robertson, Claire, and Martin Klein [eds.] (1983) Women and Slavery in Africa. Madison: University of Wisconsin Press.

Robinson, C. H. (1980) Hausaland or Fifteen Hundred Miles Through the Central Sudan. London: Sampson Low, Marston.

Robson, J.R.K. (1962) "Malnutrition in Tanganyika." Tanganyika Notes and Records 58-59: 259-267.

Rolland, J. F. (1976) Le grand capitaine: un aventurier inconnu de l'épopée coloniale. Paris: Bernard Grasset.

Romaniuk, Anatole. (1959) "Evolution et perspectives démographiques de la population du Congo." Zaire 13: 563-626.

Romaniuk, Anatole. (1980) "Increase in natural fertility during the early stages of modernization: evidence from an African case study: Zaïre." Population Studies 34: 293-310.

Rondet-Smith, M. (1911) L'Afrique équatoriale française. Paris: Plon.

Rothiot, J.-P. (1984) "Zarmakoy Aouta: les débuts de la domination coloniale dans le cercle de Dosso, 1898-1913." Thèse de 3e cycle, Université de Paris, VII.

Rouch, Jean. (1956) "Les migrations au Gold Coast (Ghana, enquête 1953-1955)." Journal de la société des africanistes 26: 33-196.

Rouch, Jean (1961) "Second generation migrants in Ghana and the Ivory Coast," pp. 300-304 in Aidan Southall (ed.) Social Change in Modern Africa. London: Oxford University Press.

Routledge, W. Scoresby, and Katherine Routledge. (1910) With a Prehistoric People: The Akikuyu of British East Africa. London: Frank Cass. (1910)

Ryckmans, M. (1953) "Etude sur les statistiques démographiques au Congo-Belge." Zaïre 7.

Sabakinu, Kivilu. (1981) "Histoire de la population et des conditions de vie à Matadi de 1890 à 1959." Ph.D. dissertation. Université nationale du Zaire, Lubumbashi.

Sala-Diakanda, M. (1980) Approche ethnique des phenomènes démographiques: le cas du Zaïre. Louvain-la-neuve: Cabay.

Sala-Diakanda, M., and L. Lohlé-Tart. (1983) Social Science Research for Population Policy Design: a case study of Zaire. Liège: International Union for the Scientific Study of Population. (Papers, No. 24)

Salifou, André. (1977) "Colonisation et sociétés indigènes au Niger: de la fin du XIXe siècle au début de la deuxième guerre mondiale." Thèse de docteur-es-lettres, Université de Toulouse.

Sanderson, F. E. (1961) "The development of labour migration from Nyasaland, 1891-1914." Journal of African History 2: 259-631.

Santandrea, Stefano. (1964) A Tribal History of the Western Bahr el-Ghazal. Bologna: Centro librario dei Missionari Comboniani.

Saul, John D., and Stephen Gelb. (1981) The Crisis in South Africa: Class Defence, Class Revolution. New York: Monthly Review Press.

Sautter, Gilles. (1966) De l'Atlantique au fleuve Congo: une géographie du sous-peuplement (2 volumes.). Paris: Mouton.

Sautter, Gilles. (1967) "Notes sur la construction du chemin de fer Congo-Océan (1921-1934)." Cahiers d'études africaines 7, (26): 219-299.

Sauvy, Alfred, with Gérard-François Dumont and Bernard Merigot. (1982) Démographie politique. Paris: Economica.

Sawadogo, M. (1970) "Le chef des terres au Yatenga, Haute-Volta." Revue juridique et politique: indépendance 24: 1153-1160.

Schwarz, Alf. (1980) "Le déclassement du villageois zaïrois: une approche psycho-sociologique du développement inégal." Canadian Journal of African Studies 14: 113-133.

Scott, James C. (1976) The Moral Economy of the Peasant. New Haven; CT: Yale University Press.

Scott, Peter. (1954) "Migrant labour in Southern Rhodesia." Geographical Journal 44: 29-48.

Seccombe, Wally. (1983) "Marxism and Demography." New Left Review 137: 22-47.

Sen, A. (1976) "Famines as failures of exchange entitlements." Economic and Political Weekly 11 (special number): 1273-1280.

Shea, Philip. (1974-1977) "Economies of scale and the indigo-dyeing industry of pre-colonial Kano." Kano Studies (new series) 1: 55-61.

Sidikou, Arouna Hamidou. (1974) Sedentarité et mobilité entre Niger et Zgaret. Paris: COPEDITH. (Etudes nigériennes no. 34)

Sidikou, Arouna Hamidou. (1980a) "Niamey: étude de géographie socio-urbaine." Thèse du doctorat d'état, Université de Haute-Normandie.

Sidikou, Arouna Hamidou. (1980b) "Population," pp. 30-33 in Edmond Bernus and A. H. Sidikou (eds.) Atlas du Niger. Paris: Editions Jeune Afrique.

Simkins, Charles. (1983) Four Essays on the Past, Present, and Possible Future Distribution of the Black Population of South Africa. Cape Town: Southern Africa Labour and Development Research Unit.

Skocpol, Theda [ed.] (1984) Vision and Method in Historical Sociology. Cambridge: Cambridge Univ. Press.

Smith, A. (1970) "Deloga Bay and the trade of southeastern Africa," pp. 265-290 in David Birmingham and R. Gray (eds.) Pre-Colonial African Trade. Oxford: Oxford Univeristy Press.

Sociologie et sociétés. (1981) Special issue: "Les femmes dans la sociologie." 13: 1-157.

Stadler, Alf W. (1979) "Birds in the cornfields: Squatter movements in Johannesburg, 1944-1947," pp. 19-48 in B. Bozzoli (ed.) Labour, Townships, and Protest. Johannesburg: Ravan.

Stent, G. E. (1948) "Migrancy and urbanization in the union of South Africa." Africa 18: 161-183.

Streicker, A. J. (1980) "On being Zarma: scarcity and stress in the Nigerien Sahel." Ph.D. dissertation, Northwestern University.

Stürzinger, Ulrich. (1983) "The introduction of cotton cultivation: the role of the Administration." African Economic History 12: 231-245.

Suret-Canale, Jean. (1964) L'Afrique noire: l'ère coloniale, 1900-1945. Paris: Editions sociales.

Tabutin, Dominique. (1978) Tendances et niveaux de la fécondité au Zaire. Louvain-la-neuve: Département de Démographie, Université catholique de Louvain. (Working Papers, 54)

Terray, Emmanuel. (1975) "Gold production, slave labour, and state intervention in precolonial Akan societies" in Research in Economic Anthropology 5: 95-129. (Special issue, G. Dalton, ed.).

Thomas, Robert Paul, and Richard Nelson Bean. (1974) "The fishers of men: the profits of the slave trade." Journal of Economic History 34: 885-914.

Thomas, Roger. (1975) "Military recruitment in the Gold Coast during the First World War." Cahiers d'Etudes Africaines 15: 57-83.

Thornton, John. (1980) "The slave trade in eighteenth century Angola: effects on demographic structures." Canadian Journal of African Studies 14: 417-427.

Thornton, John. (1981) "The demographic effect of the slave trade on western Africa, 1500-1800," pp. 691-720 in Christopher Fyfe and David McMaster (eds.) African

300 AFRICAN POPULATION AND CAPITALISM

Historical Demography, II. Edinburgh: Centre for African Studies, University of Edinburgh.

Thornton, John. (1983) "Sexual demography: the impact of the slave trade on family structure," pp. 39-48 in Claire Robertson and Martin A. Klein (eds.) Women and Slavery in Africa. Madison: University of Wisconsin Press.

Trump, Martin. (1979) "The clearance of the Doornfontein yards and racial segregation." Africa Perspective 12: 40-56.

Tshund'olela, E. (1984) "Le Kasai à la periphérie du Haut-Katanga industriel." Les Cahiers du CEDAF, 6:

Turshen, Meredeth. (1984) The Political Ecology of Disease in Africa. New Brunswick: Rutgers University Press.

Turshen, Meredeth. (in press) "Gender and Health in Africa" in Steven Feirman and John Janzen (eds.) The Social Origins of Health and Disease in Africa (tentative title). Submitted to University of California Press.

United Nations (1956) Demographic Yearbook, 1955. New York.

Unterhalter, Beryl. (1955) "A study of fertility and infant mortality in an urban African community." Master's thesis, University of the Witwatersrand.

Vail, Leroy. (1983) "Political economy of East Central Africa," vol. 2, pp. 200-250 in David Birmingham and Phyllis Martin (eds.) History of Central Africa. London: Longman.

Van de Pute, M. (1946) Le Congo-Belge et la politique de conjoncture. Mémoires, collection in-8. Volume 4, fasicule 4. Brussels: Institut Royal Colonial Belge.

Van de Walle, Etienne. (1968) "Note on the effects of age misreporting," pp. 143-150 in William Brass et al. (eds.) The Demography of Tropical Africa. Princeton, NJ: Princeton University Press.

Van Donge, J. K. (1984) "Rural-urban migration and the rural alternative in Mwasi Lundazi, Eastern Province, Zambia." African Studies Review 27: 83-96.

Van Horn, L. (1977) "The agricultural history of Barotseland, 1840-1964," pp. 144-169 in Robin Palmer and Neil Parsons (eds.) The Roots of Rural Poverty in Central and Southern Africa. Berkeley: University of California Press.

Van Leynselle, P. (1979) "Les Libinza de la Ngiri: l'anthropologie d'un peuple des marais du confluent Congo-Ubangi." Ph.D. dissertation, University of Leiden.

Vansina, Jan. (1966) Kingdoms of the Savanna. Madison: University of Wisconsin Press.

Vansina, Jan. (1981) "Lineage, idéologie et histoire en Afrique équatoriale." Enquêtes et documents d'histoire africaine 4: 133-155.

Vansina, Jan. (1982) "Towards a history of lost corners of the world." Economic History Review 35: 165-178.

Vansina, Jan. (1983) "The peoples of the forest," vol. 1, pp. 75-117 in David Birmingham and Phyllis H. Martin (eds.) History of Central Africa. London: Longman.

Vansina, Jan. (1985) "Knowledge and perceptions of the African Past," in Bogumil Jewsiewicki and David Newberry (eds.) African Historiographies. Beverly Hills, CA: Sage.

Verrière, L. (1965) "La population du Sénégal." Doctorate of law, Université de Dakar.

Verster, Joan. (1965) "The trend and pattern of fertility in Soweto: an urban Bantu community." African Studies 24: 131-198.

Vieillard, Gilbert. (1940) "Notes sur les Peuls du Fouta Djallon," Bulletin de l'IFAN 1.

Waldron, Ingrid. (1983) "Sex differences in illness incidence, prognosis and mortality: issues and evidence." Social Science and Medicine 17: 1107-1123.

Wallerstein, Immanuel. (1977) "The task of historical social science: an editorial." Review 1: 3-7.

Wauters, A. J. (1891-1895) Le Congo illustré—Voyages et travaux des Belges dans l'Etat Indépendant du Congo. Brussels.

Wilbur, C. Martin. (1943) Slavery in China during the Former Han Dynasty (206 B.C.-A.D. 25). Chicago: Field Museum of Natural History.

Williams, Eric. (1944) Capitalism and Slavery. Chapel Hill: University of North Carolina Press.

Wolpe, Harold. (1972) "Capitalism and cheap labour-power in South Africa: from segregation to apartheid." Economy and Society 1: 425-456.

Wolpe, Harold. (1979) "L'Afrique du Sud: modes de production, force de travail et armée de reserve." Tiers-Monde 20: 155-167.

Wood, Peter. (1974) Black Majority. New York: Norton.

Wright, Marcia. (1983) "Technology, marriage and women's work in the history of maize-growers in Mazabuka, Zambia: a reconnaissance." Journal of Southern African Studies 10: 71-85.

Zwanenberg, Roger van, with Anne King. (1977) An Economic History of Kenya and Uganda: 1800-1970. London: Macmillan.

About the Book and Editors

An appreciation of Africa's population history informs the delineation of its now rapidly changing demographic dynamics. In this book, the impact of contact with Europeans looms large as the catalyst for the restructuring of African societies. The contributors not only examine the effects of slavery, colonialism, and capitalism on these societies, but also mark the resistance and resilience of many African institutions and individuals. As they outline the past and present diversity of African population dynamics, the contributors illuminate the ongoing process of economic and political change.

Changes in settlement patterns, labor migration, and marriage and household structure, as well as the impact of health on fertility and mortality rates, form the major demographic themes of this volume. The case studies cover twenty African societies representing each of the major regions of sub-Saharan Africa. The population issues emerge not as external or internal variables, but as part of a dynamic system that the editors characterize as a demographic regime.

Dennis D. Cordell is associate professor of African and Middle Eastern history at Southern Methodist University. **Joel W. Gregory** is professor of demography at the Université de Montréal.